Praise for *The Race for the Triple Crown:*

"Drape, who paid for his wife's engagement ring by winning a trifecta bet, writes poignantly of his personal ties to racing—of his mother, who always bet on the gray, and his own quarter horse, Oh Desperado, who made it to the winner's circle." —*The New York Times Book Review*

"Drape follows the colts from the spring yearling sales all the way through the Belmont, painting a fascinating picture of how the high-stakes horse industry operates and introducing a cast of characters who stand out even in a business notorious for outsize personalities." —*Time Out New York*

"A fast-paced book . . . *The Race for the Triple Crown* is for everyone who loves the game." —*Atlanta Journal Constitution*

"It's a tribute to Drape's reporting skills and his easy storytelling style that he's able to keep our suspense through the road to the 2000 Kentucky Derby. . . . Drape displays a knack for in-depth characterizations of the many fascinating players, warts and all. He tackles well-known figures like the trainers D. Wayne Lukas and Bob Baffert and still manages to dish up the little-known, telling details." —*Lexington Herald-Leader*

"In this breezy, yet informative look at the highest level of horse racing, the author traces the lives of a handful of preeminent horse owners, trainers and jockeys in their preparations for the Kentucky Derby, the Preakness and the Belmont. . . . Drape's zeal for his subject and his comprehensive knowledge provide a gratifying read." —*Publishers Weekly*

"[Drape] opens up a magical, mysterious world—and he does it with equal parts humor, affection and wisdom. . . . For anyone who has ever felt that intense surge of possibilities—scratching off a lottery ticket, buying into a church raffle, crossing your fingers for a little luck—Mr. Drape has boiled it all down." —*The Dallas Morning News*

"[Drape] has penned a terrific book. . . . It gives the reader an exciting look at last year's incredible three-year-old season." —Larry King, *USA Today*

"[A] well-researched, spellbinding book . . . Whether you are a novice to the Sport of Kings or a grizzled veteran, you will find Drape's 261-page personal conversation both informative and entertaining, much like a good friend. . . . Drape's work combines humor, drama and pathos . . . there are only eleven Triple Crown winners. Joe Drape, with *The Race for the Triple Crown,* just became the twelfth." —*Lowell Sun*

"This is a sparkling kaleidoscope of people and horses told at a pace that drives us to the finish line."   —*Toronto Globe & Mail*

"Written with an engaging blend of warmth and moxie, and laced with hundreds of candid quotes from the likes of trainers Bob Baffert, D. Wayne Lukas, Neil Drysdale and Jenine Sahadi, the book doesn't candy-coat the year's sometimes bitter (and often petty) rivalries, yet manages to show a great deal of respect for everyone involved—especially the horses."   —*Louisville Magazine*

"If you've read *Laughing in the Hills,* it may be more personal than that. And this book has more meat-and-potatoes facts, and the single-malt scotch of good writing to make it all go down smooth."   —*Fort Worth Star-Telegram*

"Drape's narrative never falters. He captures the personalities that dominate the sport and documents the astounding amounts of money that billionaire owners spend at auction on the equine dreams."
                                                        —*Raleigh News & Observer*

"[A] compelling chronicle of . . . Triple Crown dramatics, and the owners, trainers and jockeys who made it such a riveting story. Drape does a splendid job on the trainers, capturing the arrogance of D. Wayne Lukas, the mischievousness of Bob Baffert, the inner fire of Jenine Sahadi, the cockeyed optimism of eighty-eight-year-old Harold Rose. There are revealing portraits of jockeys Pat Day and Jerry Bailey, both recovered alcoholics; and some wonderful, raucous inside stuff about owner Mike Pegram, who named Captain Steve after a Louisville cop who bailed him out of an airport jam years earlier."   —*Philadelphia Daily News*

"*The Race for the Triple Crown* gives the reader the excitement of a horse winning at 50–1 odds. A first-rate and absorbing account by one who knows his material—a wonderful book that leads the field from starting gate to finish line. A delight for both aficionado and novice."   —George Plimpton

"[Drape] captures the sights, smells and outrageous dreams that are a part of the thoroughbred game, and does so in a way that only a member of the initiated can."   —*Staten Island Advance*

The Race for the Triple Crown:

Horses, High Stakes, and Eternal Hope

Joe Drape

Grove Press
New York

Triple Crown is a registered trademark of Triple Crown Productions, LLC

Published simultaneously in Canada
Printed in the United States of America

FIRST GROVE PRESS PAPERBACK EDITION

Library of Congress Cataloging-in-Publication Data
Drape, Joe.
The race for the Triple Crown / Joe Drape.
p. cm.
ISBN 0-8021-3885-3 (pbk.)
1. Triple Crown (U.S. horse racing)   I. Title.
SF357.T74 D73 2001
798.4'00973—dc21   2001016044

Grove Press
841 Broadway
New York, NY 10003

02 03 04 05   10 9 8 7 6 5 4 3 2 1

I've been blessed with a loving family and true, good friends.
To all of you.

CONTENTS

NOTE ON SOURCES
AND ACKNOWLEDGMENTS

I am grateful to the owners and horse-men and horsewomen portrayed in this book who were generous with their time and candor. They allowed me remarkable access and spent probably more time than they wanted to talking horses and personal histories with me. Jim and Terry Scatuorchio, Eddie Rosen, Todd and J. J. Pletcher, and their families always saved a seat for me on their roller-coaster Triple Crown ride. Mike Pegram was an ebullient and straight-talking tour guide. Barry Irwin, Fusao Sekiguchi, his daughter-in-law Yukari, Bob and Beverly Lewis, Sheik Mohammed bin Rashid al-Maktoum, and Frank Stronach were gracious with their time. D. Wayne Lukas, Jenine Sahadi, Neil Drysdale, Bob Baffert, Joe Orseno, Harold Rose, and Bobby Frankel patiently helped me understand their craft. This is true for the riders, too—Pat Day, Kent Desormeaux, Jerry Bailey, and Roger Velez—all of whom have been gentlemen and professionals.

The same can be said of many others within the industry who, over the years, have been eager to offer insights and share their passion about their sport. Basically, horse people are nice people, and I continue to give many thanks to them for making covering the sport so pleasurable.

Two of my colleagues at *The New York Times* contributed to my understanding of Sheik Mohammed and Fusao Sekiguchi. Foreign corre-spondent William J. Orme, Jr., wrote a story from Dubai about the Godolphin operation that was an invaluable guide to the scale of Sheik's ambitions, as was a series in the *Lexington Herald Leader* by Maryjean Wall. I collaborated with our Tokyo-based correspondent, Howard French, on a profile of Sekiguchi that ran before the Preakness Stakes. Howard's interview in Tokyo with Sekiguchi was vital to this book.

There are many gifted and dedicated turf writers who have helped me understand the sport better and have been gracious in sharing their knowl-edge and friendship, especially Tim Price, Ed Fountaine, Paul Moran, David Grening, Jay Privman, Bill Christine, Bill Nack, Mark Beech, Gary West, and Cormac Gordon. Two esteemed writers went out of their way to welcome me; Joe Hirsch, who is one of racing's treasures; and my colleague at *The New York Times,* Joseph Durso. I want to thank them all.

The folks in the communication department at the New York Racing Association are tireless at keeping me informed while working and smiling when I'm not. Thank you, Glen Mathes, Fran LaBelle, Tom Durkin, Bill Nader, Jason, David, and Eric. At Churchill Downs, Tony Terry, Lane Gold, and their staff always went the extra mile. As did Chris Helein and his staff at Pimlico. I'd also like to thank Jim Williams at Keeneland and David Heckerman, formerly of The Blood-Horse, for making the world of the horse sales understandable to me. Joan Lawrence at the National Thoroughbred Racing Association, as well as Jenifer Van Deinse, Jack and Nancy Kelly at the Jockey Club, need to be thanked for their help and friendship. I'd be remiss if I didn't thank Tom Merritt for introducing me to many of these people and giving me a stall on the New York circuit.

I'm grateful, too, that Neil Amdur, the sports editor at *The New York Times,* believes horse racing is important and that our editors—all of them talented and good people—care about the coverage. They are wonderful to work with and have been very supportive. Two friends and colleagues in particular, Fern Turkowitz and Judy Battista, kept my spirits up.

In racing parlance, this book was foaled when Myra MacPherson started talking horses with Robbie Hare at a chance encounter. I thank Myra, my former mother-in-law, for putting me in touch with Robbie, my future and current agent. After putting me through my paces on the farm, Robbie delivered the project to another horse enthusiast, my editor Joan Bingham. Both these women handled the book with great care even though they sometimes had to put the whip to me.

But as I learned on the road to the Triple Crown, you need a great team of grooms, hot walkers, even a bettor or two holding a ticket on you. I did. When I stumbled out of the gate, Susan Adams, another *Times* editor, gently gathered me up and put me back in the race. Bob Curran, my friend at the Jockey Club, was called on often for his encyclopedic knowledge of the game and sharp pencil. Joan's assistant, Hillery Stone, took care of all kinds of tasks in the barn.

On the rail, clutching tickets, I had Mary Kennedy making sure I kept it together in the stretch. Without her, I may not have made it to the wire. Thank you all.

Chapter 1

ON THE ROAD TO THE TRIPLE CROWN: HOPE IS ROBUST, IT'S THE HORSES WHO ARE FRAGILE

JUNE 1999

BELMONT PARK, NEW YORK

"I once asked my dad to tell me about his life. 'Pretty simple,' he answered. 'Went to the races, got married, got divorced; went to the races, got married, got divorced; went to the races, got married, got divorced. Went to the races.'"
— *Victoria Vanderbilt about her father, Alfred Gwynne Vanderbilt, at his memorial service at Aqueduct on December 6, 1999. Vanderbilt was a onetime prep-school bookie, Pimlico Race Course president, and noted breeder.*

Every horseman and horsewoman alive, from a superstar trainer like D. Wayne Lukas to the most obscure dreamer in the backwaters of racing, wants to believe that among the babies in the barn that are just beginning racing careers there is *the* one. The big horse. That magical equine athlete who in the springtime of his third year on this earth can grow fast enough to win one—or, better, all three—of the races that make up the Triple Crown. The fact sheet on this famous series is pretty straightforward: a trio of races each worth $1 million at three different tracks contested at various distances in the span of five weeks.

The first leg, the most famous race in the world, is the Kentucky Derby, held on the first Saturday of May at Churchill Downs in Louisville at the distance of 1¼ miles. Two Saturdays later at Pimlico Race Course in Baltimore, Maryland, the distance shortens, barely, in the 1³/₁₆-mile Preakness Stakes. Three weeks after that, the 3-year-olds take on the marathon distance of 1½ miles at Belmont Park in Elmont, New York.

The stakes transcend the purse money: a guaranteed $750,000 for the Derby, $650,000 for the Preakness, and $600,000 for the Belmont. In addition, Visa USA promises a $5 million bonus to the horse that sweeps all three events. But better, a victory in one Triple Crown event can turn a racehorse bought for $17,000 into a stud prospect worth upwards of $30 million. It means fame and national coverage in newspapers, magazines, and on television.

Best of all for the people who breed racehorses, who buy them, who train them, who ride them, even who bet on them, it means being right. In the 126 years of the series, only eleven horses have won all three races and given the people who loved and developed them that once-in-a-lifetime gift.

In pursuit of all this, racing people ignore the numbers that add up to terrible odds against them. Of the 35,078 registered Thoroughbreds foaled in North America in 1997—the crop eligible for the Triple Crown in 2000—only 10,936 would make it to the track to race as 2-year-olds, about 31 percent. By January 2000 only 387 of them would be nominated to run in the rich, prestigious three-race series—that's about 1.1 percent.

By May 6, 2000, only nineteen would stand in the starting gate at Churchill Downs for the Kentucky Derby. That's .005 percent of the entire crop of foals born in 1997 in North America.

These horses had earned their spot in the Derby by competing against the best of their generation and earning enough purse money to show that they belonged. Their owners were delighted to pay the fees: $30,000 for the Kentucky Derby, an additional $20,000 each for a spot in the gate at the Preakness and Belmont Stakes.

Owners with Triple Crown dreams, which means all of them, spend big money in the hopes of finding the big horse. In 1998, 8,275 of these would-be big horses were offered at auctions in North America. They were yearlings, unproven 1-year-olds. Still, owners paid $354 million for them. Why?

Over the twenty hours I spent at Belmont on June 5–6, 1999, a period replete with pain, panic, and exhilaration, I caught a glimpse of the many reasons.

I watched Wayne Lukas board an equine ambulance van with a veterinarian and a seriously injured horse while reporters and cameras clattered along behind.

I heard the weeping of the grooms and exercise riders from Lukas's barn as his prize colt Charismatic spent a harrowing night hobbling in his stall awaiting surgery after the horse had taken a misstep in the stretch of the Belmont Stakes.

I had seen Lukas endure a morning grilling about whether or not the injury was his fault. But I also had seen how a first-time starter winning a maiden race could displace yesterday's heartache with the faintest promise of glory down the Triple Crown road.

I decided then that for the next year I would travel along this trail myself. I would discover how perilous the journey is from that first step in the winner's circle as a 2-year-old to a place in the starting gate at the Kentucky Derby as a 3-year-old the following May. Then on to the Preakness in Baltimore and the Belmont Stakes in New York in a chase of history over five grueling weeks.

I am a sportswriter. Say this in response to the question "What do you do for a living?" and it's met with a smile and the words "Do you know [fill in the name of famous athlete]?" It doesn't matter the questioner's age or gender. Just the name of the profession conjures a front-row seat to great athletic spectacles, cold beers, bonhomie, and, well, not a whole lot of real work. I do have good seats at sporting events. I am acquainted with some famous athletes, and the profession does offer good times. The cold beers, however, don't flow until the late hours of long days, usually weekends—more often than not after talking to people who really don't want to be talking to you—then furiously pounding a keyboard to make never-ending but always fast-approaching deadlines.

It is work, but I smile most of the time and have no complaints.

And it is this work that had me leaning over the rail of a paddock in the morning sunlight on June 6, squinting with other bettors at six horses like I was trying to determine the cut and clarity of a diamond. We were also looking at the tall gray-haired guy in the paddock, the one in a $3,000 suit and the bloodshot eyes behind ear-to-ear aviator shades.

He was D. Wayne Lukas, and his eyes were bloodshot because he had been up all night worrying about Charismatic. The day before, the big chestnut colt had come within a fractured foreleg of becoming the twelfth horse to capture the Triple Crown.

The terrible misstep had taken place only twenty hours before, in front of 86,000 people here at Belmont Park and millions more in TV land. The injury probably occurred at the top of the last turn as Charismatic swung wide, beginning what looked to be a determined drive down the stretch and into the record books. But out of the turn, the horse's rider, Chris Antley, felt a bobble in the horse's gait; then something he had never felt before atop Charismatic—a lack of power. Two other colts, Lemon Drop Kid and Vision & Verse, rolled by.

Antley knew instantly Charismatic was hurt. Sixty yards past the finish line, seconds after Charismatic held on to finish third, Antley leaped off the horse's back, landed on the seat of his pants, scrambled to his feet, and lifted Charismatic's left leg in his hand until an ambulance arrived, seemingly out of nowhere. Tears streaked Antley's dusty face.

I was waiting at the paddock, because that's what you spend most of your time doing when you're a reporter. Waiting. For phone calls. For a city council meeting to end. For the final buzzer of a basketball game. For a horse to get out of surgery. You wait. You watch. You ask questions. You listen. You think a lot about what you're doing. Eventually, you type it up.

On the other side of this grand old racetrack on Long Island, inside a cinder-block building atop a sterile table, Charismatic was surrounded by equine surgeons who were trying to save the colt's life. It was 1:15 P.M. and Charismatic had been in the operating room for two hours. Lukas, however, did what he does 365 days a year: readied a horse to run.

At that moment, his job entailed saddling a filly named Cash Run who was about to make a trip to the track for her very first race. At two years old—think eighth grade in human dimensions—she was rattled by this new experience. Sweat glistened on her bay coat, turning it brighter in the same way melting ice highlights the color of a fine single-malt scotch.

She resisted Lukas's attempt to hang a white bridle on her snout, shuffling back a few steps and tossing her head left and right like a boxer slipping punches. Lukas was wrung out, too, from the events of the past twenty-four hours.

Yesterday, he was the Hall of Fame trainer on the verge of celebrating that recent honor by sweeping the Triple Crown—the Kentucky Derby, Preakness, and Belmont Stakes. Today, he was fielding the edgy and familiar questions about why his horses break down so often.

Yesterday, he was his sport's most accomplished trainer, running a storybook horse in a nationally televised $1 million race that, if he won, meant a $5 million bonus to the owners of Charismatic. Today, he looked all of his sixty-three years as he tried to calm his first-time starter for a maiden race of 5½ furlongs (a furlong is ⅛ of a mile) with a purse of $40,000 before a crowd of barely 11,000.

Lukas's mind may have been stuck on that distant corner of the backside, but his eyes were appraising the half waltzing, half polkaing bundle of nerves before him. Here is all Lukas, or for that matter anyone else, knew about Cash Run: One, she was sired by Seeking the Gold from a dam named Shared Interest, and these bloodlines had been rich enough to fetch $1.2 million at the 1998 Keeneland July Sale. Two, she was, in the parlance of the game, an "outstanding individual," which meant she was muscled and had reasonably straight legs and excellent conformation, which meant visually she appeared balanced. Three, she liked to run fast in morning workouts. Four, her owner, a Florida computer magnate named Satish Sanan, was Lukas's latest deep-pocketed client; in two years, he had already spent $100 million in search of fast horses but so far had found modest success.

The business of horse racing is not much different from the "new economy" spawned by the Internet, the dot-com companies and new millionaires. Except the sport of kings is three centuries old and doesn't have as many Wharton Business School graduates or software-design-engineer basement geniuses involved. But like the new economy, horse racing is more about possibilities than past performance. As they say in breeding sheds, "Breed the best to the best and hope for the best." Another maxim of the sport is: Run them.

Lukas was preparing to follow the last directive as he gave Jerry Bailey a leg up on Cash Run. The jockey danced the filly around the saddling circle and vanished into the tunnel leading to the racetrack. Lukas broke for the owner's box, but Sanan was not even here for a first glimpse of what $1.2 million had bought him.

Once in his seat, Lukas peered through binoculars to watch Bailey move Cash Run into the starting gate. The trainer tossed his shoulders back and stood stiffly when the words of track announcer Tom Durkin echoed from the sound system: "They're all in line." Then a bell sounded and the gates crashed wide open.

Bailey hustled Cash Run out first. She hit the quarter-mile mark two lengths ahead in $22^2/_5$ seconds. Bailey had a firm hold on her as she ran a half mile still ahead by two lengths in a quickening 46 seconds. As they entered Belmont's wide sweeping turn, the jockey crouched down and loosened the reins. With parabolic precision, Cash Run's lead increased to four lengths, six lengths, and then eight lengths as she reached the head of the stretch. Bailey peeked under his arm to see who was behind him. There was no one.

His hands moved gently in rhythm from her ears to her neck as Cash Run moved ten lengths, then twelve lengths ahead of the second-place Shannonaire. Bailey never used his whip, which bent backwards in the air like an antenna on a fast car. When Cash Run crossed the finish line, she was a $15^3/_4$-length winner in a time of 1:04.27.

Lukas hustled through the clubhouse toward the track, his pace picking up as he reached the grandstand patio. The filly's groom was already out on the dirt with a bucket, a sponge, and a huge smile, waiting for Bailey to bring Cash Run to the winner's circle.

When Cash Run arrived, he grabbed a sponge and squeezed some water on the filly. Then Bailey pranced her forward, turned her sideways, and let the track photographer flash a photo. The jockey bounded off her back, patted her affectionately on the withers, and unhooked his saddle. Then Lukas and Bailey strode back though the tunnel toward the paddock.

"She's a beauty, Wayne—a real push button. Didn't have to use her much at all," Bailey told Lukas as adrenaline quickened both their strides.

The pair stopped at a television monitor hanging in the shade about halfway up the tunnel. They watched the replay of Cash Run crushing her opposition. When Bailey watched the two-length lead he took into the turn grow into eight lengths, he just shook his head. "No wonder I couldn't see anybody," he mumbled. Lukas let the corners of his mouth part as steadily as Cash Run motored off with the lead. He didn't grin until the replay showed her crossing the finish line. Nearby, a security guard whistled in amazement.

"That's one hell of a filly, Mr. Lukas," he said.

"By next year, she'll be the best 3-year-old in the country," Lukas said, matter-of-fact.

Meanwhile, back in his corner of the backside, Charismatic was being wheeled into a recovery room to sleep off the two-and-a-half-hour surgery. The displaced lateral condylar fracture, a break extending about three inches from the ankle up the cannon bone, was fixed. As was the fractured sesamoid in the ankle joint. The prognosis for Charismatic was excellent.

Lukas, too, looked mended. He hustled back to his barn, accepting handshakes and backslaps and crackling with big plans. Because Cash Run was a filly, she was a long shot for the Kentucky Derby as well as the other Triple Crown races. In 125 years, only three fillies had won the Derby. That hardly mattered to the trainer—he had trained one of them, Winning Colors, who won in 1988. He also had another half dozen expensive colts in his barn, a résumé with an unprecedented $200 million plus in purse earnings, twelve victories in Triple Crown races, as well as the odds-defying optimism possessed by all horsemen at this time of year.

I too, suffer from this same optimism because I am a horseplayer, which most of us like to think is a higher calling than being merely a gambler. Rational or not, we believe we use our brain as well as intuition to pick horses who we think—no, *know*—are going to win.

Most of the time, I travel for my work. When you're on the road, there are too many afternoons or evenings to kill in a hotel room. Movies and mall walking have never done it for me. I don't play golf. Don't shop for antiques. I can nurse a meal, a drink, and a book for only so long by myself in a restaurant.

So I go to racetracks—more than seventy of them at last count, in seven countries. I've driven two hours from New Orleans to Rayne, Louisiana, on a Sunday to watch Cajun farmers and horsemen race quarter horses and Thoroughbreds for anywhere from $300 to $10,000 of their own money at an unsanctioned track. I've drunk Budweisers, eaten boudin sausage, and learned the hard way that to collect a 3–1 bet on "daylight" meant my horse had to win by three lengths.

I paid for my wife's engagement ring by hitting a trifecta bet—choosing the three winning horses in order—in a race for Appaloosas at Arapahoe Park outside Denver.

I've been escorted by four bowler-wearing ushers to the riffraff section of the Queen of England's track, Ascot Racecourse, because I hadn't worn a morning coat. I caught a ride back to London with a cabbie deemed similarly ill attired who also didn't mind being invisible to the Royals. I had no idea how or on which horse to bet in Nairobi, Kenya, but recognized the noisy jubilation of the winning bettors as well as the international gesture favored by losing ones: ripping up the ticket.

In short, I subscribe to the sentiment attributed to an unnamed horseplayer that "A bad day at the races is better than a good day anywhere else."

My yearlong pilgrimage with a purpose was no different. Before it all was over, I got to know a New Jersey couple, Jim and Terry Scatuorchio, who were fortunate enough to experience the highs and lows of the Triple Crown with their first big horse. I enjoyed an evening of karaoke at a dive called the 100 to 1 Lounge with a Washington State fast-food baron, Mike Pegram, who won the 1998 Derby with Real Quiet but preferred the ushers and bartenders on the littered front sides of the nation's racetracks to his fellow owners who inhabited the spotless box seats and private dining rooms at the tracks. I learned about General Sheik Mohammed bin Rashid al-Maktoum, minister of defense of the United Arab Emirates, Crown Prince of Dubai, and the single most powerful global force in horse racing, as well as Fusao Sekiguchi, an entrepreneur from Japan who, in a Derby first, brought geishas and a $4 million colt to Churchill Downs.

I was struck by the odd coupling of Harold Rose, an eighty-eight-year-old Jewish owner/trainer, and Roger Velez, a forty-three-year-old Puerto Rican jockey and recovering alcoholic. Both were onetime stroke victims. Both had faith that a small-time horse would deliver their once-in-a-lifetime dream. These men were a new breed of owners far removed from the aristocrats of the past, such as the Whitneys, Vanderbilts, Phippses.

The trainers and jockeys, too, couldn't have been more different. The two most famous horse conditioners, Lukas and Bob Baffert, were graduates of quarter horse racing in the Southwest. Their rivalry shook each other up along with the once genteel business of Thoroughbred racing. Another trainer, Neil Drysdale, was an educated Englishman whose apprenticeship took him from show horses to South American breeding farms to the Hall of Fame. He was part Renaissance man, part horse whisperer.

Jenine Sahadi was perhaps the best female trainer in the history of the sport. She was thirty-seven, a veteran of racetrack publicity, and constantly subjected to rumors that her boyfriend, husband—the men in her life—actually trained her horses.

The sport's rising training star, Todd Pletcher, thirty-two, had a college degree but opted to follow the lessons he'd learned from his trainer/father as a boy tagging along the grits and hard-toast circuit of second-tier tracks.

Of the three jockeys who each captured a leg of the Triple Crown in 2000, two—Pat Day and Jerry Bailey—were in their mid-forties and had conquered addictions in time to earn spots in the Hall of Fame and reputations as the best riders in the world.

The third, Kent Desormeaux, was a young Cajun who was deaf in one ear as a result of a spill and had learned his trade as a boy in places like Rayne, Louisiana, riding in those crazy match races on the bush tracks that had come to captivate me.

Before it was all over, the road to the Triple Crown led me to horse racing's heaven: Saratoga Springs, New York, where old-world class bumped up against working-class charm. To the sport's rich, wildly thumping heart: the Keeneland September Sale, where buffed-up horses pumped up free-spending millionaires in cutthroat auction bidding. And finally to its soul: the backsides of racetracks in California, Florida, Kentucky, Maryland, and New York, where old horses, young horses, cheap and expensive horses worked alongside one another in the mornings and competed against one another in the afternoons.

Before it was all over, I would have a colt tell me—yes, a colt—that he would win the Kentucky Derby. On Belmont Stakes day, I'd dream of a midnight flight to Paris on the Concorde after picking four of four winners on a Pick Six ticket with a guaranteed $1 million pool. And I'd come to understand what every horse owner, trainer, and jockey already knows about the sport: Hope is robust, it's the horses who are fragile.

On the road to the Triple Crown 2000, I waited. I watched. I asked questions. I listened. I thought about it a bunch. I typed it up.

Chapter 2

SARATOGA:
THE BIG HORSES DEBUT

AUGUST 1999

SARATOGA SPRINGS, NEW YORK

"Thirty-two thousand foals mean thirty-two thousand stories, because a Thoroughbred never goes unnoticed or undiscussed. And most of the stories are the stuff of drama."

—*Jane Smiley*, Horse Heaven

His name was More Than Ready. He had won all five of his races at four different racetracks and had broken a twenty-five-year-old track record at Belmont held by the great filly Ruffian. Everything about this 2-year-old colt seemed to be in a hurry.

He was named just nine days before his first race when his owners, Jim and Terry Scatuorchio, picked his moniker via cell phone from the celebrated La Tour D'Argent restaurant in Paris, France. It was April 2, 1999, Terry's fiftieth birthday. As the waiters circled, Jim's trainer, Todd Pletcher, called to say that he wanted to run the colt in a maiden race at Keeneland on April 11. But first they needed a name. Terry knew Jim was excited; it was the kind of moment he had hoped for when he retired as managing director of equity trading at Donaldson, Lufkin & Jenrette a year earlier at the age of fifty. He wanted to be a serious player in the sport he first learned as a boy growing up on the Jersey shore in the shadow of Monmouth Park. And now in Paris he kept asking Todd to describe the colt's extraordinary training. Then he phoned home to Rumson, New Jersey, where his daughter, Courtney, was checking possible names against the Jockey Club's registration list on the Internet. With names for 40,853 Thoroughbreds registered in 1999 alone, it was no wonder the Scatuorchios' original choice, Ember, was already taken.

Terry, slender with thick, shoulder-length black hair and a fashion sense in harmony with Paris, was ready to get on with her birthday celebration. She was tired of batting names back and forth with Jim, tired of Jim being on the phone with Todd, tired of hearing her husband repeating a question to his trainer: "You say he's more than ready to run?"

Finally, Terry had had enough. "Call him More Than Ready because I'm more than ready to eat," she blurted.

For Jim, the moment was thrilling, symbolic of why he had left Wall Street behind. In his more than thirty years on The Street, he had worked hard enough to rise from the trading floor and to have the usual complaints, but he was grounded enough by the good fortune not to voice them. The sixteen-hour days—compounded by a commute from New Jersey by car, train, or boat—had drained him in body and spirit. He had missed countless parent-teacher conferences and football games while his daughter and son were growing up. He had been supplanted by the bottled-water, health-club crowd of younger traders. He had enough money. His daughter was at Boston College. His son, Kevin, was a year away from joining her. At around five-foot-eight and balding on top, Jim didn't see bottled water and Nautilus machines rejuvenating him. He sought a rebirth through owning and racing Thoroughbreds.

For Terry, the rush to name a horse across international time zones was irritating, comical, and all too familiar. As a little girl, she had been dragged to racetracks all over the East Coast by her father, who had owned horses. She had met Jim when she was sixteen; their first date was at Monmouth Park. In fact, much of the couple's courtship unfolded to the sound of horses' hooves, beneath the lights of tote boards. Now in a transatlantic pique, she had given the colt a name that was on the lips of everyone in a place where horses are worshiped, their names chanted like prayers: Saratoga Springs, New York.

This was where the best bred and most expensive horses in the nation usually took their baby steps on the road to the Triple Crown. Before the meet opened in late summer, Joe Hirsch, the legendary columnist for the *Daily Racing Form,* acknowledged what the fast colt had already accomplished. He laid out the challenge ahead of him. "Good 2-year-olds, very good 2-year-olds and great 2-year-olds: Saratoga has been the place to sort them out," he wrote. "There is great anticipation as the meeting opens because More Than Ready is here."

I came with more purpose than I had on dozens of previous trips to this upstate New York town of 25,000, home to the nation's oldest racetrack. Saratoga Race Course was founded by John "Old Smoke" Morrissey, whose résumé foretold his creation's enduring charms. He was a gambler, casino owner, boxing champion, and future U.S. congressman, and his three-day race meeting in 1863 laid the foundation for the town to become the Brigadoon of horseplayers. It is the kind of place where you drink too much, bet too hard, and have plenty of folks to commiserate with—whether it be about losing a photo finish in the day's eighth race or the thumping your body and soul are taking at the hands of your vices.

The heart of this town is the 350-acre racetrack. It is veined by white fences, tangled with shade trees, and embedded with rows of barns spaced far enough apart to maintain tranquillity and gentility. This time of the year, Saratoga belongs to the horses. From sunup until 10 A.M., they stop traffic on Union Avenue, steady columns of them—from Kentucky, Florida, California, and, of course, New York—as they cross back and forth from the barns to their workouts on the racetrack. I liked that the horses remained the royalty here in this village of pastel Victorian houses.

The town was given its name by British colonists trying to pronounce the Iroquois word for the area, Sarachtogoe, and the mineral springs that were beneath it. It was here in 1777 that the patriots beat back the British and turned the tide in the War for Independence. There's Civil War history, too—Union general Ulysses S. Grant's cottage at Mt. McGregor is where the bankrupt former president, near death, wrote his memoirs and restored his family fortune.

But, for most, what matters more than the 1,000-plus buildings on the National Register, the monuments, the springs, and the prime fishing in the surrounding lakes are the horses and their history. This is where the horse Harry Bassett, representing the South, beat Longfellow, representing the North, in the 1872 Saratoga Cup; where Man o' War experienced his only career defeat in twenty-one starts to a horse fittingly named Upset in the 1919 Sanford Stakes.

Some fifty years ago an elegant turf writer, Joe H. Palmer, wrote that "he was no noted lover of the horse, but of a way of life of which the horse was once, and in a few favored places still is, a symbol—a way of charm and ease and grace and leisure." And that is the reason Saratoga Springs triples in population from the last week of July to the first days of September when the Spa, as it's called, hosts a six-day-a-week meet with at least one rich stakes race on each card.

On Broadway, the town's main drag, horseplayers prepare for the afternoon races by scratching notes on the *Daily Racing Form,* from the rocking chairs on the wraparound porches of old hotels like the Adelphi, or at poolside behind chain-link fences in the more modest motels like the Turf & Spa. I like that, too. By the 1 P.M. post time, more than 25,000 people, imbued by genius from studying the *Daily Racing Form,* stream into Saratoga Race Course.

It, too, is from another time. By the paddock and throughout the track's backyard, the gazebos and white clapboard buildings, the red-and-white-striped awnings, the picnic tables and strolling brass bands bespeak a country fair. Families and habitués sprawl beneath trees and park their strollers and coolers. There are television monitors and betting windows, but the real attraction is being close to the horses. Before each race, the ponies are led into a grassy circle and saddled beneath elm, maple, and oak trees that carry hand-painted signs with the horse's number hammered to them. The wooden grandstand and clubhouse do not abandon this turn-of-the-century motif. Elegant dining is found on a balcony overlooking the track; sandwiches, beer, and merry-go-round horses in the open-air Carousel Pavilion; and champagne or whiskey in smoky, speakeasy-styled bars tucked in nooks of the track. What unites wardrobes and wallets, however, is watching a horse race and trying to pick a winner.

This place may be famous as a playground for racing's bluebloods. But the working—or barely working—people are having fun, too.

As soon as the races are over, the Springwater Inn across from the track is crowded with characters like Augustino Gugliametti, a retired carpenter from nearby Albany. He offers a business card with his photo and the title "Professional Italian," as well as an invitation to Sunday-morning keg parties at the cottage he owns, where you find grooms and handicappers and the occasional Hall of Fame trainer. Then there are George, Joe, and Taylor—all in various states of either retirement or full-time horseplaying—who come down from Vermont and New Hampshire for the whole six weeks to pick horses. Over beer, screwdrivers, and the occasional chocolate martini, they argue over the sorry state of the current jockey colony or the training patterns of certain conditioners or how Dr. Fager, the great horse of the late 1960s, would romp over these fragile fields.

By dark, those who aren't at the harness track nearby, playing the trotters, stroll the narrow downtown streets off Broadway and duck into taverns. On the corner of Lake Avenue and Henry Street is Joan Desadora's place: the Parting Glass. It's an Irish Pub run by a sixty-year-old Italian lady who, to the backstretch crowd, is what the socialite Marylou Whitney is to the owner's-box set: gracious hostess, generous benefactor, and grand doyenne. Mrs. Desadora hosts benefits for a disabled-jockeys fund, offering her stage to bands of pickup musicians that often include jockeys' agents or New York Racing Association employees. On Mondays, especially, the joint is filled with jockeys like Robbie Davis or Jose Santos or Jorge Chavez, as well as their families, along with exercise riders, hot walkers, and grooms—all blowing some steam on the eve of the one day the track is dark. You've never seen so many short people in one place.

Just to remind you of where you are and why you're here, Channel 12, the all-horses-all-the-time OTB network, flickers on virtually every TV in town. As a colleague once remarked, it offers the kind of production values usually seen on Bulgarian cable television. But its prerace programming is rich—despite the dim lighting and occasional audio wails—as upstate handicappers with names like the

Wizard chat with trainers and make their selections for the coming card with the same passion as the political pundits on Sunday-
morning talk shows.

I had discovered this wonderful place because of my father. He
grew up two hours south of Saratoga and, after my mother died in
1991, decided he wanted to spend time in the place that had shaped
him as a young boy. My father, Mike, was instrumental in my development as a horseplayer, though he never dreamed I'd become this
passionate. As a boy living in Kansas City, Missouri, the closest racetrack, Ak-Sar-Ben (Nebraska spelled backwards), was three hours
away in Omaha, and an annual weekend trip for my parents. On the
night before they left, my father always bought a *Daily Racing Form*
and then gave lessons on how to read it. He showed me what, in the
single-line shorthand that sums up each of the horses' last ten or so
races, to look for in handicapping a horse: its running class, pace and
position, the trainer and jockey statistics. Unfortunately, by the time
I was old enough to go with him, Ak-Sar-Ben had already closed. In
the ensuing years, we made trips to Oaklawn Park in Hot Springs,
Arkansas, and the Woodlands in Kansas City, Kansas.

But it was in Saratoga that I discovered not only the "charm and
ease and grace and leisure" that Joe Palmer had promised but pieces of
my father's history. The treks always started in the Beacon-Newburgh
area along the Hudson River, where my father was raised by an uncle
with the two cousins he considered sisters. We would stay with
them, eating three kingly meals a day, sandwiched around forays
into town. My father would point to a storefront and tell me it used
to be the tavern and that as a boy he had dropped off the betting
sheets to horseplayers there on behalf of a local bookie. We would
end up at the Knights of Columbus Hall where, amid strangers, I'd
hear how he traveled around upstate New York, playing softball
for a team this same Knights Council had sponsored. He told me
why I never knew my grandfather and grandmother, who were im-
migrants from what is now Czechoslovakia. His mother had emo-

tional problems and died when he was a boy. His father drank and died soon after. My father never offered up many details.

In every other way, he was expansive and fun-loving enough to earn the nickname "Easy" from old friends. I was always reminded of that when we arrived in Saratoga. He'd get coffee and a racing form in the morning so we could study outside in rocking chairs for a couple of hours. In the afternoon, he'd slip into a sport coat and knot a tie for the track. Even in his seventies, my father wandered the paddock and the backside, and would even trudge up the stairs to the roof to watch at least one race a day. It seemed that when we were six stories high with a horse-racing kingdom stretching below us, he had something he wanted me to hear.

One rooftop confession, on August 12, 1997, I'll never forget. We had just watched a turf race, which was especially striking because the grass muffled the sound of the horses, and a gusting wind blew the crowd noise in another direction. "I've had a good life," my father said abruptly. "I've raised five kids who aren't bums and can take care of themselves. I've lived to see my grandkids grow. I can't ask for anything more."

We both knew he was undergoing surgery the following week to remove a cancerous tumor in his mouth. He also was battling prostate cancer. I did not suspect that he was in immediate danger, and neither did my siblings. He came out of the surgery in decent shape physically, but the drugs and the trauma left him disoriented. Seven days later, he experienced a sudden seizure. He died in the hospital three days after that.

Saratoga was the best place I could ever think of to hear the last meaningful words of someone so important to me. I was reminded of him now not only because I was here, but because everything about More Than Ready's emergence as a possible Triple Crown contender was a family affair. The colt was plucked off paper for his bloodlines by the Scatuorchios' friend Eddie Rosen, a New Jersey real estate lawyer who really would prefer to solve the mystery of what in a horse's breeding makes for a runner, rather than practice law. The colt was spotted on the grounds of the Keeneland sales a year earlier by J. J. Pletcher, the father of More Than Ready's trainer, Todd Pletcher.

Rosen saw potential on both sides of the colt's bloodlines. The sire, Southern Halo, was the leading producer of runners in Argentina and a son of Halo, who had already produced two Kentucky Derby winners—Sunny's Halo in 1983 and Sunday Silence in 1989. The colt's dam, Woodman's Girl, was out of the great Woodman, a champion in Ireland and the son of the late Mr. Prospector, who sired thirty offspring that commanded $1 million or more in the sales ring. Before he died on June 1, 1999, at the age of twenty-nine, as the United States' all-time leader by progeny earnings with $80 million, Mr. Prospector commanded a $250,000 stud fee.

J. J. Pletcher, a salty Texan and former trainer on the bush tracks of the Southwest and Midwest, saw a nicely balanced colt with plenty of attitude in this son of Southern Halo and Woodman's Girl. "I don't know how good he is, but I'll tell you how good he thinks he is," J.J. told his son Todd.

Armed with Rosen's detective work and Pletcher's eye for horseflesh, Scatuorchio bought the colt that became More Than Ready for $187,000. He shipped him to J.J.'s training farm in Ocala, Florida, to learn the basics of racing. His wife named him. And now the colt, the Scatuorchios, the Pletchers, and the Rosens were in upstate New York dreaming of the Triple Crown.

On Saratoga's opening weekend, More Than Ready sorted himself out under the "Great 2-year-old" category and validated everyone's expectations by winning the Grade II Sanford Stakes by nearly ten lengths. In the owner's box, Jim Scatuorchio and Todd Pletcher almost knocked each other to the ground with a too violent high five. Terry Scatuorchio and Barbara Rosen cried with joy. In the winner's circle, the Scatuorchios, the Rosens, and the Pletchers crowded around their undefeated colt and practiced their Kentucky Derby smiles.

For them, the process of protecting More Than Ready from the burden of expectations was in full swing. And it was up to a very young trainer to be the voice of reason.

The sun was just beginning to evaporate the morning mist as the hot walkers removed a half dozen horses from their stalls, then led them in lazy circles. The grooms swept in with rakes and bags of straw and the mucking-out began. The horses were led back in, a half dozen more taken out, and this swift, silent square dance moved on down the barn to the soft treble of Spanish and the occasional percussion of snorting horses. In the middle stood a squarely built guy with a close-cropped haircut that old-time barbers give to young boys along with a couple of brightly colored gumballs. But Todd Pletcher's hair was brushed with blond and gray strands. His face was broad and placid. His wide stance, hands buried in the pocket of his jeans, projected gravity.

He looked older than his thirty-two years. He slowly circled a smallish black colt just back from the track. It was only a gallop, but More Than Ready's lap around dozens of other horses on the track was trailed by the eyes of every trainer, exercise rider, clocker, and jockey agent leaning over the rail. Pletcher studied the colt as his assistant and exercise rider, Cindy Hutter, described the workout.

"He still wants to look around when we get around other horses. I had to fight with him a little to keep him from running off. He's moving real easy, though," Hutter told him.

The trainer squatted to one knee and took hold of More Than Ready's right back ankle; slowly he moved his hand up the shin. He felt for heat, swelling, anything that didn't feel right. He repeated the process on each leg. He smoothed his hand over the colt's right flank, then his left flank. He used both hands to press the chest of More Than Ready, then pulled them up his neck like a doctor does to you when checking for swollen glands. Finally, Pletcher brushed the nose of More Than Ready and patted the colt's forehead above his eyes, on

the white blaze that looked like a child's drawing of a star. Pletcher
stepped back and nodded; Hutter squeezed a large sponge over More
Than Ready and steam rose off the colt's back. She lathered him with
another sponge and bath time was under way. The trainer watched
until the colt was rinsed, combed, wrapped with a blanket, and finally walked off to the shed row for more lazy circling. He turned
and had a preemptive response for an unasked question.

"He's not the next Man o' War or Affirmed or superhorse,"
Pletcher said. "He's a very talented 2-year-old who has exceeded all
expectations. He's still a baby and I believe he's still improving, but
he hasn't done anything yet."

He smiled slightly as he said it, but Pletcher knew the comparisons
to the famous Man o' War and Affirmed, who in 1978 was the last horse
to win the Triple Crown, were piling up too quickly and inevitably
would crash down on him and his colt. Devil's Bag, Time Bandit, and
Montreal Red were among a long list of young stars whose summer-
time promise failed to deliver the performance the following spring
when it counted most. Pletcher knew it was too early to place any colt
in the starting gate of the next Kentucky Derby. He understood that
More Than Ready was the "now" horse in the Juvenile division only
because he ran into the headlines first.

In the second start of his career at Churchill Downs, on the same
day that Charismatic won the Kentucky Derby, More Than Ready
romped home a four-length winner in the WHAS Stakes before more
than 100,000 people. He fought hard to win his next race by a head in
the Flash Stakes at Belmont and followed that up with the record
1:02.2 dash for five furlongs in the Grade III Tremont Stakes. It was
how More Than Ready won the Sanford—a race previously won
by Affirmed and another Triple Crown victor, Secretariat—that
prompted the dangerous talk. He tracked the leader, Dance Master,
into the far turn, then exploded past and away from the field.

Jockey Shane Sellers had climbed off second-place Mighty and
declared, "We were second best to a great horse."

Pletcher wanted to believe that, but he was bothered by how More Than Ready fought his rider, John Velazquez, in the stretch run, turning his head to look at the people in the grandstands. "This time of year is for the early developers, horses who mature and come to hand quickly. We've outrun some fast ones, but he still is green, and the real expensive horses haven't been rolled out yet," the young trainer warned in an old one's voice.

He was right. Nick Zito, a two-time Derby winner stabled right here on the grounds, had yet to debut the babies that he intended to show up with at next spring's classics. On the West Coast, Bob Baffert, who in two of the last three years campaigned colts to within one victory of the Triple Crown, had recently sent out Forest Camp and Captain Steve to impressive victories in their first starts. In California, D. Wayne Lukas had just won maiden victories with a $575,000 colt named Commendable and a $1.4 million colt named Exchange Rate. A few barns down, his first-string colt, the $1.05 million High Yield, was to begin his racing career right here at Saratoga in a couple of weeks.

Still, word sweeping across the backsides of every track from California to Kentucky to Saratoga was that there was a potential wonder horse, a son of Mr. Prospector, who fetched a sales-topping $4 million in 1998 at the Keeneland July Sale—the most exclusive of sales. He was named Fusaichi Pegasus and was supposed to be as mythical as his name suggested.

The fact was that Pletcher was as precocious as his colt and from a more proven pedigree. He graduated from the University of Arizona in 1989 with degrees in racetrack management and animal science. Better, he did his graduate work at what is considered around racetracks as the Harvard of horse training: six years as a D. Wayne Lukas assistant. It hardly mattered that Todd was posted in New York and worked more closely with Wayne's son, Jeff, or that J. J. Pletcher had him riding homebreds on his Texas ranch by the age of two and tagging along to racetracks on weekends and in the summer as a boy.

As long as Lukas dominated racing or until Pletcher started bringing home his own Triple Crown victories, Todd knew he would be
identified only as a former Lukas assistant. It wasn't the worst thing
that could be said about anyone.

On August 10, about two weeks after More Than Ready's impressive Sanford victory, Pletcher had joined four other former assistants
in presenting Lukas for induction into the National Museum of
Racing's Hall of Fame. In the course of his thirty years of becoming
the most successful Thoroughbred trainer in history, Lukas had been
called everything from visionary to villain, been hailed for redefin-
ing the sport and cussed for ruining it. Not often, however, had he
been called gracious or humble. But on the day he was inducted into
the Hall of Fame, Lukas was both. His voice cracked with emotion,
and one of the achievements he said he was most proud of was the
young trainers who came through his barn.

Lukas trainees were known for the same three qualities as their
former boss. They worked hard, were incredibly organized, and knew
how to train owners as well as horses.

When Pletcher left Lukas in 1995, he had just seven horses in his
barn. By 1998 he had fifty, had won the most stakes races in New
York—thirteen—and had captured his first Saratoga training title
with twenty victories. Lukas's influence on Pletcher was everywhere. Like his former boss, Todd Pletcher was the first person at
the track in the morning and the last to leave. Just like Lukas, his
barns could pass for sidewalk cafés with their manicured landscapes
and garden-home awnings. His horses, too, were sent to the racetrack
with Lukas-style flair; they wore satin saddle cloths and blankets with
the trainer's T.A.P. monogram.

There were differences, of course. Pletcher was neither as charismatic nor as image-conscious as Lukas. A true Texan, he preferred
jeans and ball caps while Lukas, a Wisconsin native, wore chaps and
donned his signature white ten-gallon cowboy hat. But Pletcher had
the same knack for communicating with the people who were pay-

ing him to train their horses. His three most prominent owners, Cot Campbell of Dogwood Stable, Eugene Melnyk, a biotech entrepreneur, and Scatuorchio, had called Pletcher out of the blue because he was a Lukas protégé. Each had grilled him in interviews and walked away with the impression that the young trainer had his own vision and was smart enough to break his mentor's records, as well as follow him into the Hall of Fame.

Pletcher understood that his connection to Lukas had helped him land owners and horses and spoke reverently of his former boss. But beneath the surface he chafed, partly because he was young, competitive, and proud, partly because the association diminished his father's role in his development. J. J. Pletcher and Lukas have known each other since the days when both trained quarter horses on dusty tracks in places like Sallisaw, Oklahoma, and La Mesa Park, Colorado. They are good enough friends, the elder Pletcher liked to say, that "I've known all four of Wayne's wives." Like Lukas, J. J. Pletcher evolved into a Thoroughbred trainer and one accomplished enough to win 370 times in 2,296 starts, or 13 percent of the time, for $4,268,188 in purses, from 1976 to 1989. While Lukas headed west to the California circuit to chase rich races and an even richer pool of horse owners, J. J. Pletcher stayed in the Southwest and raced in places like Bossier City, Louisiana, and Hot Springs, Arkansas, where the purses are smaller and the owners play mostly in the claiming ranks. In fact, the majority of racehorses in the nation compete in the claiming ranks, which is a sort of poker game that has affordable table limits.

It works like this. If you want to run a horse at the bottom of the claiming ladder, say $5,000, you must be willing to lose him for that price. In the minutes before the race is run, anyone can put up $5,000 and claim your horse. If the colt or filly wins, you get the purse money, but the horse now belongs to the owner who bought him. The same rules are at play for $25,000 on up to $100,000 claiming horses. It prevents owners with classier horses from dropping down to easier races and picking up first-place checks. It also means horses change barns frequently. Like the stock market, the goal is to buy low and sell high. So done properly, you buy a horse at $5,000, move it up the claiming ladder and earn a few purses, then lose him for $25,000.

Claiming isn't as glamorous as preparing expensive horses for the Triple Crown, but it is the lifeblood of the racing business. J. J. Pletcher had made a good living at claiming and developed twenty-four stakes winners along the way. He also had plenty of time to teach young Todd about horses.

The way Todd took to one of his first lessons in the racing business convinced J.J. he had a budding trainer on his hands. His son, then eight, had accompanied his father to a sale at La Mesa Park in Colorado. "One of my training buddies got drunk and bought a horse for $800. His wife got mad at him, and she asked Todd if he knew anybody who wanted the horse. So Todd says, 'I'd like to have him.' He called me and said, 'Dad, she's going to give me this horse.' I thought, Lord, he must be terrible. But we took him," J.J. said.

For two years, the Pletchers trained the horse they named Rambunctiously at the family ranch in Texas. When it was time for the colt to make his debut at Oaklawn Park in Hot Springs, Todd was ten and too young to be allowed in the track's grandstands. Still, J.J. took out an owner's license in his son's name.

When Rambunctiously won, Todd bolted from the backside and was the first one in the winner's circle. Rambunctiously won his next start, too, but he got claimed. "He was so damn mad in the winner's circle because they claimed his horse," J.J. Pletcher said.

Between the colt's earnings and his claiming price, the Pletchers had $36,000 that J.J. put into an account for Todd's college tuition. His son was going to get a college degree, and he reminded Todd of that every chance he could. J.J. wanted him to have the options that he never had. Even if Todd decided to follow his father into the business, college was only going to help.

"We're in a peculiar business. If you tell an owner that their horse can't run a lick, he's going to put him in a truck and take him to the next barn," J. J. Pletcher reasoned. "So you have to kind of encourage owners, be vague but avoid lying at all costs. It takes some skills."

Even as a good student and fraternity man at Arizona, Todd had little doubt as to what he wanted to do. The day he graduated in 1989, he and J.J. loaded the truck in Tucson and drove through the night to Elmont, New York, and Belmont Park.

Once there, Jeff Lukas handed Todd the lead of an expensive horse, one named Houston who had led the Kentucky Derby that year for a mile before fading to an eighth-place finish behind Sunday Silence. Don't let him get loose, he told him. Todd Pletcher held on to Houston with both hands, and his lessons in the Lukas finishing school were under way.

From Rambunctiously and Hot Springs to Houston and Belmont, it was all about getting to Saratoga Springs, the most important place in racing from late July to early September. His stable now was eighty strong. Before him, wrapped in a blanket and touring the shed row, was the leader of the Juvenile Division. More Than Ready was to run next in the Hopeful Stakes, a Grade I seven-furlong race on the meet's final weekend.

But the real goal was nine months off in Louisville, Kentucky. The young trainer took off his cap and ran his hand through his hair. He ticked off all the things that could prevent him from running his first horse in the Kentucky Derby. More Than Ready could get hurt. He had never been beyond six furlongs; maybe he was just a sprinter and the Derby's 1¼-mile distance was too far for him. The Scatuorchios could decide to put him in someone else's barn. He could be sold, retired to stud.

"But I'd be lying if I didn't tell you that I think he is good enough," Pletcher said. "And at the end of the day, the ultimate goal in this business is to get to the Derby." Then he pulled his cap back on his head with both hands and declared, "Yeah, I think we're going."

Chapter 3

THE MARKETPLACE: KEENELAND
SEPTEMBER YEARLING SALES

SEPTEMBER 1999

LEXINGTON, KENTUCKY

"I also was the only one who seemed to know the details about the Earl of Roseberry, who achieved the three things he wanted in life— to win the English Derby, marry England's richest heiress and become prime minister."

—*Clifton Daniel, former managing editor of*
The New York Times

Each autumn, horsemen briefly abandon the racing circuit and go to Lexington, Kentucky. For eleven days in September, those who harbor ambitions on the scale of the Earl of Roseberry's convene at the Keeneland September Yearling Sale where thousands of unraced horses are eyeballed, touched, x-rayed, then cleaned, combed, and paraded into a dimly lit ring to be bid on and bought at often knee-knocking prices.

The road to the Triple Crown begins right here in an exercise that Wayne Lukas describes as trying to spot the next Michael Jordan at a basketball bazaar for eighth-graders. The sales ring is the only place in horse racing where owners are the primary combatants and compete head to head. Race day belongs to the trainer first, jockey second, and horse third.

.There are more exclusive sales—the July Selected Yearling Sale here offers anywhere from 200 to 500 of the finest prospects breeders have to offer. It's a more exclusive big-money affair held over two days with the same sort of ceremony and seriousness you find at the baccarat table in a casino. There are more elegant sales—the Fasig-Tipton Yearling Sale in Saratoga Springs also prunes its guest list by offering only top-end colts and fillies. The buyers wear long skirts or linen suits and white bucks, which makes the occasion feel like an A-list society cocktail party. The Keeneland September Yearling Sale is more like a shopping extravaganza. All these would-be kings come: the computer magnates; captains of industry; international tycoons; retired stockbrokers; local auto-parts store owners; small-time trainers from bush tracks in Idaho and Washington State.

They fly in on Lear jets; or they drive up in pickup trucks with goosenecked trailers attached. Even the heavy hitters opt for boots or tennis shoes, T-shirts and polo shirts. They all tote a sales catalog and often have a bloodstock agent and a veterinarian in tow. They are convinced deep down that they can unearth a Kentucky Derby, Preakness, or Belmont winner. Maybe from the top-end prospects trotted out in the first two days when prices blow past the $1 million mark. Though even then their dreams defy logic: no winner of the Kentucky Derby was ever bought for more than $1 million. Mike Pegram, for example, picked up the 1998 Derby and Preakness winner, Real Quiet, for $17,000.

Barely contained beneath the casual clothes and sincere camaraderie is a whose-is-bigger streak of ego that bounces from one owner to another when bidding begins in the sales ring, and continues pulsing through conversations in the bars and restaurants that surround the sales pavilion.

Late on the afternoon of the first day, leaning on a piece of mahogany in one of the bars with the wife of an owner, I heard a pretty apt description of this testosterone-charged atmosphere. To the left of us, two owners from the Northeast slugged down beers after spending $650,000 on a horse. They drank heartily, as if the brew were going to put money back in their pockets. Their friend, another owner, downed a shot of bourbon. He had an excited tremor in his hand and a sour look on his face. "Let's see if I can get him for $1.5 million," he said tersely, then marched back to the pavilion.

My new friend was a veteran of the sales. She rolled her eyes. "I don't know what is worse—the smell of horse shit or the sound of bullshit around here," she said.

"In buying a horse or taking a wife, shut your eyes tight and commend yourself to God."

—*Tuscan proverb*

He wore jeans and a white T-shirt underneath a royal blue satin jacket with the name of his racing stable fancily embroidered over the breast: Godolphin. He was a slight man with a trim beard, and his importance was signaled less by the size of his entourage—four young men in the same stable jackets—than by how the group moved. They ambled between barns, never in a hurry, never walking in a straight line.

The rain had been coming down all morning, but he continued to roam the barn areas behind the sales pavilion to size up the horses he might want to buy. The help in the consignor's barns was dressed better—in a uniform of khaki pants and polo shirts—than the Sheik and his associates. These young men and women were responsible for bringing out a requested horse. They became more nervous as the Godolphin contingent approached.

The Sheik stopped at Barn 11, where Mill Ridge Sales kept its merchandise. He turned his sales catalog to the page where the pedigree of Hip No. 441 was listed and showed it to a young woman. She disappeared into a barn and a moment later returned with a bay colt that, not too keen on walking out in the rain, tried to back up. The Sheik nodded and the woman pulled the Red Ransom colt to a strip of grass about twenty-five feet away, then turned him around and led him back. The Sheik held his right elbow with his left hand and pressed his cheek into his right palm. He held one finger up from his face, signaling for her to make the walk again. This time he tilted his head to one side, then the other, and focused on the colt's back end. On the return trip, he dropped both hands and took dead aim on the colt's front legs.

By now, buyers on the adjacent gravel paths stopped. These owners dropped their sales catalogs to their sides and watched the Sheik examine the colt. No matter what Sheik Mohammed bin Rashid al-Maktoum sees when he is scrutinizing a horse, everyone else sees dollar signs.

He wins the "see whose-is-bigger" contest as soon as he hits town. His own Emirates Airlines Boeing 747 was parked at Blue Grass Field. You couldn't miss it driving down Versailles Road before you turned into Keeneland's gates—just as you couldn't miss the one just like it parked nose to nose. It belongs to his older brother, Sheik

Hamdan, who, though more low-key, also likes to throw some money at horses.

In fact, Sheik Mohammed beat the hell out of the Earl of Roseberry in both accomplishment and ambition. The English Derby? Did it in 1995, along with the Irish Derby in 1994 and most of the other prestigious European races—the Prix de l'Arc de Triomphe, the King George VI and Queen Elizabeth Diamond Stakes, the St. Leger Stakes, and the Oaks at Epsom.

Marry a rich heiress? No need. The Sheik set a record for the world's most expensive wedding, according to *The Guinness Book of World Records,* when he married Princess Salama in 1981. He built a stadium for the occasion, invited 20,000 guests, and spent $44 million.

Become prime minister? Why? He was the minister of defense for United Arab Emirates and Crown Prince of Dubai, one of seven Arab sheikdoms that comprise the UAE, which was founded in 1971 on 32,000 square miles, about 65 percent of it desert. Its location at the crossroads of Europe, Asia, and Africa turned Dubai into a profitable trading center for everything from gold and pearls to electronics and designer labels. Its oil reserves sprouted banking and finance centers that helped build beach resorts on the Persian Gulf, create five-star restaurants, and turn Dubai into a cosmopolitan city with the ambition of becoming the next Hong Kong.

The Maktoums, the ruling family, were aware that the city-state of 675,000 needed to transcend oil if it was to continue to prosper, because oil supplies were expected to dry up within the twenty-first century. They were trying to add tourism to their trade and, from Sheik Mohammed's perspective, horses were a natural way to make the world aware of a seafront winter desert resort with crime-free streets and duty-free shopping. It was public relations grafted on to history and a family passion. The modern Thoroughbred is a descendant of three Arabian bloodlines that date to the late seventeenth and early eighteenth centuries. The sires are Byerly Turk, Darley Arabian, and Godolphin Barb. Close to 90 percent of Thoroughbreds can be traced to the Darley Arabian line through its descendant and Thoroughbred sire Eclipse—including Bold Ruler, Northern Dancer, Secretariat, Seattle Slew, and Affirmed. The Godolphin Barb line produced the Thoroughbred sire Matchem, whose line gave the racing world Man o' War and Sheik Mohammed the inspiration to create Godolphin Racing.

The four Maktoum brothers have been coming to Keeneland since the 1980s: Sheik Maktoum bin Rashid al-Maktoum, sixty, is the vice president and prime minister of UAE, Crown Ruler of Dubai, and owns Gainsborough Stud and Woodpark Stud in England as well as Gainsborough Farm in Kentucky. Sheik Hamdan, fifty-four, is minister of finance and industry for the UAE, deputy ruler of Dubai, and owner of Shadwell Stud and the Nunnery in England, Derrinstown in Ireland, and Shadwell Farm in Kentucky. The least involved is Sheik Ahmed, forty-eight, the deputy commander of the Dubai Police Force, who owns Aston Upthorpe Stud in England. The most involved is Mohammed, forty-nine, who owns eight farms in Britain, including Dalham Hall Stud, four farms in Ireland, and Raceland Farm in Kentucky. Three of the brothers attended Cambridge University; Ahmed went to Britain's Mons Officer Cadet Training college.

Together, these descendants of Bedouin camel herders have billions of dollars—Sheik Maktoum alone was ranked the eighteenth richest person in the world, with $10 billion in net worth in 1998, according to *Forbes* magazine. The family has spent more than $1 billion on racehorses, plenty of it in the Kentucky bluegrass, more than $600 million at the Keeneland sales. At the 1989 July Selected Yearling Sale, for example, the brothers bought sixty-seven yearlings for more than $44 million, or 44 percent of the total sales.

Their relationship with the other horsemen is complicated. The old-line Kentucky horsemen, or hardboots, have a saying that "you have to save the farm." They utter it whenever they must explain why they made a lot of money doing something they didn't want to. Selling off these treasures of their heritage to Europeans, Japanese, and

Arabs—all of whom have had periods dominating the fifty-five-year-old Keeneland sales—to be raced overseas doesn't always sit well with most of the good folks of Kentucky.

The Maktoums were treated affably in public and catered to in private because their exorbitant spending was saving a lot of farms. During the sales, the Maktoum brothers are set up in the Director's room off the adjacent racetrack with a closed-circuit television beaming in the sales ring; an on-site spotter with an open phone line relays their bids.

In the 1980s, they drove the market to record heights, often bidding against one another. Then they were considered ostentatious bidders who, even better, were often overpaying for poor racing and breeding prospects. In the 1983 July sale, Sheik Mohammed paid a then world-record $10.2 million for a Northern Dancer colt eventually named Snaafi Dancer, who never raced and proved to be infertile in the breeding shed. Although there was resentment from the Kentucky hardboots, it was tempered by a smugness that the desert lords did not have a clue as to what they were doing. In the early 1990s, when the economy tailed off, and with it the horse market, the Maktoums were simply resented. Between the Gulf War and tighter times, American and European buyers, once exhilarated by knocking heads with the Sheiks in the sales ring, now grumbled that it was hopeless to go head to head with the too secretive and too rich Arabs.

Now the attitude toward the Maktoums wavered between respect and fear. The Maktoums, especially Sheik Mohammed, knew exactly what they were doing in those years of free spending at the sales. They were building the most powerful racing operation in the world, and it coalesced in 1994 when Sheik Mohammed formed Godolphin Racing Inc. The idea was simple: Build the finest training facilities in Dubai, bring the game's brightest minds there, then train the best of the family's horses over the winter in the desert kingdom's temperate climate before sending them around the globe to race in the sport's biggest races.

As always, money was no object. Under Sheik Mohammed's direction, the Maktoums built the state-of-the-art Al Quoz Racing Stable with amenities such as a private track, irrigated lawns separating walking tracks, tile-shaded paddocks, ten screened barns, a world-class feed mill, and a 250-foot single-lane Thoroughbred swimming pool. For the more than one hundred Thoroughbreds, most worth $1 million or more each, the Sheik lured former jockeys from Ireland, England, and the United States to exercise them, as well as blacksmiths and veterinarians from Kentucky and grooms from Pakistan to care for them. The help are paid handsomely, given five weeks' vacation, put up rent-free, and given four-wheel-drive vehicles.

Simon Crisford, a savvy Brit with an international track record of success, was installed as racing manager. Saeed bin Suroor, a former police officer, was named head trainer.

Yet there's no doubt that Sheik Mohammed is in command. He is an avid sportsman who owns racing camels, as well as an expert falconer who employs the regal birds in hunts. But he is first a horseman who is a frequent competitor in the World Endurance Championships held on road courses at distances of up to a hundred miles.

Any doubts about Sheik Mohammed's vision and commitment to horse racing were dispelled when Godolphin horses won the Irish and English Derbies right out of the box. The 1995 English Derby winner, Lammtarra, is a particular point of pride for Sheik Mohammed; the colt was bred in Maktoum family stables and sold for $30 million after consecutive victories in major European races. Also noteworthy is Almutawakel's victory at the Dubai World Cup in the spring of 1999 over the best Thoroughbreds in the world, including 1997 Kentucky Derby and Preakness winner, Silver Charm.

If forming Godolphin was the first step in building name recognition for a new tourist destination, bankrolling the $5 million Dubai World Cup was the second. Owners and trainers applauded the rich purse and were eager to compete against an international field with horses from as far away as Japan and Australia. They also embraced the third phase of the public relations blitz—the Maktoums' $15 million investment over three years for an annual "World Series" of nine Thoroughbred competitions in eight countries, from Ascot to Hallandale, Florida, to Hong Kong, culminating in the Dubai Cup in March.

It was the fourth phase, however, that scared the hardboots and was beginning to bring the old resentments to the surface. Sheik Mohammed and Godolphin had recently set their sights on winning the Kentucky Derby.

In the fall of 1998, Godolphin paid $5 million for Worldly Manner, a colt that had won three of four races and earned more than $250,000 as a 2-year-old racing in the United States. Sheik Mohammed also paid $3 million for Comeonmom, another promising American 2-year-old. He shipped them both back to Dubai for training and pointed them to the Kentucky Derby with an unusual strategy. The colts would skip the traditional American prep races such as the Florida Derby or Bluegrass Stakes and, after a pair of trial races in Dubai, would ship into Louisville for the Derby. Comeonmom never got fit enough and did not make the trip to Louisville for the Derby. But Worldly Manner and an unfazed Sheik Mohammed showed up. He shrugged off any questions about preparations.

"Transportation is getting much better, and the world is getting much smaller," he said. "I know some people in America think it is strange, these horses coming out of nowhere, running in their best race. They can't understand that we are thinking globally."

When Worldly Manner came out of the far turn in second place in the 125th running of the Kentucky Derby, it looked like Godolphin was going to kick sand in the bluegrass. The colt battled in the stretch before tiring to finish a creditable seventh. Sheik Mohammed was far from discouraged and not only promised to return to the race but vowed one of his horses would win it within four years. For many hardboots, it was scary but not implausible.

Here for the sales, Sheik Mohammed softened his grand pronouncements with some personal touches. On the first two days of the sale, he often left his private room for a seat inside the sales pavilion. His first appearance sent a stampede of owners and spectators pouring through the doors and into the sloped auction theater, looking for seats. They paged through their catalogs, making the current of anticipation audible as they tried to figure out which horse the Sheik was about to make a sales legend. The other big players already knew. They were after Hip. No 153, a son of Unbridled out of the dam Missy's Mirage.

Unbridled was the 1990 Kentucky Derby winner and 3-year-old champion who had earned $4,489,475 and already given life to Grade I winners Banshee Breeze, Unbridled's Song, and 1996 Derby winner Grindstone. In the currency of horse trading, a Grade I victory was the gold standard. There were all kinds of stakes races, but the crème de la crème ran in graded stakes, either Grade III, II, or I. There were only 475 of them in America, out of tens of thousands of races. These were the most prestigious races with the biggest purses. Winning a Grade I race meant a horse beat the very best of its peers. Multiple Grade I victories meant a horse consistently competed at the top levels of racing. For owners, each Grade I victory enhanced the stud value of a horse by millions.

In five foal crops, Unbridled had sired 243 foals; 125 of them made it to the races, 71 were winners—including 11 in stakes races—and his offspring so far had earned more than $9 million. This son of Unbridled was the half brother to Sasha's Prospect, who brought a sale-record $2.3 million in 1997, and a foal of Missy's Mirage, a Grade 1 winner. He was bred to race. He was bred to breed. He was bound to be expensive.

As soon as the colt waltzed through the sliding doors and took his place in a small dirt patio behind shrubs and a braided rope fence, the Keeneland sales staff began doing what they did best: taking money from the buyers at the rate of thirty-five to forty horses an hour.

Spotters in green blazers, white shirts, and rep ties were in position in front of each section of the semicircled arena. Behind the auctioneer's tower, more spotters watched buyers who preferred the anonymity of the back waiting area, camouflaged by a long line of horses waiting their turn to enter the sales ring.

Three auctioneers, eight feet or so above the ring, were responsible for keeping the beat and prices pounding. They worked in shifts and were accompanied by the "Haaahs" or "Eeeeres" of the spotters who punctuated the bids with punches in the air.

In the middle of the arena, the Sheik barely paid attention as his bloodstock agent did the bidding. A section to the left of him, Lukas was going a hundred thousand for a hundred thousand with him by almost imperceptibly lifting his index finger from his ankle, which was resting on his knee. On the other side, the Thoroughbred Corporation—a consortium of horsemen headed by Saudi prince Ahmed bin Salman—was keeping the lights of the tote board blinking upward. There also was a fourth bidder, somewhere in the back, shielded by the press stand and the comings and goings of people entering the ring. But a Keeneland spotter knew exactly where the buyer was and relayed his bids.

"Two million," rumbled head auctioneer Tom Caldwell in a rich baritone. He learned his craft from his father, Colonel H. J. Caldwell, and had been selling at Keeneland for forty-three years, which was long enough to have sons Scott and Cris follow him into the business and onto the podium as part of the auctioneer team. Tom Caldwell let it hang there for a few seconds before bringing down the hammer. The Sheik got up and left. He didn't buy the Unbridled colt.

Heads turned toward Lukas and then the Thoroughbred Corp. contingent. Both groups stayed in their seats, and neither had the satisfied look of a winner. The victors, bidding imperceptibly from the back, now were out in the hallway introducing themselves as new players in the loftiest levels of horse trading.

They were a father-son team, Bob Hess, Sr. and Bob Hess, Jr., and had won the horse trainer's lottery: a rich, committed owner. It was actually Junior's deal. He was thirty-four and an up-and-comer on the West Coast circuit after having played baseball and earned a degree at Stanford University. He had thick dark hair and polished country-club looks. He accepted congratulations while speaking on a cell phone to the owner who had just bankrolled this purchase, a California computer entrepreneur named David Shimmon.

Hess Sr. wore jeans and a ball cap and looked like any other hard-knocking horseman on the claiming circuits, which he was in northern California. Like J. J. Pletcher, Hess Sr. put his son to work on the backside and insisted he get an education. He had done the bidding on the colt, but directed the attention to his son. "I've had my day. All I did was follow instructions. Mr. Shimmon said to keep our hand up until we got him," Hess Sr. said.

So the father leaned against a wall and watched the son explain the rush he had experienced in bidding against the Sheik, of buying a $2 million horse, of having a chance now to compete in the best races. Hess Sr. grinned as his son flashed a boyish smile. Before he walked off, I asked the elder Hess if he had ever bid on such an expensive horse. Had he felt any pressure?

"This game anymore belongs to young, articulate guys who are businessmen as much as horsemen," he said. "I've never come close to talking anyone out of that much money. You want pressure? Try buying a horse with a guy's last $35,000. That's harder."

Shimmon and the Hesses should have felt grateful that the Sheik wasn't passionate about the Unbridled colt. However, the gentleman from Dubai was just getting warmed up. Before the eleven days were over, the Maktoums bought thirty-nine yearlings for more than $24 million to outpace the next highest spender by almost 3 to 1. Sheik Mohammed not only bought the Red Ransom colt he had scrutinized for $650,000, but in ten dizzying minutes in the sales ring he resurrected in horsemen the giddy memories of the high-spending '80s as well as the stomach-churning fear that, once again, they could not compete with the Sheiks.

It was late in the second day when Hip No. 503 was led into the sales ring, a bay colt by Kris S. out of a Mr. Prospector dam, Mr. P.'s Princess. He was a half brother, by Kris S., to Fasliyev, the current leading 2-year-old in Europe. Mr. P.'s Princess was a half sister to Menifee, the 1999 Kentucky Derby and Preakness runner-up. Kris S.'s line was among the most efficient and lucrative sires in the world: 618 foals, 492 winners—48 of them stakes—earners of more than $30.1 million in purses. There's no such thing as can't-miss prospects in the horse business, but on paper, as well as in the balanced frame and rippled flesh of the colt standing before the auction tower, this was as good a gamble as you could hope for.

The bars and hallways were empty and the sales arena packed for what everyone suspected would be a high-stakes poker game. In addition to the Sheik, international intrigue was heightened by the cluster of men gathered in the far back corner. They were the principals of Coolmore Stud, perhaps the preeminent stallion station in the world, with operations on five continents. In 1975, the original partnership of Britain's leading international owner Robert Sangster, trainer Dr. Vincent O'Brien, and stallion master John Magnier took over a 350-acre existing stud farm in Ireland. They spun off other partnerships and established farms in Kentucky, Japan, South America, and Australia with the revenues from such sought-after sires as Sadler's Wells, Danehill, Southern Halo, Alzao, Peintre Celebre, Royal Academy, El Gran Senor, and Woodman.

Sangster and company were among the first to, literally, get more bang for their bucks by shipping their Irish-based stallions to Australia for the Southern Hemisphere breeding season. So instead of being limited to 75 or 100 matings per year, Coolmore stallions could double that number, as well as the farm's fees, by going south in the month of July.

In the early 1980s, Coolmore, particularly Sangster, was involved in epic bidding battles with the Maktoums. They won some. They lost many. They got outspent. They overspent. Led by Magnier, the Coolmore guys dug in at the back of the arena looking very much like some ranch gang ready to rumble with the Maktoums. Their emotional stake in the Kris S. colt was greater, too, because Coolmore had already purchased Mr. P.'s Princess and another of her colts for $800,000 in a private deal with a breeder from Georgia named Harold Harrison.

Before the Kris S. colt flicked his ears back for the first time in the sales ring, Caldwell had serenaded the bidding past $1 million. The audible interplay of the spotters bounced rapidly off the arena's wood-paneled walls as the price ratcheted up in $100,000 increments from the Sheik to Coolmore to Lukas to the Thoroughbred Corporation past $2 million. Lukas threw in the towel at $2.9 million. The Thoroughbred Corp. dropped out, too. The bidding slowed as the Coolmore group waited to respond to the Sheik's bid. They huddled and spoke among themselves. "There's an awful lot of noise back there, but nothing is getting through," Caldwell singsonged as the price reached mid-$3 million.

The Coolmore crew bid again, but now they were running out of steam. Once a defiant knot in the back of the arena, now they stood with space between them, their shoulders hunched, anticipating defeat. When the price hit $3.9 million, the Coolmore guys turned and walked out of the arena. Caldwell brought down the hammer and applause erupted. "Let's wait for the colt to leave," Caldwell gently scolded. "That's one expensive piece of horseflesh."

It was a record price for the Keeneland September Sale. Harold Harrison was at home in Bethlehem, Georgia, when he received a phone call informing him of the windfall for the colt he had bred. At first, he thought his farm manager was kidding him, then he almost fainted. Finally, it occurred to him what had happened. "I thought

the Arabs and the Irish must have gotten into it again," said the
seventy-nine-year-old retired poultry-processing owner.

They had, and it was the 1980s all over again, but with a new,
important turn-of-the-century goal for Sheik Mohammed. As he
walked out to the barn to look at his new purchase, he repeated his
goal to win the Kentucky Derby and the other Triple Crown races.
He held his hands behind his back and explained how he had fallen
in love with the colt's pedigree and how the horse showed championship motion even while standing still. The Sheik spoke deliberately,
reaching for a clear explanation to an intuitive decision.

"It's just a feeling," the Sheik said. "It's not a car. It's more like
discovering the right woman."

*"I'm a compulsive buyer. You walk a good-looking saddle pony in
front of me and I want to buy it."*
—D. Wayne Lukas

The only thing more satisfying than winning Triple Crown races
for D. Wayne Lukas is spending money, most of it other people's, in
the sales ring. The problem early in this sale was that Lukas was bidding without his usual bottomless war chest. Bob and Beverly Lewis,
the owners of Charismatic and one of the trainer's primary owners,
were absent because Bob Lewis was at home recovering from heart
bypass surgery.

Lewis was a hard-nosed businessman who watched his equine
investments closely. He built a beverage company from a couple of
delivery trucks that he himself used to drive into one of the nation's
largest Budweiser distributorships. By splitting his horses between
Lukas and rival trainer Bob Baffert, Lewis made sure he kept the
upper hand in the owner-trainer relationship. He knew better than
to bestow blind trust and his money on anyone when it comes to a
horse. Lewis thought competition and accountability, like moving

units of beer, made for incentive-motivated managers. In turn, that meant more profit.

Who Lukas really missed here was Satish Sanan, the owner of Cash Run and the latest in a long line of colorful, committed, and extravagantly rich neophytes the trainer brought into the horse business. Sanan was still colorful and committed, but the week before the Keeneland sale, his Florida-based company, Information Management Resources Inc., was battered on Wall Street. Its stock dropped by nearly 33 percent in one day with volume more than ten times the daily average. As the sale opened, the company, which supplied computer and outsourcing and software services to firms to solve the Y2K problem, was trading at a fifty-two-week low and Sanan, chairman, CEO, and a major shareholder, was not in Kentucky.

They were missed—or at least their money was—especially by Lukas. The Indian-born, English-educated Sanan, along with his wife, Anne, had created Padua Stables and been among the leading American buyers of yearlings, spending more than $44 million on seventy-two of them since 1997.

The stress on Lukas was compounded by the fact that he had gone into business with Sanan on a 586-acre stallion, broodmare, and training ranch near Ocala, Florida, that so far had cost $15 million. Still, the trainer tried to put the best face on his top client's suddenly shaky finances. "The thing about that Satish is he wants to buy every damn horse that walks in the ring," Lukas said lightheartedly. "We have other orders to fill here, too."

But after the first day, sitting for hours with his ankle crossed over his knee and raising that index finger without landing a single horse, Lukas was frustrated. He was especially aggravated when Pletcher, his former assistant, outbid him at $1.3 million for a colt fathered by A. P. Indy. Pletcher was acting on behalf of a Canadian owner named Eugene Melnyk, who was stepping into the new-money void created by the absent Sanan.

"I hit him hard, too," Lukas said of his aggressive bidding. "I taught the kid too well."

The casual atmosphere and poor lighting in the Keeneland pavilion robbed Lukas of his majesty. There was no need for the tailored suits he wore at the racetrack. No need for the buckskin chaps and spurs he donned in the morning for training. Without the white ten-gallon hat and ever-present shades, Lukas blended in with the other horsemen in his jeans and western shirt. Even so, he still was the most recognizable figure in horse racing, though his famous coif was more salt than pepper now. He also had his reputation—for better or worse.

Still, he looked lonely without a big-time owner to squire around, like a high school prom king who had the crown but came to the dance alone. He had plenty of clients, but most had been with him for a long time and left it to him to make the purchases at the sales. One of his stalwart suppliers of racehorses, W. T. Young, kept him company, but the founder of Overbrook Farm owned the premier stallion of his generation, Storm Cat, who commanded a $300,000 stud fee, and Young was more of a seller than a buyer these days. Another long-time client, Bob Baker, along with his wife, Christina, and the couple's dog, Brandy, occasionally took a seat next to him, but mostly he was on the aisle alone.

When Lukas returned to the Marriott Griffin Gate after the first day, he dialed up some owners. "We need to turn up the volume and go after some horses," he told them.

Lukas was aware that his legend, if not notoriety, had as much to do with how he bought horses and trained owners as it did with his accomplishments on the racetrack.

He attributed to himself an "eagle eye" for sizing up horses, a gift he first discovered as a teenager growing up in Antigo, Wisconsin, ninety miles northwest of Green Bay. He would await the knackers bringing in wild horses from the Dakotas for slaughter to feed the minks raised in the region. He eyed the horses as they were funneled from the trucks to the pens, and bought the ones he deemed sound and visually appealing. He cleaned them up, marked them up, and sold them to local farmers. At the sales, Lukas acted as his own blood-stock agent, which not only was a tribute to his own skill but also allowed him to charge a 5 percent commission on the purchase of a horse. He studied the catalog and inspected each horse on the grounds. Lukas knew what he was looking for—he calls them box-office horses, superstars that can put a stable on the racing map.

He had a keen nose for box-office horses and enjoyed talking about the riches and reputation it had won him. He found his first winner as a quarter horse trainer twenty-six years ago in a gray mare named Native Empress whom he had claimed for $3,500. She was one of seven horses Lukas showed up with at Los Alamitos racetrack in California. Native Empress was a 5-year-old, which by quarter horse standards meant her peak earning years had passed. Lukas was broke and unknown, just in from El Paso, Texas, desperate to go big-time, which Los Alamitos is on the quarter horse circuit. For Lukas, Native Empress ran to the Los Alamitos horse-of-the-year award in 1973. The real accomplishment, however, was that he sold her eight times, the last for $250,000, but she always remained in his barn with him as the trainer.

Lukas's résumé is at once odd and pioneering for a Thoroughbred trainer. He earned a master's in education from the University of Wisconsin. He was a high school basketball coach and teacher, and also served as a graduate assistant coach for Wisconsin. He came to Thoroughbreds from the quarter horse ranks, which in class and cache is like leaping from being a door-to-door encyclopedia sales-man to mergers and acquisitions on Wall Street. In the 1980s, Lukas wove lessons from each of these phases into a personal narrative he delivered in an upbeat Tony Robbins–speak that resonated with the self-made money men in the Greed is Good and a Whole Lot of Fun decade.

He demonstrated his ingenuity and drive by reciting how, as part of his master's thesis, he designed a basketball shoe weighted with

BBs in its sole that, when worn in practice, would strengthen leg muscles and provide more lift when replaced with a regular shoe on game day. Lukas tested it on the Wisconsin freshmen team he was coaching. He patented it and sold it to the Converse shoe company, which eventually marketed it as the All Star Blue toe, and paid him about $20,000 in royalties. Now Lukas pitched a vision that borrowed from the lexicon of coaches—build a program, be a part of a team. He quoted everyone from UCLA basketball coach John Wooden to the Green Bay Packers' Vince Lombardi.

He pointed to his quarter horse days as credentials for his street smarts. From the Wisconsin fair circuits to the South Dakota straight-aways to the red clay of Oklahoma and Texas, he boasted that he had "traded horses with every thief in the world."

What Lukas ultimately was selling was his unwavering belief in himself. The proof that it worked was tangible in the arc of his ca-reer: climbing from $350 races in the hinterlands to the top of the na-tional quarter horse rankings and, in 1980, only his third year with Thoroughbreds, into the Triple Crown history books when a colt named Codex won the Preakness Stakes.

In this way, Lukas had always commanded the best tables in the turf clubs of racetracks. He dressed more elegantly than the own-ers. He stressed the positive. He talked anything from basketball to construction-cost overruns. He adhered to the Golden Rule of Retail: The customer is always right. Lukas was—still is—able to pull off a difficult seduction: He strokes the owners' egos but commands their respect as an equal.

There is a story often told around racetracks by trainers to show how owners are a cause of more headaches than any sore-legged bottom-level claimer. It involves the late Hall of Fame trainer Charlie Whitting-ham and the award-winning composer and longtime horse enthusiast Burt Bacharach. Whittingham was revered as the most astute horse-man ever to walk a backside. A former Marine, he was beloved as a wry, sometimes gruff, and always-there-for-you man's man who put his horses' health first. Whittingham did things his way.

One day, after one of Bacharach's horses ran poorly, the composer asked Whittingham for an explanation. The trainer was in no mood to offer one. So Bacharach allegedly blurted out, "Maybe he needs to get dewormed."

Whittingham was said to give the composer a long look and then reply, "Burt, when you write a terrible song, do I tell you to get your piano retuned?"

From the Lukas perspective, the composer, or any other owner, deserved an explanation. He respected Whittingham immensely, but he also believed that the retelling of that story, or any other that conveyed the prevailing sentiment that horse racing was an insular or insolent world, threatened to ruin the industry. He knew that owners by and large lose money, that the most successful ones win races at a 25 percent clip, and that trainers shouldn't compound those dismal numbers with poor communication or strained relations. Otherwise, owners leave the game.

Like it or not—and most traditional horsemen didn't—Lukas's fresh approach brought fancy, fresh money to the game. His roster of new clients in the 1980s demonstrated his broad appeal. In 1984, Lukas hooked Eugene V. Klein, an equally driven Bronx native who had evolved from "Cowboy Gene," pitching used cars on television for his southern California automobile empire, to part owner of the San Diego Chargers. Klein had sold his interest in the National Football League franchise, was flush with more than $50 million in cash, and was looking for action. Lukas also trained horses for W. T. Young, who founded W.T. Young Foods Inc., which manufactured peanut butter. Young's career as an industrialist was behind him, as was a stint in the Kentucky cabinet of Governor John Y. Brown, Jr. He had owned horses since the 1970s but had just established Overbrook as a breeding operation. Later, Lukas became the trainer for the rap artist Hammer, from Oakland, California, whose millions from gold records financed his family's Oaktown Stable.

They all had two things in common. They believed in Lukas and they spent a lot of money on horses. From 1985 to 1990, Lukas's owners bought 337 yearlings at a cost of $104.6 million, according to the Jockey Club's Equine Line computer service. By then, Lukas flew in his own corporate jet to racetracks across the nation to check on his 250 horses. He drove his Rolls-Royce to meet with owners. Lukas led the national training standings for earnings over ten consecutive years, from 1983 to 1992; he set a single-season earnings record, winning $17,842,358 in purses in 1988, the same year he captured his first Kentucky Derby with the filly Winning Colors. In 1990, he became the first trainer ever to earn more than $100 million when Criminal Type won the Pimlico Special.

"We were living in a fairy-tale land" is how Lukas explained that glorious stretch.

Lukas also was a principal in the most audacious moment in the history of any horse sale. In 1985, at the July Sale, there was a colt by Nijinsky II, a leading sire in England, that was rumored to be the certain sales topper. The Maktoums, a group led by Sangster—pre-Coolmore—that included the Greek shipping magnate Stavros Niarchos, and Lukas were all interested. Between his new clients and the success of his horses, Lukas was flush as well and had taken to investing with his owners in a percentage of the horses. So he formed his own syndicate with Gene Klein and two of his most loyal owners who had been with him in quarter horses, the Texas oilman Bob French and the Oklahoma rancher and builder Melvin Hatley.

"We were going to take on the British Empire," Lukas said.

The bidding started at $1 million, but within one minute jumped to $9 million, where it began to stall. When it inched past the previous top dollar paid for Snaafi Dancer or any horse in the world, a mumble went through the packed sales pavilion. "But none of us batted an eye," Lukas said. The numbers began increasing at intervals of $100,000 and $200,000 and reached $12.5 million. Bob French ripped a page out of his sales catalog and scrawled a note. He handed it to Hatley. Hatley grimaced and said he was out. Klein took a look.

"So Gene says, 'I'm out,'" Lukas related. "But he was hard of hearing and like most people who can't hear, he says it real loud and keeps repeating, 'I'm out. I'm out.' I look at the note and it says, 'Go to $15 million.' My mind starts racing. I started with four partners and 25 percent, and now two have dropped out and I'm in for half. I start trying to calculate what my three ranches in Oklahoma are worth."

Lukas bumped the bid $500,000 to $13 million in the hopes of scaring Sangster off. The Brits instead countered with another $100,000. "I couldn't pull the trigger," Lukas said. The hammer fell on the world-record price of $13.1 million.

"French looked at me and said, 'What did you do? We had them on the ropes,'" Lukas said. "My heart was racing. I was nearly out of breath."

The colt was subsequently named Seattle Dancer and went to the races only five times. He won twice, finished second once, and third once, earned $150,000, and was retired at the age of three, yet another example of the overwhelming odds owners face. Chew on this: In the past forty years of the Keeneland July Sale, just four sales toppers have earned their purchase price at the racetrack.

Not long after that, Lukas's free-spending fairy tale began to unwind and became a parable about living too large and too loud. When an Oklahoma City bank failed, Lukas had to pay $1.8 million to the FDIC to satisfy $4 million in loans he had received from the bank for a quarter horse partnership. Like many people of the 1980s on a roll, Lukas went public with a stock offering for Mid-American Racing Stable Inc., a company he ran to train and race quarter horses and Thoroughbreds. The new cash got him out of his hole, but after three years, that company failed, too, costing investors $4 million. In 1989, Klein was dying and sold his horses; Lukas lost his primary owner. When Calumet Farm went bankrupt in

1991, Lukas lost another $3.1 million on horses he had owned with Calumet.

It didn't take long for the Rolls-Royce to be traded in for a pickup truck, the private jet for commercial flights. Not long after, this financial backlash led to the savaging of his integrity and horsemanship. It came to a head in 1993 at the Preakness Stakes when Union City, a horse some believed was not sound, fractured a leg during the race. The colt did not survive.

It was W. T. Young's horse, and the owner wrote a letter to the *Racing Form* defending his trainer and insisting the colt was sound before the race. Still, other breakdowns by Lukas star horses followed. So the charges grew louder that the trainer was too hard on his horses.

The 1994 Preakness winner, Tabasco Cat, was retired with a leg injury at the age of four; the 1994 champion juvenile filly, Flanders, broke a bone in a Breeders' Cup race and was retired. The 1995 Preakness winner, Timber Country, strained leg tendons and was retired on the eve of the Belmont; and the 1995 Kentucky Derby winner, Thunder Gulch, fractured a cannon bone in his foreleg five months after the Derby at the Jockey Club Gold Cup and was also retired. In 1996, the Derby winner, Grindstone, was injured and retired while preparing for the Preakness.

When Charismatic fractured his foreleg a half mile from sweeping the Triple Crown in 1999, Lukas heard it again—though moments after the injury, the track veterinarians said the colt merely took a bad step and absolved the trainer of any responsibility. The following morning at his barn, Lukas's wife, Laura Pinelli, who also is a trainer, blasted reporters who asked about the injuries.

"Do you people think we are butchers?" she said.

Lukas, however, calmly answered every question. He's heard them often enough to have a stock reply: that his stable's large size increases the overall number of injuries and that his high profile brings greater scrutiny. That his owners are geared to winning the lucrative races for 2- and 3-year-olds, when horses are still developing and fragile.

Besides, he says, he knows some people don't like him, especially the news media.

This was in some instances true, but also disingenuous. Lukas didn't court the media so much as he held court. He was accessible, but he did the talking always aware of the myth he had built and was now trying to maintain. Along with his eagle eye for runners, he boasted that he never used a stopwatch to time his horses in the morning and never read the papers to see what anyone said about him. Amazingly, though, Lukas always knew how fast his horses worked and was quick to confront writers who were critical of him or his horses. He kept score, with the media as well as with other trainers.

In the previous year's Triple Crown, trainers Edward Plesa and Baffert had entered fillies in two of the races. Both had troubled trips—Three Ring in the Kentucky Derby and Excellent Meeting in the Preakness—and were never quite the same.

"If I had trained those horses, I would have been absolutely barbecued," Lukas said. "Just ripped up because, I guess, I rub people the wrong way."

He did, and in the gossipy and competitive circle of racing his name was among the first to pop up as a perpetrator for every sort of nefarious practice. It happened again here the week preceding the sale when Ray Paulick, the editor of the breeding industry's bible, a weekly magazine called *The Blood-Horse,* wrote a column about the potential for fraud at horse sales and a thesis that the horse business is not always a nice one.

His column was careful to point out that there were more honest people than dishonest ones. He quoted a passage from an article printed in 1926 by England's *Horse and Hound* addressing the issue to show historical perspective. He acknowledged that "no one wants to go on the record and talk about pre-sale deals, run-ups, and kickbacks and how unsuspecting owners can get fleeced. But anyone who maintains that these practices are not taking place in the Thoroughbred marketplace is out of step with reality . . ."

Paulick laid out how it worked. "Say, for example, there is a pre-sale agreement to buy a horse for $300,000, but the hammer price is pushed up to $400,000. The buyer, who doesn't know that his representative had an agreement with the seller to purchase the horse for $300,000, writes a check to the auction company for $400,000. After the auction company gets its 5% commission, it passes the balance on to the seller or sales agent. The seller, in turn, gives the person representing the buyer an amount equal to half the difference between $300,000 and $400,000. That's a nice piece of change. It also qualifies as fraud."

The article was generating great buzz throughout the sales pavilion, and Lukas's name was among the list of suspected violators. One of the trainer's strengths, however, is addressing issues head-on. No matter how combative his relationship with the media has been over the years, Lukas has always shown up to answer the hard questions. He has never ducked them. Lukas took this one on, too, outside the sales pavilion. He grimaced and was agitated because he was there to buy horses and his plans weren't going too well.

"No owner has ever accused me of that. I've had guys with me ten or twenty years. I work for them. I am as loyal to them as they are loyal to me. One of the things I'm proudest of is how many new guys, how much new money, I've brought into this game. They are the only people I have to answer to," he said. He started to walk away, but stopped.

"Look at my record. None of this ever gets said about guys who aren't on the top."

There was no doubt that Lukas was on top. His horses had won twelve Triple Crown races, he had trained an unprecedented twenty champions, and he was the only trainer in history to earn more than $200 million in purses. His barn was full of Triple Crown prospects. His purchase of the first-string Triple Crown horse, High Yield, was as much an example of his business sense as it was of his horsemanship.

The colt was out of Storm Cat, who was owned by Young's Overbrook Farm—a loyal Lukas client. To buy the $1.05 million colt, the trainer partnered the Lewises with Michael Tabor and Susan Magnier. The Lewises had owned Charismatic, the 1999 Derby and Preakness winner; Tabor and Magnier had owned Thunder Gulch, the 1995 Derby winner. So Lukas got two sets of owners a good deal on a top prospect, made a nice commission, and kept a potential Triple Crown horse in his own barn. The trainer had another box-office horse and another cut of the box office. Already High Yield had rewarded his owners by winning his first two races by a combined 13¾ lengths.

Now Lukas was thinking about the Triple Crown races coming up in 2001. He put on his wraparound shades and pulled his white cowboy hat down low on his head.

"I got to go shake some money loose and get some runners in my barn," he said.

"The one thing you can't tell about a horse is his heart. Don't worry about what you can see, you better worry about what you can't see."
                    —Keeneland cofounder Hal Price Headley

Team Scatuorchio sat on a bench under a canopy outside Barn 32. This is how they found More Than Ready at the 1998 Keeneland Sale. This is how they intended to find another Triple Crown horse.

Eddie Rosen, a mite of a man at five-foot-two, called out the roll. He was buried in catalogs and clipboards and leafs of paper that looked ready to blow away as he shuffled through them. He twitched and bounced on the bench.

"One-oh-six-eight?"

"Six-plus. Like her body," said Todd Pletcher.

"One-oh-eight-four?"

"Crooked," said J. J. Pletcher.

"One-one-four-four?"

"Six," answered the team's veterinarian, Scott Hay.

"I didn't like him, good or bad, but there's a higher chance he's bad," countered J.J.

"One-two-three-four—the El Prado?"

"Six-plus, smallish, I'll look at him again," promised Todd Pletcher.

"One-three-oh-six?"

"Not enough hind leg," said Todd.

"One-three-one-one?"

"Crooked—no use wasting any more time on that one," said J.J.

"One-three-seven-two?"

"Little filly, nice hind leg," Todd said.

"We're destined to get another Southern Halo," added J.J.

"Whenever they see Eddie coming, they put them on the corner to tempt him," jibed Hay.

"Then we're going to get One-one-seven-six. He just licked me in the face and sealed the deal," chimed in Jim Scatuorchio.

"One-three-three-five?"

"That's my filly. I love the silver tail. She looks like a merry-go-round horse," said Terry Scatuorchio. "We'll name her Carousel."

"Then I give her seven-plus," said J.J., winking.

On it went, with numbers followed by curt comments: "Swayed back, New York–bred," "plow horse," or—J.J.'s all-purpose dismissal—"J-A-H, just another horse."

Hay looked at his list. He shook his head. "You had a lot of bad ones on this list. I don't know how you do it, Eddie," he deadpanned.

This is how they had unearthed More Than Ready the previous September, as a team with each member assigned a role that reflects his personality.

Eddie Rosen was the pedigree guy. He traced genealogies in the same fidgety and determined manner that he attacked the *New York Times* crossword puzzle each morning. In pen, of course. He was a real estate lawyer in Freehold, New Jersey, who discovered the racetrack when his father, also a lawyer, accepted an interest in a racehorse in lieu of a fee. The mare, Craftiness, won some important New York stakes races in 1961 and Eddie, then sixteen, became a committed racetracker who read the *Racing Form* every day of his life. He was a very good race handicapper, but a cautious $2 bettor.

He saw angles and possibilities in a dense paragraph of a horse's past performances, but putting down big money at the betting window contradicted his disciplined mind-set. Consuming and processing information was excitement enough. He began devouring bloodlines and, by the time he was twenty, was talking daily with the Hall of Fame trainer P. G. Johnson about which well-bred horses might make for good claims. Rosen picked out a few racing prospects for himself at cheaper sales in Maryland.

Rosen maintained his law practice, but twenty years ago he began charging a bloodstock agent's fee, usually 5 percent of the purchase price. He made a little money and sometimes thought about doing this full-time, but for the time being contented himself with the rush of the hunt.

"When I'm focused, things will just leap off the page. It's like reading the Talmud" is how he explained it.

It was through an astute selection that Rosen sealed his friendship with Scatuorchio. They were racetrack buddies from Monmouth, for years meeting in the bar to exchange tips and shuttling between each other's boxes to needle the other about their failures. In 1995, Scatuorchio and ten other partners hired Rosen to identify a couple of colts that might someday develop into stallions. They needed pedigree, as well as an athlete.

Among the colts Rosen picked out was one by Storm Cat that the partners, under the banner of Phantom House Farm, named Tale of the Cat. They paid $375,000 for the colt, who won five races in nine starts. They sold him as a stallion for $11.6 million.

Suddenly, Rosen had a reputation that he solidified when he found More Than Ready. The angle that Rosen was playing then was that the sire, Southern Halo, would be regarded suspiciously after standing the past eight years in Argentina. Rosen always focused on the female side of the bloodline, figuring if the second and third dams threw multiple stakes winners then the odds were pretty good that their offspring would continue to do so.

The summer success of More Than Ready had not only given Rosen a boost but had legitimized Southern Halo as an American sire. The stallion's stud fee increased to $30,000 from $15,000, and a Southern Halo at this sale went for more than $700,000. Rosen was proud of his discovery, but shrugged off any talk that it was an act of genius.

"Jackie Mason plays the Catskills forty years before getting a show on Broadway and they call him a genius, too," he said.

What the pedigree consultant came up with on paper was gone over by Todd and J.J., then Hay took a look. It was a tricky business sorting through the cosmetics of a horse, identifying the natural stunners from the made-up beauty-pageant contestants.

Consignors worked all sorts of sleight of hand. Feed supplements and low-level exercise gave the horses well-defined muscle. Corrective hoof trimming and surgery could obscure their conformation flaws. A procedure called periosteal elevation, for example, can encourage legs to straighten through an incision in the periosteum, the elastic tissue that covers bone, promoting additional growth on that side of the bone. A cool stall away from the afternoon heat helped cure bleached or scorched coats. A little dishwashing liquid mixed into a bath could give the horses a healthy sheen. The Pletchers and Hay had seen it all.

Each had his own ranking system and applied it in ways that reflected his approach to horses. Theoretically, Todd worked on a scale of 1 to 10, though it seemed about every horse he graded was in the 6 or 6-plus range. He had other clients he was buying for as well, so he roamed the barns purposefully and alone. He had extensive notes in the margins of his catalog but doled the numbers gingerly. He kept expectations low and the fact that it was a crap shoot right on the surface. J.J. shared his skepticism and was loath to give out numbers.

He provided running commentary on every horse from memory, dismissing most of them, but was an enthusiastic advocate when he came upon a horse he fancied, as he had More Than Ready last year. He saw the colt first, noted how its legs were slightly turned out, but insisted he had found the group's real runner.

"He looked smart and had presence. He reminded me of probably my best horse, Uncool. I found him for $15,000 and he went on to win the Oaklawn Handicap. Sometimes they talk to me," J.J. said, altogether serious.

Only Hay's grades seemed clear-cut. He employed a 3 to 8 scale and gave detailed accounts of physical flaws and possible infirmities. These were aided by X rays of the sales horses that were on file at a medical repository on the grounds. They were of help, but before the team decided to bid on a horse, Hay was dispatched to vet the horse himself with fresh X rays and scopes. It wasn't cheap, about $500 per horse. Ultimately, the final decision was up to Todd Pletcher.

As the trainer now called off the Hip numbers of the prospects he wanted Hay to vet—five of them—Jim Scatuorchio sat silently while more of his money was being spent. He was the boss, but not really, and that offered up its own blend of frustration and helplessness. He was able to retire at fifty by being disciplined on Wall Street. He intended to approach the horse business the same way. He had come a long way from the night twenty-six years ago when he'd purchased his first horse, Shoot-n-Dash, for $3,000 after a night drinking red wine and eating pasta. The dinner led to a trip to Garden State Park and the impulsive buy of a low-level claimer he could barely see in a dark corner of a stall.

The Phantom House Farm partnership that yielded Tale of the Cat taught him a couple of things. First, that the real money was in stallion prospects. Second, that too many owners with opinions can take the fun out of the game. It had happened with his syndicate even as they were hitting the lottery with the $11.6 million sale of Tale of the Cat. He vowed then to make his next horse his own horse.

But Scatuorchio was in limbo at the horse sales. The businessman in him recognized he had nothing to contribute to the discussions about individual horses. It was why he had assembled this team. The action guy in him, however, was stymied. He wasn't the Sheik. He wasn't Bob Lewis. He was on a budget. Scatuorchio was willing to spend $1.1 million—or about twice the amount he did the year before—on three, four, or maybe even five horses. So far, however, he barely had the opportunity to put his hand in the air. Earlier in the afternoon, he went to the sales arena to bid on a Hennessy colt that his team valued at $300,000. He was inside only minutes before bounding back through the door with a sour look on his face.

"He was up to four hundred grand before I could take a sip of my beer," he said, his cup still nearly full.

Scatuorchio was wrestling with a common horse-owner conundrum. On one hand, you devise a plan and stick to it. On the other, it's not much fun not spending money in the sales ring. He had only to look to last year to show the advantages and dangers of both.

He patiently waited for More Than Ready and plucked the colt for a bargain $187,000. But he was too eager to buy a colt out of Mountain Cat and paid $200,000. Team Scatuorchio recognized their mistake soon enough to name this new colt the self-deprecating Advantage Overbrook. The significance? The horse was bred at W. T. Young's Overbrook Farm, which clearly got the better of the deal. The horse never won a race and was eventually sold.

Scatuorchio had more distressing things on his mind. Two days before the Hopeful Stakes, More Than Ready spiked a fever and had to be scratched from the race. Setbacks like that are common, but this one occurred at a most costly time. The owner was on the verge of selling the colt to stallion farms. The buzz of his five of five starts combined with his breeding suddenly made him a hot commodity among breeders like Coolmore. Scatuorchio had bids of $10 and $12 million with a $1 million bonus for each Grade I victory, as well as another

$1 million if More Than Ready captured titles such as being named Juvenile Champion.

Scatuorchio also would be allowed to race the colt through a 3-year-old Triple Crown campaign and keep the purse money. The breeders were betting on the come, and the owner was trying to do what he vowed he would. Run his horses like a business. No ego. No sentiment.

But Scatuorchio was still spooked by how difficult it was to follow this course. He remembered how he got news of the fever via cell phone while playing golf. It was September 2 and he was lining up a twelve-foot putt on the thirteenth hole when the phone rang. It was Todd Pletcher. His barn at Saratoga was surrounded by producers and cameramen working on a feature on the wonder colt for the race-day telecast of the Hopeful Stakes.

The colt had just returned from the track and Pletcher knew something was amiss. More Than Ready quietly stood in the corner of his stall. Besieged by reporters, Pletcher didn't want to show he was alarmed. As soon as he finished the interviews, the trainer called the veterinarian. More Than Ready's white cell count was up and he had a temperature. The vet advised waiting a day, but Pletcher wanted to scratch him even though he knew a great deal of money was at stake.

"My heart dropped to my feet," Scatuorchio remembered. "So many things went through my mind, but none of them were about the money. He had won five times for us, giving me my *first* win ever at Saratoga, and brought a lot of joy to so many people. Our families—Eddie's, Todd's, J.J's—had gotten so close. I was afraid the colt might never run again or, God forbid, die. When I got home and told Terry, she broke down and cried. It was shattering."

Just as quickly as it appeared, the fever disappeared. The next day More Than Ready attacked the feed barrel and nickered and pranced in his stall. Their minds, however, were made up: More Than Ready would not run in the Hopeful, and Scatuorchio delayed any sales deals until the winter. He remembered what the Hall of Fame trainer Leroy Jolley had told him one morning alongside the fence at the Saratoga training track.

"You do right by that horse. He's a special one," Jolley had said.

Scatuorchio did. But it was not an altogether comfortable choice. He knew a dispassionate business approach toward More Than Ready wasn't going to work. The colt was now his third child and damn well better be his first Kentucky Derby horse. He had broken his rule, but he swore never to do it again. He sat there under the canopy and listened to his team talk horses and grew more frustrated that they had nothing to show for it.

Then his cell phone rang. It was his broker. Scatuorchio leaped to his feet, grateful for something to do.

"Sell fifteen thousand shares," he told him. Then he looked at his wife, Eddie Rosen, Scott Hay, and the Pletchers. He smiled.

"There's some things I know about. Besides, I got to pay for these damn things."

Chapter 4

THE SYNDICATE: SPREADING THE RISK

LATE SEPTEMBER 1999

"In this game, only the fools are positive of anything."
—*The late Humphrey S. Finney,*
former head of the Fasig-Tipton auction company

Barry Irwin was aware of Finney's pronouncement; he had even quoted a version of it himself during his eighteen years as a racing journalist for publications like *The Blood-Horse* and the *Daily Racing Form*. But sometimes he couldn't help himself, especially since he has a five-star track record as an investment banker in horseflesh, and Irwin believes in his own instincts with a client list that is accustomed to his being right. Ready to ignore the words of Humphrey S. Finney, Irwin was about to put pen to paper and write a remarkable letter on behalf of an obscure colt named The Deputy.

Granted, Irwin, fifty-six, was no longer a journalist chained to objectivity. In 1987, he hooked up with another Californian, a turf writer and longtime friend, Jeff Siegel, to do what you do when you've spent too many years handicapping and writing about horses. You try to figure out a way to own and race them. The pair had one undeniable strength—know-how; and one potential obstacle—not enough financial wherewithal to play where they wanted to, which was at the highest level of the game. So they decided to syndicate racehorses, which means find them, manage them, and own them with the help of other people's money. They understood not everyone had the cash, or time, or the knowledge and passion to ferret out prospects at the Keeneland sales. Most of these people didn't know what to look for in a horse's training or how to find the races that had the best chance of winning a maximum purse. But Irwin and Siegel had been around tracks long enough to know there were plenty of people who'd like a piece of a racehorse that could compete in the best races with the richest purses and most prestige. Stakes races. So they hit on the idea of forming Limited Liability Corporations for each horse, selling ownership interests of anywhere from 2½ to 10 percent. They found the horses, bought them, marked up the price, and collected a management fee.

Irwin and Siegel looked the part of racetrack swells, with their tweed European touring caps and natty sweaters and sport coats. Over the years, they had built followings on various radio and television shows in California. They had a combined sixty years of experience as horse-players, public handicappers, and insiders in the game. They were once journalists, after all, with access to the best trainers, owners, and breeders in the sport, access they used to shake down the sharpest minds in the business. They understood how the press worked and had a flair for attracting it. They called their syndicate Team Valor and spelled out right there on the letterhead what they were about: "Identifiers of Class, Managers of Talent, Providers of Sport."

Most important of all was that they lived up to their letterhead. Of more than 156 starters from 1987 to 1999, Team Valor had won stakes races with 41 of them, and 5 had brought home Grade I victories, the most coveted at the highest level. Their horses averaged one stakes win for every four starts and had earned more than $21 million in purses. Team Valor had yet to capture a Triple Crown victory, but in three tries the syndicate had never finished less than third. In each instance, Irwin and Siegel discovered and purchased the horses in unlikely places.

In 1997, they found Captain Bodgit in Maryland competing on the minor Mid-Atlantic circuit, bought him for $500,000, and then syndicated him for $540,000. The colt had an ugly bowed tendon in the lower left portion of his left front leg that could be spotted at fifty feet. But respected Kentucky veterinarian Alex Harthill determined it was more unsightly than fragile. They told potential partners of the ailment up front and still managed to put together thirty-two dreamers who included a retired congressman from Delaware, a radio talk-show host from Wisconsin, an engineer from Hawaii, and a Liberian ambassador. The partnership was rewarded when Captain Bodgit won the Grade I Florida Derby, the Grade II Wood Memorial, and lost the Kentucky Derby by a head to Silver Charm, as well as finishing third in the Preakness. Team Valor followed that up the next year by running third in the Belmont Stakes with a Texas-bred named

Thomas Joe who had run previously in the $25,000 claiming ranks, or in the tenement district of horse racing.

Like everyone else in the sport, Irwin and Siegel became intoxicated with the Triple Crown races. In 1999, Irwin, the syndicate's president, moved to Versailles, Kentucky, in the heart of bluegrass country to focus on winning these classic races for 3-year-olds. Team Valor's strategy, however, remained the same: Buy wholesale; sell retail; find a racing prospect, not a breeding one.

"We prize heart first, talent second, conformation third, and pedigree last. We are always after the athlete, not the printed page." Irwin often waxed with the pithy dramatics that made for good sound bites.

What was indisputable about Team Valor's track record was that Irwin and Siegel had many friends in the Thoroughbred business. They were constantly being tipped off to look over horses found in dark stalls in remote locales of the racing world. In fact, The Deputy, the colt Irwin was about to memorialize in a letter, had much in common with the syndicate's first Triple Crown horse, My Memoirs.

In 1992, Team Valor had bought My Memoirs in England just five weeks before the Belmont Stakes. He had won only three of eight starts in Great Britain. On videotape, however, My Memoirs looked impressive when he charged from last place to first in the stretch.

The syndicate purchased My Memoirs too late to nominate the colt to the Triple Crown for the nominal fee of a couple hundred dollars. So Team Valor paid a $50,000 supplement—or late fee—to get him a starting spot in the Belmont Stakes.

Three days before the race, Irwin and Siegel flew the horse seventeen hours to New York. The partners knew My Memoirs had to run at least third to make money. Bettors weren't backing him; they sent My Memoirs off at 18–1.

But in the stretch of the 1½-mile race, My Memoirs displayed a late kick and almost caught the favorite, A. P. Indy, who was subsequently voted Horse of the Year. My Memoirs lost by three quarters of a length, but he earned Team Valor a $168,256 purse.

In September 1999, Irwin believed he had found another off-the-beaten-path bargain in plenty of time to prepare for all three Triple Crown races. The Deputy was a 2-year-old Irish-bred who was bought for a paltry $24,000 when sold as a yearling. The colt had won only once in five starts. Still, Irwin believed.

He batted out a letter, announcing Team Valor's intention to syndicate The Deputy for $500,000, and mailed it to 150 clients.

It began: "From time to time—whether in conversation with a prospective client or in an interview with the press—the question that inevitably and invariably arises is as follows: 'The big horses you've had, do you know they are going to be the top ones when you buy them?' The answer is 'yes.' A big, resounding YES."

He continued describing the look and performance of The Deputy. Irwin admitted the colt had yet to win in a stakes race. He reasoned that the colt's England-based trainer took his time with young horses and that was why The Deputy was described in European racing publications as carrying a "surplus of flesh." Irwin wrote that The Deputy didn't like the soft footing on the grass—virtually all of European races are run on the turf—and "the tricky up-and-down-course of Epsom Downs." Irwin said the conditions thwarted the colt's best effort.

Irwin wasn't afraid to let some purple blotch his prose. The Deputy was "our hero"; his pitch on behalf of the colt was "bullish" and "bold." Eventually, the president of Team Valor got to the point. Just like with My Memoirs, Irwin had discovered something extraordinary on videotape. It was the effort The Deputy displayed in his most recent race on September 8, 1999, the $330,000 St. Leger Yearling Sales Stakes in Doncaster.

"The Deputy finished third, beaten by a nose and a head, after racing behind early and still being 10th, some 7 or 8 lengths back with less than 2 furlongs to go," Irwin wrote. "He made an electric run from along the rail to reach a contending position, then exploded in the final 100 yards to just miss. A step past the wire he was a winner. If he had stayed straight instead of drifting over to find his competitors, he may have won by as much as a length . . ."

Even better, Irwin had gleaned from the English racing publications that a "huge bet" had been laid on The Deputy. The colt was running just five days after winning his first race—a terribly quick turnaround—against a field of twenty at the distance of six furlongs. Somebody knew something. Now so did Irwin.

"For Team Valor's purposes, the colt is ideal," Irwin concluded to his clients. "He has the tactical speed to track, press and pounce routing in America," which meant The Deputy could race at distances beyond a mile. "And in the Doncaster effort, he showed the turn of foot possessed by the world's top Milers."

If anyone doubted his ardor for the colt, Irwin announced he was en route to England as his clients were receiving this letter. Irwin did indeed fly to London on September 24, 1999. He drove to Newmarket to look at The Deputy. He circled him once. "I looked at him for maybe forty-five seconds," Irwin said. "He looked like a Triple Crown athlete."

Irwin made the deal, got back in his car, and returned to Heathrow International Airport. Meanwhile, back in Versailles, Kentucky, his wife, Becky, was filing the partnership.

In just five days, The Deputy had fifteen new owners under the Team Valor umbrella. Irwin's clients believed, too. One of them was a new partner named Gary Barber. He asked for and received 50 percent of The Deputy. Barber was a native of South Africa and a movie producer. He was already having a good year. His latest movie was on its way to grossing $650 million and being nominated for an Academy Award.

It was named, fittingly enough, *The Sixth Sense*.

Chapter 5

FUSAICHI PEGASUS: THE FLYING HORSE

OCTOBER 1999

LOS ANGELES

"Never say anything about a horse until he's been dead for ten years."
—Charlie Whittingham, the late Hall of Fame trainer

They met for lunch at the Peninsula Hotel in Los Angeles to discuss an extraordinary colt, one that had cost $4 million at the 1998 Keeneland July Sale; a colt that had seduced some of the sharpest minds in horse racing with its almost human curiosity. This quality became apparent minutes after he dropped out of his mother, a mare named Angel Fever, on the night of April 12, 1997, and shimmied to his chest to eyeball everyone in his stall at the Stone Farm near Paris, Kentucky. A colt that, despite not running in a single race, his owner and trainer believed had prodigious talent. Enough talent for them to feel certain he was not only a Kentucky Derby horse, but surely a winner of the famous race on the first Saturday in May.

The colt's name was Fusaichi Pegasus. He was owned by Fusao Sekiguchi, a freethinking Japanese entrepreneur. The owner named the horse by adding the suffix "-ichi," which meant "number one" in Japanese, to his own first name. Just to make sure everyone knew that he expected greatness, Sekiguchi attached the name of the winged horse of myth, Pegasus, to the colt's. The owner was in Los Angeles for lunch to hear how his trainer, Neil Drysdale, intended to fulfill the owner's prophecy of greatness for his high-dollar purchase. Since Sekiguchi did not speak English, Drysdale explained through an interpreter that Fusaichi Pegasus would continue to be handled patiently, that the colt was eccentric, high-strung, and given to fits of boredom. Fusaichi Pegasus was obstinate even when asked to do things that he had done before. The colt would be lightly raced, perhaps starting only once as a 2-year-old and not beyond the sprint distance of six-and-a-half furlongs, which was short of seven eighths of a mile.

This cautious approach to preparing for the Triple Crown not only contradicted conventional wisdom, but also was contrary to historic precedent. Wayne Lukas, for example, brought eventual 1999 Kentucky Derby winner Charismatic to Churchill Downs with fourteen starts, seven of them as a 2-year-old, and one at a distance of a mile.

The last colt who had not run as a 2-year-old and won the Derby was Apollo in 1882. The last Derby winner who ran as a 2-year-old but did so without a victory was Proud Clarion in 1967. Still, Drysdale told Sekiguchi that Fusaichi Pegasus was the trainer's boss, not the owner, and that he'd listen to what the colt told him and do the right thing—by the horse, not the owner. This wasn't hubris or a threat.

At fifty-two, Drysdale was among the most accomplished horsemen in the sport. He had trained five champions and consistently was at the top of the national trainer standings for purses earned. He was thought to be destined for Thoroughbred racing's Hall of Fame. But in twenty-five years of conditioning, Drysdale had saddled only one horse in a Triple Crown race, a colt named A. P. Indy, who won the Belmont Stakes in 1992.

The defining moment of Drysdale's career, however, occurred five weeks earlier than that Belmont victory when the trainer scratched the heavily favored A. P. Indy from the Kentucky Derby on the morning of that race. The colt had bruised his foot. A. P. Indy was owned by Tomonori Tsurumaki; the Japanese businessman was in Louisville to see A. P. Indy race in person for the first time. The owner's presence at the most famous race in the world did not sway Drysdale. He decided the horse should not run and scratched him.

Drysdale skipped the Preakness, too, before returning to the racetrack and winning the Belmont Stakes. In the fall, after A. P. Indy won the Breeders' Cup Classic—a 1¼-mile race that is often the first time the 3-year-olds take on the best older horses—he captured the Eclipse Award as Horse of the Year. Drysdale had demonstrated caution before in his career: He scratched his first high-profile horse, Forceten, on the morning of the 1975 Travers Stakes.

But a Triple Crown race is different. It's the one time of the year that the sport transcends the world of horse enthusiasts and gains a national audience. What Drysdale did by scratching A. P. Indy was like keep-ing Reggie Jackson, Mr. October, on the bench during the World Series.

They were, perhaps, a mismatched pair, Drysdale and Sekiguchi. The trainer was an Englishman, a son of a British Royal Marine of-ficer, who studied at the University of Barcelona and took a circui-tous route to southern California and Thoroughbred racing. He began in Florida, training show horses, which is as much about appearance as it is precise performance. Drysdale switched to Thoroughbreds for the money, working under John Hartigan at Tartan Farms, which bred great horses like Dr. Fager and Ta Wee. It was Hartigan who gave him a memorable lesson on how serious the horse business was.

Late for work one morning, the then twenty-something Drysdale was pulled into Hartigan's office and issued an ultimatum: Either "work at work or play at play," and if Drysdale chose the latter, "Don't let the door hit your behind on the way out."

Drysdale stayed at Tartan two years before moving to Argentina and then Venezuela to manage a stud farm. By 1969, however, he was back in America as assistant to Roger Laurin at Belmont Park. The following year, Drysdale moved to California and went to work for a man who would shape his philosophy both in training horses and in handling owners: Charlie Whittingham.

At lunch with Sekiguchi, Drysdale demonstrated what he had learned in the four years under his mentor. It was the same thing Whittingham was taught sixty years earlier by his mentor, another Hall of Fame trainer named Horatio Luro. "Patience. You've got to let the horse tell you when he's ready," Whittingham once explained of the Argentinean's influence. "Listen to anyone else, and you're in trouble."

By the time Whittingham died in April 1999, he had won three Eclipse Awards as the best trainer in North America, as well as more than 2,400 races and 650 stakes. He led all trainers in purse money seven times and had trained eight champions. But it was Whitting-ham's presence and principles on the backside that made him per-haps the most beloved trainer on the West Coast. He was tall and lanky, with a clean enough pate to earn the nickname the "Bald Eagle," and he was utterly devoted to his horses. He got to the barn before dawn, stayed until dark, fed his horses peppermints, and treated them like they were his children.

Whittingham had little use for the Kentucky Derby and the Triple Crown, believing that too many good young horses were sacrificed to the grueling preparation. The trainer had tried the race in 1958 and 1960 with Gone Fishing and Divine Comedy, who finished eighth and ninth respectively. So it was startling when Whittingham returned to Louisville in 1986 with a colt named Ferdinand who didn't win his first race until his fourth start as a 2-year-old.

Ferdinand was a bull of colt whom Whittingham worked long and hard and fast. He gave the mount to jockey Bill Shoemaker, then fifty-four and already the winner of more than 200 stakes races for Whittingham. Still, Ferdinand was sent off as a 17–1 long shot. In a ride for the ages, Shoemaker and Ferdinand ran a half mile in last place before slipping and cutting past fifteen other horses and on to a two-length victory. At seventy-three, Whittingham had his first Derby triumph.

"It took me twenty-six years to get here because I said I wouldn't come till we had a good horse," he told the horse's owner, Elizabeth Keck, in the winner's circle. "We've got one now."

Three years later, in 1989, Whittingham became the oldest trainer to win a Derby when Sunday Silence beat Easy Goer in the first of two stirring Triple Crown race duels between great rivals. In the Preakness, Sunday Silence caught Easy Goer in the stretch and outlasted him by a nose to move one victory away from the Triple Crown. But at the Belmont, the New York–based Easy Goer turned the tables and routed Sunday Silence by eight lengths.

"I'm trying to feel bad," Whittingham said afterward. "But they handed me this check for $1 million, the horse is fine, and I plan on waking up tomorrow. Anyway, we beat the other horse two out of three. We just couldn't handle him on his home ground."

Drysdale didn't have the charisma or knack for witty pronouncements that his mentor did, but he had an impish smile and a way of holding his head sideways with his nose angled up that made him look constantly deep in thought and battling puzzlement. He intimidated most at first meeting—especially during the mornings at the track when he was focused on his horses. The stone face he put on in the morning as he hurried between his barn and the racetrack with his horses turned the cheeky smile into a frown. He was absolutely absorbed by how they moved, even if a colt or filly was just grazing on a grass patch in front of the barn. This was his craft, his profession, and it cast a spell on him that sometimes was impenetrable. Drysdale had little patience for the media attention that was part of campaigning a talented horse in the big races. One of Whittingham's many famous bits of wit and wisdom—any funny racetrack axiom that carried a bit of truth was universally attributed to this trainer—was something he often told Drysdale.

"I taught you all that you know, but not all that I know," he'd say.

His protégé took this one better. He despised talking about horses, his or anyone else's. Drysdale was unfailingly polite, but routine questions about a horse's training were more often than not met with a blank stare, or an earnest "I don't understand the question." The former English teacher, and perhaps the Englishman in him, demanded precise language.

Even then, his reticence was apparent as he'd toss off a monotone answer or two, then, with a warm smile to mask the impending abruptness, he'd ask, "Do you have your sound bites?"

None of it was about arrogance. It was perhaps about embarrassment; Drysdale either didn't know how or didn't care to talk about his lifetime passion. He was uncomfortable reverting to the usual blend of racetrack fatalism and clichés—"You know, one out of every six phone calls in this game is bad news," or (another Whittinghamism) "Horses are like strawberries, they can go bad at any time."

He also didn't want to sound like one of those box-office stars on *Inside the Actor's Studio,* soulfully speaking about his craft. Drysdale couldn't explain exactly what he was doing with a horse; if he could, he didn't believe you would understand it anyway.

In 1992, when A. P. Indy was in Louisville preparing for the Derby, the trainer tried to extricate himself from a media session like Whittingham might have. "I don't mind what you write," he deadpanned, "as long as you have the grammar correct."

When it showed up in print as if the trainer actually meant it, Drysdale was amused but even more wary of the media.

It was a shame, because the trainer is a warm conversationalist on topics beyond horse racing. He was seldom without a book and his reading list included anything from Michael Ondaatje's *The English Patient* to mysteries, including, yes, fellow Englishman Dick Francis's racetrack stories, which he favored for cross-country air travel: "I'm finished when the wheels hit the ground."

He was a gourmand, wine connoisseur, and frequent habitué of Venice Beach restaurants, which he argued were some of the finest in the world. He kept his home in Playa del Rey—because he claimed it was "the last funky beach town in L.A."—and his stable at nearby Hollywood Park on the edge of South Central Los Angeles near the airport rather than the more pastoral and suburban Santa Anita Park to be closer to the city's playhouses and movie theaters. He spoke Spanish, traveled the world, and was fairly successful at leaving his worries about his horses back at the barn.

His heart also beat closer to the surface than he normally showed. On the day Whittingham died, Bill Christine, the turf writer for the *Los Angeles Times,* reached Drysdale in his barn for a reaction. The trainer hadn't heard the news of his friend and mentor's death and broke down in tears. Unable to speak, he also kept his silence at a memorial service for Whittingham, which was a warm, rollicking mélange of funny stories and poignant moments in the life of an American original.

"It was a great service, a great party, a real celebration of Charlie. But I didn't dare say anything. I couldn't have handled it," Drysdale said.

Sekiguchi, the man sitting across from him at lunch, was a mystery. In his sixties, he wore a ponytail and dark, round glasses. With his bold charcoal pinstripes or the yellow leather jacket he often wore, the owner projected a character out of a Hollywood classic, perhaps from the Los Angeles of *Chinatown* or the Las Vegas of *Casino.*

No one in America knew much about him. Not Drysdale, who was meeting the owner for the first time. Not John Ward, a third-generation Kentucky horseman who was the owner's consultant in America and the man who led Sekiguchi to the $4 million colt. Not Arthur Hancock III, who bred and sold Fusaichi Pegasus and who had nicknamed him "Superman" almost as soon as he was born that night in Kentucky.

In Japan, however, Sekiguchi was notorious as a self-described rebel, which was not necessarily a good thing in a culture that values teamwork and anonymity. There, he is a member of a loose class of men who are referred to as "bubble gentlemen," a label attached to those who built dizzying individual fortunes in the booming 1980s. It also implies that the source of one's wealth is never quite clear, though signs of it are everywhere.

Sekiguchi collected modern and vintage racing cars, and two of them—a blue 1935 Bugatti and a blazing-red Formula 1–style machine built by his own engineers—grace the lobby of his new company, Venture-Safenet, near Tokyo Bay. He orchestrated extravagant spectacles to welcome new employees to his company, a high-tech temp service that sends engineers and computer programmers to other companies. In 1998, he imported matadors from Spain and bulls from Mexico to stage the country's first bullfight. Another year he rented a disco, piled 100 million yen up on the stage, and exhorted his new employees to "aim high and be a player."

In 1991, Sekiguchi wrote a book titled *Challenge to Japan Dream* that became a best-seller. It offered a vision for success that challenged the country's traditional approach of devoting a career to one company as the only way to succeed. The book stated that even the world's most formidable corporations needed help from outside problem solvers.

The example for the book was Meitec, the business he started in 1974 that, much like his current venture, trained engineers and then leased them out to companies.

Sekiguchi had been involved in horse racing in Japan since the early 1970s, but by the 1990s he decided to head down the high-dollar horse path. He wanted to conquer American racing. The Japanese owner has been fascinated and appreciative of Western culture since the age of ten when American GIs occupied his hometown in the Kobe area as World War II was coming to an end. They fed him. They told him stories about the States. They told him about the Kentucky Derby. In 1992, Sekiguchi donated $2 million to the U.S.O. Later, at a dinner the organization held on his behalf at the Madison Hotel in Washington, D.C., Sekiguchi insisted that a glass of milk and a Hershey bar be placed at each setting. When it was his turn to speak, he remembered the American soldiers who had confounded his community's expectations by bringing food and aid to his town.

"He said what he remembered most was the milk and chocolate," recalled General Bill Dyke, a U.S.O. board member at the time. "So he asked everybody to raise the glass of milk and toast their kindness. There wasn't a dry eye in the place."

Sekiguchi had met and befriended Dyke in 1987 when the general was commander of the U.S. Army in Japan. Dyke was not surprised when Sekiguchi asked him to find a representative in Kentucky so he could establish a U.S. presence in horse racing. The general, now retired and an international business consultant, introduced him to John Ward and his wife, Donna, successful breeders and trainers.

In 1995, Sekiguchi came to central Kentucky where the Wards showed him horse farms, the Kentucky Derby Museum, and, most memorably, feted him at sundown with Japanese food on the lawn of the famed Calumet Farms overlooking the gravestones of seven Kentucky Derby winners—including 1941 Triple Crown winner Whirlaway.

"He was moved," Ward said. "He believes in history and tradition. But he also had a game plan; he wanted his horse business in five years to be at the top."

It was an expensive climb that cost him the business he had built. Shortly after Sekiguchi won the 1996 Japan Derby with a horse named Fusaichi Concorde, the Meitec board did something rarely done in the staid Japanese business culture—they ousted him. The reason? His love for expensive horses.

The new president, Mitsuo Otsuki, told a leading newspaper, the *Asahi Shimbun,* that Sekiguchi had told him he wanted "to invest one billion yen or more in the horse racing business." The dispute was tied up in the Japanese courts, but a lawyer for Meitec said that Sekiguchi was in effect draining the company of its resources.

"Mr. Sekiguchi was earning 27,500,000 yen per month," said Junichi Tsutsumi, which is approximately $250,000 a month at today's exchange rates and three quarters of what the entire board of directors was making.

The timing was unfortunate—Sekiguchi had just bought seven yearlings for $5.75 million at the Keeneland sale. Now he was forced to return them for resale and a promise that he'd make up any shortfall the resale incurred. This was substantial, but he did pay it off.

So Sekiguchi was hardly embarrassed when he returned to Keeneland in July 1998 with Ward. Sekiguchi gave the bloodstock consultant a mandate and a promise: Find the single best horse in the sale and he would buy it no matter the cost.

Ward didn't even have to roam the sales grounds. He knew the colt he wanted. He'd been keeping an eye on him from the day he was born. The colt was a son of Mr. Prospector out of a Danzig mare named Angel Fever and had been the brightest jewel of Hancock's farm from the moment he was born that April night the previous year.

At the time, Mr. Prospector was the all-time U.S. leader by progeny earnings and stakes winners and was so sure a sire that thirty of his offspring had commanded $1 million or more as auction yearlings. Ward had heard from Arthur Hancock that this foal surpassed his royal pedigree and was supernaturally put together with smarts to rival his cover-boy looks.

"He has the look of eagles. If he can't run, I'll never make another prediction," Hancock told Ward and anyone else who stopped by the farm.

Now, this was a noteworthy label to be attached to a foal by a man who had learned the business from his father, Bull Hancock, who founded North America's preeminent breeding operation, Claiborne Farm—where Nasrullah begat Bold Ruler who begat Secretariat and . . . all of whom had made a perpetual impact on American racing.

Hancock once described his younger self as a "a freewheeling, hard-drinking, guitar-picking, bar-brawling, skirt-chasing fool," which were all attributes that had led a committee, named by his father, to choose his successor after his death, to pass over him in favor of younger brother Seth, in 1973. But Arthur Hancock abandoned every vice except guitar playing and started his own operation, Stone Farm, down the road from Claiborne.

There, he bred 1982 and 1989 Derby winners Gato del Sol and Sunday Silence. Neither of whom, he insisted, had left him in as nearly as much awe as this Mr. Prospector baby.

"You'd come out into the field and this colt would always come out to investigate. I'd scratch him under the jaw. He'd like it and follow me around for some more. He was fearless, too. When he was a yearling, we had twenty-seven inches of snow fall on us. I'm bringing all the horses in and they can't wait to get to the barn," Hancock said. "By the time I got to Superman, the snow had drifted waist deep. But he wasn't in a hurry to go anywhere. He was studying that snow—wading through it, sticking his nose in it. He was as curious as I'd ever seen a horse."

Early on, Ward was skeptical. Sure, the foal was impressive visually, with the straightest legs he had ever seen in forty years of looking at tens of thousands of foals. Still, Mr. Prospector had a reputation for producing babies with legs Radio City Rockettes would kill for, only to go off center as they grew into yearlings and 2-year-olds.

"He was about as perfect as you could get. But I was afraid maybe those straight legs might go haywire as he got older," Ward confessed.

As the months passed, Ward kept finding reasons to go by Hancock's Stone Farm and take a look at Superman. His legs remained straight. Ward had a chance to buy him as a weanling; Hancock asked $1.5 million, or half of him for $750,000. Ward, among the many others who passed, thought the asking price was too high.

Ten months later at the Keeneland Sale, however, that price looked like a bargain. Sekiguchi came to Lexington and went straight to the barn to see the horse Ward had told him about: Hip No. 228. He wasn't there long. "When I looked at him, I felt this enormous power, and that's when I made up my mind," Sekiguchi remembered.

Later that night in his hotel room, Sekiguchi asked Ward what it would take to get the Mr. Prospector colt as his own. The consultant ticked off a detailed analysis of the colt's rich bloodlines, flawless appearance, and vouched-for smarts. He was probably worth $2.2 million, Ward told him, but because of the buzz surrounding the animal, Sekiguchi would probably have to pay $3.2 to $4 million.

"I want this horse," Sekiguchi said. "I don't care how much he costs."

Sekiguchi wasn't alone in his desire for the colt. Lukas had put together another one of his consortiums—this time he partnered Satish Sanan and the Coolmore group. Ward sat out the bidding until it reached $2 million. He countered each of the Lukas groups' bids as the competing interests volleyed briskly back and forth and the price passed $3 million.

The poker game was in full swing. Lukas was ready to pull the plug, but Sanan and the Coolmore contingent of John Magnier, Michael Tabor, and Demi O'Byrne wanted to keep going. While they caucused between each bid, Ward barely looked at Sekiguchi, sitting at his elbow, and kept upping the ante. When Ward bid $4 million, he glanced at his owner, who nodded to say keep going. Lukas saw the exchange, too. He told his group it was time to get out because Sekiguchi would keep going until he got the colt.

"I would have gone to $5 million," Sekiguchi confirmed. "This was the only horse we were interested in. My first impression when I saw him was an inspiration."

Drysdale was in the sales pavilion that evening, had liked the look of the colt, but had no indication that he would ever train the horse. In July 1998, he didn't know Sekiguchi or his racing plans. The owner got back on a plane to Tokyo. The Wards took the colt to break, first at their farm in Lexington, then to their winter base in Palm Beach, Florida.

The colt, now named Fusaichi Pegasus, didn't show up in Drysdale's barn until March 27, 1999. Ward picked Drysdale because Sekiguchi wanted the colt to compete in the United States, and a West Coast training ground made more sense for an owner based in Tokyo. And Drysdale had already demonstrated that he had the patience and communication skills to handle an absentee Japanese owner with his work on A. P. Indy for Tomonori Tsurumaki. Owners may not have liked everything he told them, but Drysdale did make the phone calls and send the faxes that kept them in the information loop.

Finally, Ward discovered for himself what Hancock had told him— Fusaichi Pegasus was an uncommonly smart horse, which in turn made him eccentric, frustrating, and difficult to train. He needed very special handling.

In Florida, sometimes he'd refuse to leave his stall; other times he would bolt through hedges. Ward cured these tendencies by assigning a mare named Beautiful Pleasure as his escort. She was no ordinary saddling pony but a lightning-quick runner who had earned well over a million dollars and, after winning the 1999 Breeders' Cup Distaff, was voted the nation's champion mare.

"There wasn't a mean bone in his body, but he was a dominant personality. He liked to sleep late and roll around in his stall. When he got to the track he was exceptionally brilliant and did what was asked of him right from the beginning. But he hated repetition," Ward said. "He was like a gifted child that you put in public school. He knew his ABC's and wanted to do something else. You couldn't be heavy-handed with him. You needed to outwait him and more often than not outsmart him. Hell, he was a classy horse, and his attraction to Beautiful Pleasure showed he liked classy company. He was a challenge."

Not only had Drysdale earned his nickname "The Turtle" by embracing a deliberate regimen, he had won many races with horses that kindly could be called head cases. The trainer was as innovative a horse shrink as there was. The first four months of the trainer's relationship with the colt were merely introductory sessions, with Drysdale asking Fusaichi Pegasus for little beyond growing and acclimating to new environs. The observation period also had been predicated on physical reasons. The colt had some minor surgery conducted on his ankles, work Drysdale had characterized as a routine cleaning out of the joints, though in the following months of the Triple Crown trail, it would become one of the many sources of intrigue surrounding the wonder horse.

By August, however, Drysdale was comfortable with the colt on his couch and moved him to a training facility in San Luis Rey Downs in Bonsall, California. Fusaichi Pegasus, he discovered, was high-strung, impatient, and needed to be occupied. So the trainer took the unusual step of putting a rider on his back twice a day, once in the morning and again in the afternoon, for walks or jogs. But it wasn't until August 17 and the colt's first workout that Drysdale saw what Fusaichi Pegasus could do in any sort of racetrack situation. Even then, it was a slow, controlled quarter-mile gallop completed in 24 seconds. But it was enough for Drysdale to know that he had a very talented horse in his barn.

Like all trainers, no matter how articulate, Drysdale had a difficult time explaining what a fast horse looks like. They talk about a colt or filly's "action" and flail their arms in front of them trying to approximate the front view of a horse's staggered stride. The smoother, more symmetrical the movement—think the silent, hypnotizing firing of the pistons in an engine—the more efficient the stride. Or they murmur about stride length or quick turn of foot or the effortlessness of it all. Or they sputter and ask that you take their word for it. True to his nature, Drysdale never tried to answer the question. It was like the notorious definition of pornography—he knew it when he saw it.

He saw it in Fusao Sekiguchi's colt and told the owner about it at lunch simply by laying out a series of races he hoped they would run over the next five months, the last being the Kentucky Derby.

Chapter 6

THE VIEW FROM THE OWNERS' BOX

*"I bet a horse once at 10 to 1 and he came in at a quarter
to four."*

—Henny Youngman

I understand the optimism of owners, because for two glorious, frustrating, and money-losing years, I had myself a racehorse. Granted, mine was a quarter horse, and he never got within a thousand miles of a Triple Crown racetrack. But he did run in a $100,000 race once in a Futurity in Kansas, which is the breed's equivalent of a big-money race. So I get it, I really do, about how you can look at a horse that has never been raced, or in our case saddled, and see a champion.

His name was, appropriately, Oh Desperado, and we purchased him in a private sale—if that's what you call your co-owner's parents agreeing to sell him to you cheap.

He was a son of Batir and daughter of Ooh Tra La, which made him a half brother to Oh A Sensation, a filly that won more than $96,000 at the best quarter horse meets in the nation, as well as capturing the Shebester Futurity, an important race at Blue Ribbon Downs in Sallisaw, Oklahoma. The parents of my childhood buddy, Alex, owned Oh A Sensation and had bred Oh Desperado. They had high hopes for the colt until he had an accident as a foal.

One day, running wild in the field, Oh Desperado got tangled in a fence and suffered a nasty gash to the tendon above his ankle on a back leg. Surgery repaired the severed tendon, and the colt returned to his carefree life in the field just fine and grew into a strapping 2-year-old. He was a massive 17½ hands and a good-looking jet-black colt, except for that back leg. The tendon had healed, but not aesthetically—Oh Desperado looked as if he was lugging a couple of bean bags above his ankles. Vets had assured Alex's folks that it wouldn't affect his performance, but it pretty much eliminated him from the sales.

Someone had offered them $1,500 with the intent of turning Oh Desperado into a jumper, but they decided to keep the colt in the family. For $750, they would sell him to Alex and me to own and race.

They showed us the vet report and warned us there were dozens of things that could go wrong and that, ugly tendon or not, the odds on him matching Oh A Sensation were awfully long. It didn't matter—we were in. We both had just turned thirty and were enamored with the sport. He practiced law in Kansas City and, with his wife, Debby, whom I also grew up with, was raising three boys. I was a reporter at the *Atlanta Journal Constitution* and was just married.

The difference between quarter horses and Thoroughbreds is immense. For one, quarters are a bigger, brawnier breed that run short distances—usually 250 to 500 yards—at full-out speed, while Thoroughbreds are leaner and are bred to parse out their speed at distances anywhere from three quarters of a mile to 1¼ miles. Think Olympic sprinters versus Olympic distance runners.

But most important to us was the cost difference—the quarters were less expensive. We paid $18 a day in training fees versus the $75 to $95 a day Thoroughbred trainers get today at top-end tracks. The purses, of course, were smaller, too, and, as with Thoroughbreds, we'd be obligated to give 10 percent of our purse winnings to the trainer, another 10 percent to the jockey, and at least 1 percent of the winnings to the stable to be split among grooms and hot walkers. But fair is fair and there were opportunities to run for big purses—especially in a horse's third year, when the Futurities are contested.

These are like Triple Crown races but more egalitarian and with a playoff component. Every owner nominates their horse in at least two or three Futurities with fees running anywhere from $600 to $2,000. The payments are incremental and spread out.

For instance, in a Futurity with a $2,000 nomination fee, six months before the race your payment is $200, at four months it doubles to $400, two months $600, and on to $800 to enter the starting gates. Anytime before that, if a horse gets injured or you decide he's just not good enough, you quit paying—though there's no refund on what you've already put up. Inevitably, however, anywhere from eighty to more than a hundred quarter horses make it to the race.

This is partly because breeding is not as specific as it is in Thorough-breds; partly because in a short, intense sprint anything can happen—a stumble at the start can eliminate all chance—and partly because that's where the money is. So Futurity races offer trials or qualifying heats, where the winner of each heat gets a starting gate in the final. If there are less than ten heats, then the next fastest times fill out the field.

In other words, $750 horses can, and do, win the biggest races.

So Alex and I put Oh Desperado in training, paid the nomination fees, and tried to keep our goals modest. It was realistic for us to be-lieve we had a chance to be named champion Missouri-bred, which was at least worth a trophy. How many Missouri-breds could there possibly be? The Show Me state isn't exactly horse country.

We had plenty of help keeping our expectations grounded. My family thought I was absolutely nuts. The first time I laid eyes on my new purchase, I made the mistake of taking my brothers, their kids, my sister, and my father to the farm Oh Desperado was training at in Greenwood, Missouri. The ankle and bulging tendon were indeed noticeable enough that the group, whose knowledge of horses stopped at childhood pony rides, was skeptical, to say the least.

"You should name him Tripod," my younger brother suggested.

My mother would have understood. She took credit for my gam-bling nature, pointing to a long line of dreamers on her side of the family. Her father was an amateur inventor turned ad man. His wife was ad-dicted to sweepstakes and raffle giveaways and was one of those people who cashed in tickets for a couple of hundred dollars here and there or won a television set or box of steak knives at church ice-cream socials. When we were kids, my mom often told us her palm itched, which she said meant she was going to come into money. Like her mother, she was a soft touch for a raffle ticket. But my fixation on the horses she blamed on my aunt May, who lived in California and was a fre-quent patron of Hollywood Park.

In fact, Aunt May was responsible for my first hazy memory of a racetrack some thirty years ago, when, in the great Midwest tradition of family vacations, my folks took all five of us west to see the Grand Canyon, the California beaches, and, of course, Disneyland. It was a long trip; I was maybe five years old, my little brother three, and predictably we got on everyone else's nerves. On one of our final days in California, an excursion was planned for Knotts Berry Farm and my older brothers and sister—probably my father, too—couldn't bear to have us whine and cry our way through another theme park. So we were left behind with Aunt May and Uncle Bass and my mother, which at the time was about the most insulting thing you can do to someone who believes he is every bit as grown up as the big kids. However, Aunt May assured me that we were going to have more fun, that she had a surprise for us that my siblings would be jealous of. But it had to remain our secret.

Uncle Jack drove while Aunt May sat quietly in the passenger seat poring over a big tabloid-sized newspaper. She had to be in her seventies then, stooped over, wrinkled, and with flaming red hair. I had been scolded earlier in the trip for saying out loud that I thought Aunt May looked like an old baboon. When we arrived at the racetrack, however, Aunt May got a whole lot younger. She grabbed my hand and led us to the rail at Hollywood Park. She dispatched Uncle Jack to get us ice cream, told my mom to watch us, and scurried away. In front of us, giant horses were passing by in a line. They had men balled up on their backs, wearing bright green, pink, and yellow hats, and jerseys with stripes or diamonds or triangles on them, and white pants that were swallowed by knee-high black boots. One by one, they disappeared into this green structure that looked like a jungle gym. Soon the horses and bright colors were hard to see, though you could hear the clatter of metal and the voices of men hooting and hollering. It got still for a minute, then a bell went off and, out the other end of the starting gate, the horses thundered by and the colors blurred. Just as suddenly, they disappeared around a turn.

By then Aunt May had returned to the rail. She still had her newspaper in one hand, and a couple of small pieces of paper in the other.

She told me to look to my left and up to the other turn in the race-track and promised me the horses would be back. I looked and I waited for what seemed a long time. Then there they were, the colors getting bigger as they ran toward us. Aunt May tapped the newspaper on the fence in front of me, hitting it faster and harder the closer the horses got.

"Yes, yes, yes, yes yes yes yes," she said to the quickening rhythm of the slapping newspaper. When the horses blew by us, she kissed me on the cheek and said, "Good work."

Then I had no idea what had happened. Now I understand she had picked a horse from the *Daily Racing Form*, bet it, and won. Before a couple of races, Aunt May read the names of the horses and asked which ones I liked. She'd disappear for a few minutes, then return with a little piece of paper, a betting ticket, for me to hold. After the slapping newspaper, yeses, and horses thundering by, she'd give me a kiss, tell me good work again, and take the ticket away. I'd like to think I picked a winner or two, but I doubt it. Still, on the way back to the car, Aunt May put a wad of bills in my hand.

"Who had more fun today? Us or the big kids?" she asked.

"Us," I replied and meant it.

"Remember, it's our secret," she said.

And it remained our secret. I honestly don't remember telling my siblings about it when they returned from their day with my father.

But in the summer of 1991, my mother reminded me of our day at the track with Aunt May. She insisted she had kept the secret. At the time, my mother was dying and bedridden with pancreatic cancer gnawing her from the inside out. There was nothing to do but keep her company, and we all did. She had loved going to Ak-Sar-Ben with my father when we were growing up. While her cancer was in remission, she was always game to go to the Woodlands, the newer track that had opened in Kansas.

With nothing more to do than sit by her side, I often had the *Daily Racing Form* handy for when she drifted off. On good days, she'd even

ask to see it and pick out a horse or two she wanted to bet. I knew
that it was her way to break up a gloomy vigil. But she feigned enthusiasm and I was always relieved to have a reason to escape.

My mother understood. Just as she would have understood that
deep in my soul I *knew* Oh Desperado could run. How? Because no
one who has ever bought a horse believes he has bought a slow one.

When Oh Desperado rolled home a winner in his training race, a
practice heat required by Oklahoma racing officials, I was certain I
was destined for many a winner's circle. On April 8, 1993, he was to
make his debut at Blue Ribbon Downs in the trials of the Black & Gold
Futurity. We knew it was a tough spot to begin a racing career, but
certainly there were going to be other first-timers, and hell, we paid
our nomination fees. Why not start out our owners' career with a big
win?

I flew from Atlanta to Tulsa, where I met Alex. We rented a Cadillac
because we believed horse owners should look the part and be comfortable for the hour-and-a-half drive southeast to Sallisaw near the
border of Arkansas. It didn't take long to experience the first perk of
ownership. When we checked into the Best Bet Motel, the nice woman
at the front desk asked if we owned a horse running in the trials. We
told her in fact we did, with ear-to-ear smiles, one named Oh Desperado, who was running in the eighth race. In that case we deserved
the horsemen's rate. Instead of $22.95 a night, our accommodations
cost $19.95.

Next we headed to the barn to take a closer look at our champion
and learned a lesson in communication, or sometimes the lack of it,
that is always a quandary in an owner-trainer relationship. Oh Desperado looked terrific: He had filled out after several months of training, and his coat was stretched and glistening above sculpted muscle.

But the colt seemed a little dull, less spirited than he had in the past.
When I asked our trainer about that, he told me the colt was no longer
a colt: Oh Desperado had been gelded, which means clipped or spayed.
His fondness for the fillies had proved difficult in his training.

I absorbed this explanation, felt bad for my horse, and rationalized that those were the kind of decisions we were paying Rick eighteen bucks a day to make.

It is a gratifying and altogether strange feeling to stand in a barn with your horse and try to communicate to him how happy he already has made you and how you are looking forward to sharing many victories with him down the road. Oh Desperado had already made me a player, albeit in the minor leagues, of a game I love.

I scratched his neck, patted his long nose, and stumbled to find something to say. All I managed was: "See you in the winner's circle, big boy."

Well, there were seven races before ours, and all were qualifying heats in the Futurity. It was a chance to size up our competition, and we eagerly trudged through the dust to the front side of Blue Ribbon Downs. The track was tiny, with a concrete apron and some splintered bleachers. In other words, closer to a high school football stadium than Churchill Downs. There was a small crowd, mostly owners and mostly cowboys—or at least they wore their ten-gallon hats, jeans, and boots like they were the real thing. Most knew one another, which is not unusual since quarter horse owners often are breeders or ranchers themselves. There was a lot of hat tipping and nodding and smiling going on in the grandstand.

The races themselves were noisy, visceral, and over in 13 seconds, give or take a tick or two. These 2-year-olds were running 250 yards, most for the first time, and not all were eager to get in the starting gate. In heat after heat, one balky horse would start crashing against the walls, setting off a chain reaction of bucking and snorting and rattling in the starting gate. The poor starter had to wait for the first brief moment of stillness to pop the gates and send these runners down the lane.

In quarter horse racing, the break is everything, and everything sometimes goes wrong—especially in the baby races. Over seven heats, I saw one horse refuse to leave the gate, another bobble to his knees

and toss his rider, and another, breaking from the 10 post, make a
sudden right turn to land almost in the grandstand. In each race, at
least two and sometimes up to six banged off one another like pinballs,
creating easy victories for the lucky horse who hustled quick enough
out of the gate to avoid trouble and get a bead on a clear path.

Yes, the start was everything, and both Alex and I worried that Oh
Desperado might be too big and not agile enough to clear the starting mayhem.

But Lord, he looked good in the paddock. He sauntered into the
walking ring with his head upright and his ears perked like a TV
antenna. He was tuned into his surroundings but not at all intimidated—the colt in front of him stopped suddenly and reared, but all
Oh Desperado did was sidestep him casually and passed right on by.

"He's a professional son of a buck, ain't he?" asked a paddock
attendant as we stood outside his stall. Alex and I swelled at the
compliment.

"What's the deal with the ankle?" he asked, deflating us
immediately.

In what felt like seconds, Oh Desperado had a saddle and a jockey
on his back and disappeared through the tunnel and onto the track.
On the tote board, he was the 8–1 fourth betting choice. Alex stopped
me as I headed to the window.

"It's bad luck to bet him," he said.

There was no way that I was going to let my horse go off without
any of my money on his nose. What kind of vote of confidence is that?
I ignored Alex and went and did something stupid. I plunked $50 on
Oh Desperado to win. My sentiment was correct; it was my calcula-
tion that was flawed. It isn't exactly a high-rolling crowd at Blue Ribbon Downs, and this relatively big bet dropped my horse's odds. The
next time the tote board flickered, Oh Desperado was at 2–1. In betting parlance, I had just made my horse into a very vulnerable favorite.

We found a spot on the rail at the finish line and focused our binoculars on the starting gate. It was only 250 yards away, but we were

certain we'd know if Oh Desperado had a chance to win at the break. He had drawn the No. 5 post and had maintained stoic demeanor as the horses were loaded.

This was by far the most well-behaved bunch I had seen all afternoon, and the assistant starters popped them into the gate like they were bullets in a gun. When the gates fired, the field exploded together—all except Oh Desperado. He didn't pause and he didn't bobble; he was just a sneeze slow coming out of the gate. By the time I dropped my binoculars, I had no idea where he was. I didn't even really see who won—all I felt was a herd of horses stomping toward me, then a roar as they passed by. The winner, Second Effort, inhaled the 250 yards in 13.80 seconds—the best human sprinters go 100 yards in a just under 10 seconds.

I knew we didn't win, but it took the replay to sort out what had happened. Oh Desperado did indeed hesitate at the break, spotting Second Effort, on his inside, about three lengths and Real Ducky, on his outside, another two. But our gelding got in gear at the hundred-yard mark and made a late rush to finish a nose behind Real Ducky and a length and a half behind Second Effort. His time of 14:07 seconds didn't get us to the winner's circle; it got us third place and $100. It was a solid effort for a first start, but I confess I was bummed—until I got back to the barn and saw our gelding.

He was dripping sweat and gobbling air as a groom walked him around in circles trying to cool him out. The muscles on his flanks twitched and his head bobbed up and down, as if he were agitated and replaying the race. I imagined him beating himself up for not getting out of the gate quicker and feeling desperate to run it over again. Oh Desperado had heart, I decided then and there, and there would be plenty of opportunities to get my picture taken with him in the winner's circle. Hell, Alex and I had a cooler of beer, the horsemen's rate at the Best Bet Motel, and a Cadillac with plush leather seats. Later that night, we two-stepped at a country and western bar and toasted the fact that life didn't get much better than this.

We owned a horse—a good one, too.

Oh Desperado won two of his next three races at Blue Ribbon Downs. Unfortunately, I wasn't there. The best I could do was listen to the races on the phone. The publicity director at the track agreed to hold a phone up during the race so I could hear the call. Each time I gathered my friends at the office into a conference room and put the race on speakerphone. Yes, it was silly, because in a 300-yard race (Oh Desperado was going longer) about all the track announcer has time to do in sixteen seconds is say, "They're off," try to name a few horses, then call out the winner. As long as his final words were "Oh Desperado at the wire," I was perfectly content to bounce giddily around the newsroom a shrewd horse owner. And I did.

I experienced my greatest thrill and biggest heartbreak and learned my most important lesson as a horse owner all on the same day: August 25, 1993, the trial heats for the Woodlands Futurity. The day was already special enough because I was back in Kansas City with Oh Desperado, and dozens of friends and family members had come out to see the three-legged horse. We knew we were a legitimate contender off the back-to-back wins and a second-place finish, but on the day of the race we learned just how legitimate.

In the morning at the barn, our trainer offered to buy Oh Desperado from us for $5,000 cash. Now, this happens more often than you think in both quarter horse and Thoroughbred racing, especially before big races with ripe purses. There were eighty-nine horses competing in the Futurity for a purse just over $100,000. The winners of nine trial races advanced to the finals, as would one second-place finisher with the fastest time. In the finals, last place paid $10,000. Rick had sized up the competition and done the math. He assured us that he was serious and Oh Desperado was certain to move on.

Now we had our first real ownership dilemma. So far Oh Desperado had paid for himself and our fun by winning about $3,600 in purses. If we took the money and walked away, we would accomplish something 90 percent of horse owners are never able to do: turn a pretty decent profit.

On the other hand, if Oh Desperado was that live a horse, why not swing for the fences—hell, he might win the finals and bring home close to $50,000. We'd certainly lock up the Missouri-bred championship, and we could take him to California or New Mexico or back to Oklahoma for bigger-money races. Needless to say, we didn't sell him to Rick.

In fact, the whole episode turned up the pressure on an already stomach-churning day. Again, Oh Desperado was in the eighth race, the last qualifying heat. There were too many people to entertain, too many beers to drink, and too many cigarettes to chain-smoke for me to see clearly what we were up against.

I was a wreck and barely paid attention to the races. In the paddock before the eighth, I stood off by myself and tried to communicate with Oh Desperado telepathically. He was even cooler than he had been in the paddock at Blue Ribbon Downs. He stood perfectly still when our jockey's tack was plopped on his back, stared straight ahead, and, I swear, looked a little sleepy. The slow start in Sallisaw played on my mind.

I stood with my arms folded as he circled the ring, and tried to bore fast thoughts into his head. I closed my eyes and tried to visualize the end of the race, a flashbulb going off and cheers from our entourage as Oh Desperado was led from the winner's circle. I also murmured a prayer of intercession to my mother and Aunt May.

I had learned my lesson in Oklahoma and chose to watch the race inside the clubhouse on a television monitor by myself so I could observe his every step. The one constant about Oh Desperado was that he never freaked out at the starting gate. He ambled into the No. 3 slot and stood still, as if in a coma, as the last six horses loaded in.

I could hear myself breathing. Lo and behold, Oh Desperado catapulted out of the gate first. His jockey immediately went to the whip to keep him at full drive; he fanned Oh Desperado's fanny like he was strumming a banjo. At 100 yards, we had a length on the nearest challenger. At 200 yards, it had grown to two and Oh Desperado was rocketing down the dirt in an easy, straight path. At 300 yards, he looked like a certain winner.

"Get there wire, get there wire, get there wire," I kept saying as I leaned toward the television monitor, almost losing my balance. Then.

"Noooooooooo," I moaned.

Our rider had put away his banjo and was pulling the reins up close to Oh Desperado's neck. He thought he had it wrapped up and could hand-ride him home. But coming on next to him was a colt named Benny Bullion, and his jockey was slapping the hide off him. They were rump to rump with Oh Desperado when our rider realized his mistake. He went back to the whip. It was too late. They crossed close enough together that a photo finish was required. But I knew Oh Desperado had lost. Three minutes later or so, the photo appeared on the monitor and showed Benny Bullion had gotten him by a neck. I couldn't move. I didn't want to find anyone. I went to an empty corner of the clubhouse and paced. Finally, Alex found me. He was shaking and his eyelids looked pinned to his forehead.

"He got a shitty ride. He had it won—it ain't O's fault," I spit with a malice that startled even me.

"It was a pretty fast heat. He may be the fastest second-place finisher," Alex said.

No matter how well intended Alex was, at the moment that perhaps was the cruelest thing anyone has ever said to me. Here I had just made the first step in getting over the disappointment by adopting the time-honored right of owners: blaming the rider.

Now Alex was resurrecting hope. We bolted for the racing office to see if Oh Desperado indeed had captured the last spot for the finals by running the tenth fastest time of the day. We got there in time to see a secretary pin the list on a bulletin board. We nearly bumped heads trying to read the list. I ran my finger down the names until I found Oh Desperado. I noticed a line above it, but it didn't register with me. He had run 400 yards in 20.630.

It was the eleventh fastest time *by one hundredth of a second*. I wanted to cry. And I did on the way home, along with pounding my steering wheel and screaming at the jockey who cost me and Oh Desperado the victory.

My career as an owner went pretty much downhill from there. The following week, Oh Desperado finished third in the consolation finals, for which he earned a $3,500 check. It was some comfort for not selling him to Rick, knowing we didn't leave much money on the table. Overall, his 2-year-old campaign was deemed a success. In nine starts, he had two victories, two second-place and two third-place finishes, and earned $6,689.

He was awful as a 3-year-old, however, a problem that Alex and I compounded by selling half of him to two other friends who wanted to live the large life of horse ownership. We told Larry and Grant all of the possible things that could go wrong, about the unsightly ankle, just about everything except that our bighearted Oh Desperado might stop running. Which he did. In eight starts, he managed only two third-place finishes, and those were at the lowest claiming levels on the Oklahoma Fair Meet circuit.

His last race was at the Woodlands, where once again a large hometown contingent turned out. Fortunately, I wasn't there. By that time, I had taken to listening in on the speakerphone by myself. It was September 1994, and we were desperate enough to enter him in "hook races," which are contested at longer distances, this one 870 yards, and run partially around a turn. For much of the race I thought Oh Desperado had gotten scratched. Not once did I hear the track announcer call his name. But then it echoed: "And in the footsteps here comes Oh Desperado to finish last."

I saw our gelding one last time on the farm in Kansas City. We were about to sell him for $1,500 to a couple who intended to make him a hunter-jumper. I went to say good-bye and to thank him for the hard tries and big times he gave me. He ate carrots from my hand and prodded my shoulder playfully with his nose. Maybe he knew his racing days were over.

Six months or so later, Alex called to tell me that Oh Desperado had indeed turned out to be a champion. The couple who bought him had turned him into a dressage horse and they had just won the Kansas title. Now Oh Desperado was going to the nationals.

It turned out he danced a hell of a lot better than he ran.

Chapter 7

THE TRIPLE CROWN PREVIEW: THE BREEDERS' CUP JUVENILE CHAMPIONSHIPS

NOVEMBER 1999

HALLANDALE, FLORIDA

"Horses have never hurt anyone yet, except when they bet on them."
—*Stuart Cloete*

Mike Pegram was leaning against a rental in ratty gym shorts, still sweating from his six-mile walk that began on the backside of Gulfstream Park, where the Florida sunshine stirred the smells of hay and liniment and horse manure into a steamy, pungent aroma. It was the smell of money, in any case, because it emanated from some hundred horses from around the world, worth hundreds of millions of dollars, tucked in a city block's worth of stalls here.

In two days, on November 6, these horses—from Dubai, France, England, Ireland, and from across the United States—would compete in eight races for a combined $13 million in the sixteenth Breeders' Cup Championship. The day was the equivalent of the Super Bowl for horse racing and was held at different tracks each year. It was that rare afternoon when nearly a full card of horse racing received national exposure on NBC-TV.

The Juvenile Fillies and the Juvenile race were for 2-year-olds going 1¹⁄₁₆ miles. They were a pair of Grade I, $1 million races and an opportunity to assess the young horses who were pointed toward the Triple Crown.

There were other divisions, too: The Distaff was at 1⅛ miles for older mares, the six-furlong sprint open to speedballs of either sex, and three turf races, which drew the bulk of the overseas invaders. Finally, the 1¼-mile Classic was worth $4 million—one of the richest purses in racing—and the most important race of the day.

Pegram figured to be a player here throughout the day of championship races. His filly, Silverbulletday, had won eight of ten races, earned more than $1.7 million, and was the favorite to win the $2 million Distaff; he also had an interesting colt named Captain Steve entered in the Juvenile.

But at this moment he had a cell phone pressed to his ear and was more concerned about a cheap race in Phoenix, Arizona, at Turf

Paradise, where a horse of his who couldn't run a lick was entered in a $12,500 claiming race for a purse of $4,000.

"I know we're going to lose Fat Eddie, Mike, that's the point," he told his Arizona-based trainer. "He ain't worth a shit and we need to get rid of him."

There was a pause.

"Of course I'm going to get you more horses. But we got to cut our losses. I paid too much for that son of a bitch."

Pause.

"No, it ain't your fault. He just ain't fast," Pegram said. "I'll see you."

He snapped shut his cell phone and let out a long, good-natured laugh that was echoed by his friend, and the namesake of his next Triple Crown horse, Captain Steve Thompson.

There was no other owner in horse racing quite like Pegram, and the scene unfolding now pretty much explained why. He was forty-seven, a self-described redneck from Princeton, Indiana—home to Red Skelton and Gil Hodges—who played a little baseball at Indiana University and made enough money as a bookie there to indulge his life-long passion for horses.

On November 13, 1975, Pegram opened a McDonald's franchise in Mount Vernon, Washington. It was financed 100 percent by a banker in his hometown at a time when Pegram's assets consisted of a re-frigerator, a washer, and a dryer, which Kmart held the paper on.

He turned that single McDonald's in Washington State into a string of more than twenty, began developing property, and bought homes in Phoenix and in southern California overlooking the Pacific Ocean and Del Mar Race Track, the whole time continuing his pursuit of horses.

Pegram is a prodigious beer drinker who once shifted brand loy-alties from Budweiser to Coors because he could fit more of the thin-ner Coors cans in his cooler. The daily walks were a recent habit to combat this particular vice, which, he explained in an affable drawl, was a "twelve-pack swing—it's one six-pack I'm burning off and another six-pack I'd be drinking if I wasn't walking."

He had a thicket of red hair, the sure smile of a man who knows something good is about to happen to him, a generous spirit that begat a devoted coterie of friends, and an uncanny nose for mischief. All these qualities brought Captain Steve Thompson to Florida and put a 2-year-old colt named after him on the Triple Crown trail.

Captain Steve had met Mike Pegram in the Louisville jail. It happened the morning after the 1997 Kentucky Derby, when a woman Pegram was dating at the time, now and forever known as "Annie Oakley," packed a gift in his luggage. She told him he probably ought to check the bag at the counter, but Pegram was late getting to the airport and he didn't do it. His first surprise was the sound of the X-ray machine. His second was the police suddenly on the scene. His third was the .357 Magnum in the box they fished out of his bag.

It didn't help that Pegram had $50,000 cash on him, the proceeds from a significant winning bet on Silver Charm, the Derby winner trained by his friend and horse trainer Bob Baffert.

"They didn't know me from Adam and thought I was a drug dealer. So they took me downtown and locked me up," he said.

The police failed to confiscate his cell phone, however, and from the Louisville lockup, he reached Baffert at the trainer's barn at Churchill Downs. More fortunate than that was the fact that Baffert was standing next to Julian Wheat, who is the track's liaison to trainers and owners and who happened to know: a) Pegram was not a drug dealer, and b) Captain Steve Thompson, Louisville's chief of detectives. So Thompson vouched for Pegram and sprung him from jail. On the ride back to Churchill Downs, the two got to talking and Pegram apologized for the incident while Captain Steve in turn asked that the owner not have any hard feelings for the city.

"When Captain Steve dropped me off, he told me that I seemed like a nice enough guy and that someday he was sure he was going to see me in the winner's circle at the Derby," Pegram said.

At the time, neither one of them really believed they would see each other again. And Pegram didn't believe he was anywhere near to having a horse good enough to compete in the Triple Crown. He had had stakes winners, but he wasn't playing the game at the top level by buying expensive horses. "When the Learjets leave and the farmers with the gooseneck trailers roll in, that's when you see me buying horses," he liked to say.

But a year after spending the morning in the Louisville jail, Pegram indeed had a horse competing in the Kentucky Derby, one that had such a puny, convex-shaped chest that Baffert had nicknamed him "The Fish." The colt also had had his knees wired twice before the Keeneland sales just so they sort of looked straight. When Baffert told Pegram he bought the colt for a mere $17,000, the owner replied, "What's the matter, does he have cancer?"

On the first Saturday in May 1998, however, that colt, Real Quiet, rushed home a 1½-length winner in the Kentucky Derby. Pegram, who had grown up ninety miles from Louisville, had watched this miracle unfold through tears in his eyes on a television monitor in the paddock area of Churchill Downs. He watched it there alone, away from his family, Baffert, and dozens of friends from Princeton, and he didn't know how to get to the winner's circle. As he pushed through the crowd, the first familiar face he saw was Captain Steve Thompson. He, too, was crying.

The two men hugged and the police officer led Pegram to the winner's circle. In turn Pegram dragged Thompson into the photo. Two weeks later, the captain was at the Preakness when Real Quiet won again. Three weeks after that, he was in New York among the more than 80,000 people at Belmont Park to witness the colt's bid to become the first Triple Crown winner since 1978. Real Quiet, however, came up a nostril short to Victory Gallop in a photo finish.

"You can call it fate or whatever you want. But I've been blessed with good people and cheap colts and I wouldn't trade, either," said Pegram.

The pair have been friends ever since, and the following fall, after the sales, the owner gathered Captain Steve and Churchill Downs' horseman liaison, Julian Wheat, together and insisted that to commemorate their friendship they could each pick out a colt and Pegram would name him for them. Wheat went first and selected the $144,000 offspring of Dayjur; Thompson chose the $70,000 son of Fly So Free. Now Captain Steve was in Florida for horse racing's richest day and to see whether or not his namesake was Triple Crown–bound. Where was Wheat's colt? Pegram and Captain Steve cackled again.

"Hopefully, he's going to be sold today at Turf Paradise. It's Fat Eddie. Once I found out he couldn't run a step, I changed his name. I couldn't let him be named after Julian," the owner said.

Partly because he had come to horse racing through the front side, or by pushing money through the betting windows, and partly because he thought of himself as a hick who made it on his own, Pegram had an iconoclastic approach to the game that was frowned upon by some old-line owners—especially some hardboots from Kentucky.

Not all, but many saw him as "common" and bristled at his "affectations." He always wore jeans in the winner's circle and often showed up with a beer in hand. They whispered about rumored antics such as the brawl he'd gotten into following the previous year's Belmont Stakes, after the filly Silverbulletday tried to take on the boys with disastrous results.

It is true Pegram got into a bloody melee on the backside, as it is true that he was in a foul mood after losing a $20,000 bet on his filly. It's also true that one of his best friends from his hometown of Princeton, Indiana, was wearing a clip-on tie, which saved him from a severe choking from a bigger foe. The reason for the fight, however, was that Pegram was defending his security officer, who was black and a friend and was being baited and insulted.

But in fact it seems other owners were jealous of Pegram because he was winning with modestly to cheaply priced horses they were missing at the sales. He knew he wasn't the most popular of owners and stayed away from the clubhouse set. Still, he was pleasant to everyone, shrugged off the unflattering talk, and insisted that he appealed to a different constituency within the sport: the everyday players. And he did.

At the Preakness with Real Quiet, the infield crowd at Pimlico Race Course roared for Pegram as he passed. He obliged them by chugging a beer a patron handed in through a chain-link fence. He knew where he came from in the racetrack hierarchy and stayed there.

His late father owned cheap horses that ran on second-rate circuits at tracks such as Ellis Park in Kentucky. One brother was a jockey's agent in California, while another brother owned a bar in Seattle that had a state license allowing him to take offtrack bets.

From Emerald Downs in Washington to Santa Anita Park in California to Turf Paradise in Arizona to Churchill Downs in Kentucky to Belmont Park in New York, Pegram was on a first-name basis with the ushers, the bartenders, the program salesgirls, and especially the most hardened fans. They passed him beers, shook his hand, and saw a guy who loved the sport as much as they did. He was the horseplayer who had made it. His stable had grown to more than seventy horses and he damn near won the Triple Crown. Still, he wasn't too big to race and bet on cheap horses at Turf Paradise.

"Only so many people can own the New York Yankees. But in racing it's like owning your own franchise. You pick the level and compete," he said. "Slow-pitch softball and golf don't do it for me. This is my way to compete. The beautiful, fair thing about it is that it's simple: It's not the man with the most money who wins. It's the man who has the fastest horse. The only thing you can do as an owner is stay the fuck out of the way."

In matters of horses, the man Pegram stayed clear of and let do his job was his trainer, Bob Baffert. In the days leading up to the Breeders' Cup, the backside of the track was transformed from a placid resort for tightly wound and expensive horses into a busy stage for the egos and the entourages of the biggest names in horse racing and the reporters and camera crews that trailed them.

Not far from Pegram and Captain Steve, Baffert was holding court on everything from the eight horses he'd brought here, four of them certain favorites, to his recently released autobiography—*Baffert: Dirt Road to the Derby.*

He was telegenic, with a mop of snow-white hair and John Lennon–shaped lavender-tinted sunglasses always perched on his nose. He preferred the pressed jeans and starched shirts sported by fraternity men, which he once was, over the cowboy look. At forty-seven, he was an entertainer with an exuberant personality and practiced media savvy.

He let any television network that asked wire him with a microphone while he watched his horses train or race. He gave them a good show even if it meant throwing up his arms and yelling "Goooooooaaaaaaal!" after a particularly good workout of one of his horses in the exaggerated manner of a South American soccer announcer.

He was quick—memorably intoning, "Houston, we got a problem" into the microphone at the 1996 Preakness when his horse Cavonnier was on his way to a fourth-place finish. He was irreverent. Baffert put the trophy bowl on his head when Silver Charm followed his 1997 Derby win with a Preakness victory. He dressed himself and the horse in Arab garb and got on Silver Charm's back for a photograph to commemorate their victory in Sheik Mohammed's $4 million Dubai World Cup. He once appeared on a network telecast dressed in the psychedelic duds and wig of the movie hero Austin Powers and uttered his best "Yeah, baby" impression over and over. He had turned himself into a celebrity beyond the horse racing world; network cameras dwelled on him—just as they did on movie stars like Jack Nicholson and Dyan Cannon—when he attended a Los Angeles Lakers game.

Three years ago, nobody knew his name. Baffert was just another quarter horse trainer trying to follow Lukas into the bigger-money, higher-profile Thoroughbred circuit. It was Pegram who gave him the push, as well as $300,000 to make the switch. The owner had met Baffert through some friends in the mid-1980s and had raced a few

quarter horses with him. They didn't really get to know each other,
however, until a few years later, when they found themselves together
at a horse sale in Ruidoso, New Mexico.

They had let a horse that they wanted get away because of tenta-
tive bidding. In a rush to get out of town, they headed to the airport
in El Paso but too late to catch a flight to Los Angeles. There was only
one flight leaving and that was to Las Vegas—a city that Baffert had
never been to but that Pegram knew all too well.

To hear Baffert tell it, he knew he had made a friend for life when
he saw the croupier write Pegram a voucher for $50,000 after just
twenty minutes at the craps table. To hear Pegram tell it, he knew
the pair would be going places when he saw Baffert in their hotel
room's Jacuzzi with a cowboy hat on his head, a beer in his hand, and
two young women amid the bubbles.

They were indeed meant for each other, which further aggravated
some of the old-line horse people. But Baffert had not been an over-
night success. It took him twelve years as a quarter horse trainer, many
of them lean, before his horses surpassed the $1 million mark in earn-
ings. At one point in the late 1970s, he quit after his father, tired of
his son not winning, took a horse away from him to train himself.

He got off to a modest start on the Thoroughbred circuit, saddling
thirty-six winners for more than $882,000 in 1990, and steadily worked
his way up the training standings in California. In 1992, he won his
first major race, the Breeders' Cup Sprint, with Thirty Slews, a horse
he gave a third of to Pegram to thank him for staking his move to
Thoroughbreds. In 1995, he won seventy-nine races and more than
$2.5 million in purses.

Still, Baffert was an unknown trainer when he showed up at the
Kentucky Derby in 1996 with Cavonnier, a gelding who had won the
Santa Anita Derby. The trainer was determined not to leave that way.
He wanted attention. He wanted to attract new owners, and after
twenty years as an anonymous quarter horse trainer, he thought he
had something to say.

He and Cavonnier shared a barn with Unbridled's Song, who was the favorite to win the race but who had a foot problem. Unbridled's Song was the center of the prerace attention, so Baffert worked the edges of the crowd, soliciting interviews from media members who found his preppy look (he had left the cowboy hat with the quarter horses) and quick wit refreshing. Basically, he gave good quotes.

Even better, he went back to the hotel at the end of each day and watched himself so he could give better the following morning. He also had a horse that merited some attention, especially with the troubles plaguing Unbridled's Song.

Baffert's premeditated seduction of the media was a success. By the time the Derby was run, most fans had read or heard about some of the life and times of a white-haired joker named Bob Baffert. How, as a boy, he'd sold eggs from the family farm. How he was a determined former jockey, but not a very good one. How he wasn't really a morning person and didn't understand why most trainers thought it was necessary to be at the barns at dawn. He didn't.

When Cavonnier was caught at the wire in the Kentucky Derby by Grindstone, a finish so close that in the photo Grindstone's decisive nose looks like it may be a shadow, there wasn't a more lovable loser in all of the world. Baffert handled the loss gracefully, even slipping W. T. Young, the winning owner, the secret grip they shared as onetime members of the Sigma Alpha Epsilon fraternity. But he was ripped up inside.

He had been beaten by Lukas, a trainer he had idolized as a boy, who had offered him advice when he was shifting to Thoroughbreds but whom he now was beginning to feud with. Earlier that Derby day, Lukas had confronted him in the President's Room of Churchill Downs about some comments Baffert had made in the Louisville newspaper. Grindstone was one of five horses Lukas had run in the Derby, and Baffert was quoted as saying Lukas did it to satisfy his outsize ego. Baffert denied he said it. Still, Lukas wasn't satisfied, and words were exchanged and threats made about going head to head in the press.

In truth, however, Baffert was terrified that he'd never again have another horse good enough to run in the Kentucky Derby. He didn't have rich owners to prospect for the expensive horses as Lukas did. He was convinced that he had missed a once-in-a-lifetime opportunity.

But he was wrong. In 1997, he returned with a colt named Silver Charm and won. He did it again the following year with Real Quiet. It took Lukas eight trips to Churchill Downs before he made it to the Derby winner's circle for the first time. Baffert did it on his second appearance and became only one of six trainers in the 125 years of the race to win the Derby in consecutive years.

With both Silver Charm and Real Quiet, Baffert also had come within a half length of capturing the Triple Crown. In 1997, more than 70,000 people were at Belmont Park to watch Touch Gold swing wide and sneak past Silver Charm in the last fifty yards to win by half a length; a year later, more than 80,000 were left breathless when Victory Gallop caught Real Quiet at the wire in a finish so close the margin might best be described as by a nostril.

After Cavonnier's loss, when Baffert feared he might never run a horse in the Derby again, his stable in the next two years tripled in size from thirty-five horses to more than ninety as new owners flocked to the sport's engaging new star. His horses won $8.8 million in 1997 and $15 million in 1998 and both years he was awarded the Eclipse Award as the nation's outstanding trainer. Baffert was suddenly rich and famous.

Now, standing in the Florida sun at Gulfstream Park, however, he made it clear he wasn't too happy, even though he was about to have eight horses running in six races of the Breeders' Cup races.

Baffert was still on top of the national training standings and, with a good Breeders' Cup day, had a chance of surpassing $17 million in purse earnings, which would break the record held by Lukas. What nettled him was that he was no longer the little-trainer-who-could. He was expected to win.

"This is my bread and butter now. It takes the fun out of it. I have a huge overhead. I have ninety horses in training I'm responsible for," he said. "I'm working on next year's Derby. I'm looking for horses to buy for the Derbies down the road. The part I like best is actually training the horse, and that's just a small part of my day."

His charmed Triple Crown streak had run out the previous spring, and with it much of his personal charm had evaporated. He was trying to become the first trainer in history to win three consecutive Derbies, and he had three chances to do so. He ran Prime Timber and the cofavorites Excellent Meeting and General Challenge. They finished fourth, fifth, and eleventh. His filly, Excellent Meeting, ran in the Preakness, but she had trouble breathing in the back stretch and was pulled up by her rider, Kent Desormeaux, and didn't finish the race.

Out of capable colts for the Belmont, Baffert decided to run another filly, the one Pegram owned, Silverbulletday. She had won eleven of twelve races at five different tracks—including eight in a row—each time as the odds-on favorite. Still, Baffert was taking on one of horse racing's most fundamental tenets: Fillies don't belong with the colts. History said so.

Thirty-seven fillies had run in the 125-year-old Kentucky Derby and only three had won, the last being the Lukas-trained Winning Colors in 1988. Of the 927 Belmont starters in the 130-year history of the race, Silverbulletday would be the twenty-first filly. Only two had ever won, the last one, Tanya, in 1905.

No one is quite sure why a filly can match a colt's time on a stopwatch but needs extraordinary talent to beat the opposite sex in head-to-head competition. The evidence was anecdotal and ranged from males being bigger and stronger to fillies becoming intimidated when they drew eye to eye with a colt. In any given race, horses must overcome a variety of factors—including post position, track bias, pace, and racing luck. For fillies, there's one more factor: During spring and summer, they come into heat every twenty days.

About the only thing anyone on the backside can agree on, in the most politically incorrect way, is that the great fillies, from Ruffian to Genuine Risk to Winning Colors, were masculine and hard to handle. They also didn't make very good brood mares. This was dramatically illustrated when Genuine Risk, the 1980 Kentucky Derby winner, produced only two live foals in more than fifteen years of breeding, neither of which made it to the racetrack.

Still, Baffert knew he had an exceptional horse. He also came from the quarter horse circuit, where the boys and girls competed against one another all the time, and he insisted a $1 million race is a $1 million race no matter who is running. Baffert had tried to run Silverbulletday in the Preakness, but scratched her after she drew an outside post. The gambler in Pegram was tired of his filly going off at 2–5 odds. It wasn't worth muscling up on a bet if all he was going to get back was $2.40 for every $2 he put up.

But there was a stronger motivation to run the filly in the 1½-mile Belmont, which is about the only time in a horse's career that they are ever asked to go that far. Lukas and Charismatic, after winning the Derby and Preakness, were poised to capture the Triple Crown. By the time of the Belmont, the feud between the two trainers was fairly public; one couldn't bear to be surpassed by the other. The rub was that Charismatic was owned by Bob and Beverly Lewis, the same couple who owned Silver Charm and whom Baffert had taken to the brink of history two years earlier. It is not uncommon for owners to divide horses among multiple trainers, though Baffert had the Lewises as clients before Lukas did. But it was to Lukas that the couple gave money to buy the more expensive horses at the yearling sales.

Baffert now felt like the Lewises' second-string trainer even though he had damn near won them a Triple Crown. In the days leading up to the race, Baffert boasted that he had the best 3-year-old of any sex and that Lukas and the Lewises should not count on the $5 million bonus that Visa USA promised the winner of all three races. Lukas fired back that the filly crop was weak and that Silverbulletday had beaten a "cupcake" schedule.

But Baffert didn't relent. Finally, the seventy-five-year-old Lewis had had enough. He publicly offered to bet Baffert $200,000, horse to horse, Charismatic versus Silverbulletday, in the Belmont. The Lewises had become known as the first couple of horse racing. They had been married fifty-two years, were unfailingly polite, and had sunny dispositions that they took to tracks across the country in support of the sport. But Lewis didn't build one of the nation's largest beer distributorships by letting people show him up. He was genuinely hurt by Baffert's impetuous behavior and wanted to take him to the "woodshed for a spanking." The challenge embarrassed Baffert and put Pegram in the difficult middle.

Pegram felt a kinship to Lewis—they shared the same trainer and saw each other often at Baffert's barn. He also was grateful that the Lewises had made him a part of their Kentucky Derby celebration when Silver Charm won. Pegram believed that he was doing the sporting thing by running Silverbulletday in the Belmont. His filly was a monster who beat all comers and had earned $2.1 million. It was a horse race, after all.

He thought Lewis understood that, too. He also wasn't the one who had been sounding off. Pegram played conciliator behind the scenes and Baffert didn't accept the wager. Still, the skirmish made two of the most high-profile people in horse racing look foolish.

In the Belmont, Silverbulletday finished seventh after leading the race for one mile with Charismatic pressing her every step of the way. Baffert believed this was per Lukas's instructions and was more about intimidating the filly than winning the race. Not a quarter of a mile later, Charismatic took his bad step, fractured his condylar bone, and had to be retired.

The rocky spring apparently had taken its toll, because here in Florida, Baffert was more introverted, sober, his natural zest tempered.

He was downright contemplative about his recently released book, which he said was "about a guy who had no idea what he was doing.

"I never had a game plan," he said.

The book was the furthest thing from a prettied-up rags-to-riches tale. Baffert talked about his own experimentation with hallucinogenic drugs while a bell-bottomed teenager, his adventures as a second-rate jockey at third-rate tracks in Arizona, and how, early in his training career while he was still attending the University of Arizona, he had served a one-year suspension from California horse racing authorities. One of his horses tested positive for a painkiller after a race at Los Alamitos, and in the book, Baffert admitted giving the horse something, partly out of ignorance and partly out of desperation to win.

He also acknowledged that his recent success had taken a toll on his marriage. Baffert bemoaned the time he had missed with his wife and four kids, which basically foretold his current situation. He was in the middle of a divorce.

"You really do have to make a tremendous sacrifice. There are a lot of trainers out there who are happily married and have time to spend with their children," he wrote. "But most of them cannot compete at the level we're competing at . . ."

In Baffert's telling, his rivalry with Lukas reached a breaking point in the summer of 1996, when he twice ran Silver Charm against the Lukas-trained Gold Tribute. Both were owned by Lewis. Baffert's Silver Charm was modestly bred and cost $80,000 as a yearling; Gold Tribute was a son of Mr. Prospector and cost $725,000. Silver Charm beat Lukas's colt both times—the last by a head in the Del Mar Futurity, a Grade II, which on the résumé of a stallion prospect can mean up to $2 million in additional resale value. According to Baffert, the next time he saw Lukas, his rival grumbled that by running Silver Charm against Gold Tribute, Baffert had cost Lewis two or three million dollars.

What irritated Baffert even more is that before the race, one of Lukas's clients, Michael Tabor, had offered to buy Silver Charm from

Lewis for $500,000. Baffert advised against it and Lewis declined the offer. The thought of Lukas winning the Derby with a colt he had trained was too much for Baffert.

It was inevitable that Baffert and Lukas would end up at each other's throats. They were the same type, separated by only seventeen years and a few style points. Both had scrapped their way up from the quarter horse circuit. Both liked to think of themselves as outsiders who had to learn from their own mistakes because when they first arrived on the Thoroughbred scene, their peers shunned the former cowboys. Both were intensely competitive and obviously could train horses. In the pursuit of horses, both had failed marriages, Lukas three of them.

They were both showmen, too. Baffert remembered first setting eyes on Lukas in Sonorita, Arizona, and being dazzled by his presence. Baffert was just out of high school and even called the trainer to ask for a job galloping horses. Lukas didn't have any openings but was gracious to the teenager on the telephone. "When Wayne rolled into town he was like Barnum and Bailey. He was a showman to the max and I really liked that," Baffert wrote.

Each chose different ways to be larger than life. In appearance, Lukas opted for an Old West polish; Baffert went for Sunbelt cool. Lukas trumpeted his no-drinking, no-smoking, no off-hour-fraternization-with-owner habits. He was all horses, all the time. Baffert projected his night-crawling, late-sleeping, and my-owners-are-my-running-buddies attitude. He was all fun, all the time, though he worked just as hard and ran as tight a barn as Lukas.

Both were good for the sport—they took horse racing beyond the *Racing Form* and into the mainstream media. Lukas and Baffert were going to bring out the best in each other on the racetrack and the worst in each other off it. There were only so many good horses and so many well-heeled owners who could afford them. Baffert believed he lagged behind Lukas in this aspect.

These Breeders' Cup races were important to Baffert's client campaign as well as to his Triple Crown aspirations. He was sending out three horses for two new and very rich clients. In the Juvenile Fillies race he had Chilukki, owned by Robert and Janice McNair, a Texas couple who had just been awarded a new Houston franchise from the National Football League. In the Juvenile race, along with Captain Steve, he had Forest Camp, who was owned by Aaron U. Jones, an Oregon timber baron. The McNairs were new to the sport. Jones, however, had been in and out for years and had a reputation as a demanding owner who had gone through some of the most accomplished trainers in horse racing, from Hall of Famer Laz Barrera to, more recently, Neil Drysdale.

Leaning against a wall near his barn, Baffert already looked tired. The fun-loving guy who had no idea what he was doing and still twice came within feet of winning the Triple Crown was nowhere to be found. He had a game plan, now, though he didn't look too comfortable with it.

"I get a little bored and that's why I got out of quarter horses," he said by way of explanation. "Now I want to buy good horses and watch them develop. I've won the Kentucky Derby and Preakness. My goal now is to win the Triple Crown."

"I rode that horse better than that horse ran."
  —Ray York, sixty-six, on January 13, 2000, at Santa Anita Park
    after finishing tenth on Culebra and becoming the first
    jockey in history to compete in seven different decades.
    He won the 1954 Kentucky Derby aboard Determine.

The radio guys rushed the small man as soon as he turned the corner outside the Lukas barn. He was wearing cowboy boots, jeans, and a white western shirt with brown piping—an ensemble that looked small enough to be plucked out of a boys' department. Only a silver oval-shaped belt buckle, which popped from his navel like a manhole cover, looked like it belonged on an adult. A ball cap was pulled down low on his forehead, but not enough to hide a forty-six-year-old face cracked like well-worn leather. He was just four-foot-eleven and barely a hundred pounds, but there was no mistaking the strength of Pat Day—his arms and legs were corded as if he had been stuffed with steel cable. He squinted at a cue card the radio guy thrust in front of him along with a microphone. It was an endorsement for a radio station in San Diego.

"I'm sorry. I can't read that on air because I never listen to your station. I don't get there much," Day told him politely.

The radio guy shuffled through his promo cards and produced a more innocuous spot, one that didn't suggest the jockey was an avid listener of the station. "That will be fine," Day said. He then recited the promo in a single take and walked off to shake Lukas's hand.

"How's our horses?" he asked.

Lukas put his hand on the rider's shoulder and ticked off what had become a common refrain on the days before big races.

"Now, Pat, you just go ahead and sleep late in the morning. You get up and have some bacon and eggs, watch the *Today Show,* and spend some time with your wife and daughter. You say your morning devotionals and don't worry about a thing," he said with a big grin. "I've got them right where I want them and they're going to run for you."

"You know that's what I like to hear, Coach," said Day, grinning back.

It was their routine, the Coach or D. Wayne and Saint Pat or Patient Pat or Pat Wait All Day—all nicknames attached to the pair, more often than not with expletives muttered in between, by bettors who either loved or hated them. Lukas had won more Breeders' Cup races, thirteen, than any other trainer, and Day had ridden more winners, ten, than any other jockey. Lukas was running seven horses in this Breeders' Cup, and Day would be aboard three of them.

Why not? In the past fifteen years, they had paired up for more than 310 victories worth more than $21 million and had gotten to the winner's circle 30 percent of the time.

Still, they treated each other as respectful colleagues rather than friends, and the cheerful banter buffered the always complicated relationship between trainers and riders. The nature of the business dictated that they treat each other suspiciously. The most common practice in horse racing was to blame the rider for a loss. Often it was done publicly, moments after the race; usually it was more subtle: A jockey would be "taken off" a mount for the following race with a vague explanation such as "Jerry Bailey fits this horse better." Lukas had used both tactics in the course of his career and was more outspoken than most trainers about jockeys. He rarely let them work his horses in the morning, a common practice especially before the marquee events, and, even with Day standing next to him, he didn't hesitate to explain why.

"They either screw them up or screw themselves up. I know where I want the horse to be. Just because you get on him today and he's one way, doesn't mean that when you ride him in a race a week from now, or six months from now, you're going to have the same horse," Lukas explained. "I don't want any test-drives. I don't want Pat or anyone else to have any preconceived notions of how a horse runs, what he likes or doesn't like to do. Too many damn riders think too much. They believe they know more than you do. I don't fall in love with jockeys. The best you can hope for is to strike a balance that is like a marriage. It's hard to do and takes a lot of work. When you're winning it's easy, but there are times when you have to have the heart-to-heart or do something to shake things up."

The Lukas-Day union was no different. The jockey was in the Hall of Fame, third on the all-time victory list with more than 7,500 winners, behind Bill Shoemaker and Laffit Pincay, and, for the past fifteen years, had been considered along with Jerry Bailey the finest rider in the nation. Over that span for Lukas, he had won the 1985 Preakness with Tank's Prospect; ridden Lady's Secret to the 1986 Horse of the Year title; won the 1994 Preakness and Belmont with Tabasco Cat; and won the Breeders' Cup Juvenile with Timber Country and the Juvenile Fillies with Flanders in 1994 as well.

Over that same span, Lukas had replaced him with Bailey, Gary Stevens, and, perhaps most insulting of all, Donna Barton, a very good rider but not nearly as accomplished as Day.

By 1996, Day had exercised a top jockey's prerogative and told his agent that if Lukas didn't have an odds-on horse for him, he should walk away. Day was no longer going to cultivate their relationship.

"It was a tough thing to do, because this is a business and it's one built on relationships. But we were at a point where Wayne had lost some faith in me and I had other clients with good horses they wanted me to ride," said Day.

By 1998, however, Lukas and Day were back making cheery talk at the barns in the morning and winning races together in the afternoon. The reason? Lukas finally valued the rider's strengths over his perceived weaknesses. What had frustrated Lukas and everyone who had ever ripped up a betting ticket on a horse Day rode was the jockey's deliberate style. He waited. He waited. And he waited until he could put his horse in position for one sustained run. Day was unwavering in his belief that no matter how talented a horse, it could run its top speed with maximum efficiency for only a quarter of a mile. His job until then was to get the animal to relax, keep him clear of trouble, and gauge the pace of the race to know when and where to uncork that run. To watch Day early in a race was like watching a jazz drummer sizing up his fellow sidemen and deciding when to pick up the tempo and command the spotlight himself. He had what Lukas called "baby hands," and they brushed and tapped around a horse's neck as gently as a father adjusting a blanket around his sleeping infant. The difference was that Day was doing this to a 1,100-pound animal at 35 miles per hour with dirt flying in his face and between equally powerful horses in spaces with barely enough room to slip a watermelon through. While his hands were working, however, his body remained perfectly still. He stretched out parallel to the horse's back, as undisturbed as a bee on a flower. His record was proof that his patience was successful. But Day often looked too passive, especially when that one run came up short. When that happened, he drew the curses of bettors and questions from trainers. For Lukas, the doubts arose in 1995 when Day finished third with Timber Country at the Derby. He told the rider so, and they came back to win the Preakness, but it was the beginning of the estrangement between rider and trainer.

What Lukas valued now as much as Day's talent was that he was settled, sober, and professional. Of course, every tale of addiction is shaped by its own particulars, and there is no evidence to suggest race riding is disproportionately rife with substance abuse. But in recent years, jockeys' struggles with addiction have often been very public and frequently driven by the nature of their unforgiving work. It afflicts young riders who suddenly make big money in a grueling year-round sport. It hits jockeys who are forced to be obsessive about their weight, men often struggling with lifelong concerns about being undersized. It grows out of a need to numb oneself after another day courting catastrophic injury.

In the past five years, state racing commissions around the country have investigated and taken action against at least 160 jockeys for alcohol or drug abuse. There are roughly 900 licensed jockeys in the United States, although not all of them are active at any given time.

This dark corner of horse racing found its way into the public eye during the 1999 Triple Crown campaign of Charismatic. The colt was a former claiming horse and late bloomer who wasn't expected to do much in those races. It wasn't just the bettors who thought so; Lukas couldn't find a rider willing to go to Kentucky and race in the Derby.

Except for one—Chris Antley. Just thirty-two, Antley had recently returned to riding after another stint in a drug rehabilitation center and a battle with his weight. He had once won nine races in a single day, riding afternoon and night at two tracks. He guided Strike the Gold to victory in the 1991 Kentucky Derby and was a savvy enough player of the stock market that he turned the $6 million he had earned riding racehorses into a fortune big enough to ensure that he would not have to work again. When he won with Charismatic, a 31–1 shot, in the Derby, his story was told and retold and became emblematic of the rough life of riders.

It was a harrowing tale of how, in 1988, he tested positive for marijuana and cocaine and soon surrendered his racing license. Of how, in 1997, he felt the addictions overwhelming him again and, after refusing a drug test at Hollywood Park, entered a clinic for a scheduled eighteen-day stint but ended up staying four months because he was more comfortable among recovering addicts than pretending he was not one around his fellow jockeys. Of his career's long battle to keep his weight in the 114- to 117-pound range necessary to get mounts, Antley had resorted to "flipping," or sticking a finger down his throat to induce vomiting, or eating laxatives and wilting in a sauna for hours, even ingesting Lasix—a diuretic that is often used on horses to reduce internal bleeding.

He broke hearts telling of how he returned home to his parents in South Carolina and hid out in a bedroom filled with newspaper clippings of his accomplishments as a rider. He was so overwhelmed by self-doubt that the highlight of his day became making the morning coffee. "I thought nobody would like me," said Antley, whose weight rose to 147 pounds. "I thought everybody hated me. I got big old fat cheeks. I wore extra-large T-shirts. I was crying inside."

Still, Antley had made it back and came very close to taking Charismatic to the Triple Crown. Lukas appreciated that and also knew that the jockey's decisive action to leap off the colt's back when he injured himself near the finish of the 1999 Belmont Stakes and hold the foot of Charismatic aloft until the ambulance arrived probably prevented further injury. In fact, Antley was going to ride two horses for Lukas in the Breeders' Cup.

But their relationship was cooling. Lukas was irritated with the media coverage of Antley's comeback, especially what he perceived as the forced connection between the overachieving Charismatic and the troubled jockey. He had recently stopped the filming of a piece

that was scheduled for a network newsmagazine when he thought
the reporter was trying to put words in his mouth.

"The first time he ever saw the horse was in the paddock at the
Derby. Chris never came by the barn once to take a look at the colt.
Don't tell me they needed each other," he explained later.

Lukas also was not satisfied with the quality of the rides Antley
had recently given to his horses. In fact, he believed the ride Antley
had given Charismatic in the Belmont was horrible. The colt had
won the first two legs of the Triple Crown by stalking the leaders
on the outside of the racetrack. At Belmont, Antley gunned Charismatic to the front to chase Silverbulletday. Lukas didn't know if
Antley got too excited or what, but the trainer says he did not want
Charismatic running in the front. Lukas believed Antley was becoming distracted again and, in Lukas's mind, was close to blowing his second chance.

"I'm not here to be the Red Cross of the backstretch, giving out
third and fourth chances," he said. "I'm looking for one thing, and
that's steadiness. There may be better gate riders than Pat, and better
finishers than Pat. There may be a guy who has a better sense of pace
than Pat, a guy who can pick one up and ride through holes better
than Pat. But I don't think there is anybody who can blend all those
things together any better than Pat."

The Antley story was familiar to Day, who began his career as a
hard-drinking teenage bull rider from Colorado. He worked his way
up through the minor tracks in Arizona to the Midwest circuit and
on to Kentucky. The more races he won, the more he drank. By the
1980s, he had graduated to smoking dope and snorting cocaine. He
was headstrong, mean, and miserable. He believes now he knows
why.

"You leave the nest pretty early and begin to fly pretty quick,"
Day said of the life of a jockey. "We're competitive people, maybe
because we've always been small and the brunt of jokes coming up.

There's a macho element, too. We don't talk about problems and our addictions."

It wasn't a rehab clinic or injury or the loss of his license that straightened out the rider. It was, he says, the Lord. It was a January night in 1984 and Day had just flown to Miami to ride in a big race. He checked into the Howard Johnson's near the airport and turned on the television. The evangelist Jimmy Swaggart was conducting a revival. Day watched for a few moments and then clicked off the television and went to sleep. Soon, though, he awoke to the sound of the television. Swaggart was still on. The jockey felt the spirit of something overwhelm him. He fell to his knees and wept. He became a born-again Christian at that moment. "I turned my life over to the Lord because I was tired of being numb," he said.

The story is the genesis of the nickname Saint Pat. It was also the beginning of his sobriety and the string of successes that led him to the Hall of Fame. Lukas, as well as other trainers, recognized this clarity, as they did in the nation's other top rider, Bailey, another Hall of Famer. He was four years younger than Day, but Bailey experienced a similar career renaissance after admitting he was an alcoholic and giving up drinking in 1989 at the age of thirty-one. No one—not the two riders, nor any trainers—thought it was an accident that they were the best in the business.

Lukas was riding them both in each of the 2-year-old Breeders' Cup races. Bailey was on High Yield in the Juvenile and Cash Run in the Fillies. Day had the mount for Millencolin in the Juvenile and for Surfside in the Fillies race. Surfside had won four of five of her starts and was so well-bred—the daughter of Seattle Slew and Flanders— that the trainer had said she was "like the child of Richard Burton and Elizabeth Taylor."

"And Pat and Surfside go together like peanut butter and jelly, like ham and eggs," he said, once more reverting to the happy talk.

The rider just smiled. He had heard that one before, too.

"Bet my name. I'm hopeful. I was a long shot once, too."
—Hugh Hefner on November 6, 1999, at Gulfstream Park
before his namesake colt finished fourteenth in the Breeders' Cup
Juvenile at 40–1. Afterward, however, neither the Playboy
founder nor his three barely dressed Playmates looked
too downcast about the setback.

Hef came to have a good time, as did the crowd of 45,124 who showed up to see the world's best horses go nose to nose. It is always my intention to enjoy myself, especially at a racetrack. I usually succeed even on afternoons when picking the winners proves elusive, and the Breeders' Cup is hands down the most challenging day for handicappers—like trying to capture soap bubbles in the wind.

For me the Breeders' Cup is a melancholy affair, and it has nothing to do with the event or the races or the horses. My mother died on the eve of the 1991 Breeders' Cup, a year it was held at Churchill Downs, which also was the first year a Pick Seven was offered with great fanfare to bettors. The proposition was straightforward: Pick the winners of the seven championship races; collect millions of dollars. It's strange what you choose to remember.

What I recall about the moment of my mother's death was sitting in a sticky vinyl chair in the corner of her dark hospital room, poring over the past performances of the Breeders' Cup horses. They had been copied from the *Daily Racing Form* and faxed to me. She was in a coma after a long and debilitating illness. The machines had been turned off and the length of our vigil was measured by her breaths, which became fewer and further between as each day passed. So I buried my eyes and pen in my scroll of past performances and, with one ear cocked toward her bed, waited for a breath *not* to come. Every time another one did, I focused harder on the charts.

I had never played a Pick Six, the bet available at most tracks, and the one that was the model for this Breeders' Cup Pick Seven, but I sure as hell was going to give this one a whirl. I began to believe I was owed a consolation million, that I was going to pick the correct seven horses and Mom was going make sure they came in. When my mother's final gasp did come, about 8 P.M. on October 31, I did in fact want to hear another.

Instead, all I got was a list of errands to execute before the funeral and a combination of horses that I believed were divinely inspired and certain to memorialize Mom and me at the Breeders' Cup. The next morning I went about my duties and slid by the track and made my bets. I stopped by my childhood parish to light candles and pray for my mother. Conveniently, it was across the street from the Corner Cocktails, the one place in Kansas City where horses are discussed and worshiped and which has been, for twenty years, the unofficial church basement for folks who grew up with my family. I settled in to watch the races. By dusk, I believed I'd be lighting candles with hundred-dollar bills.

Word had already spread about our family's loss and condolences were sent over by way of cold beer, kind words, and raised glasses. That, unfortunately, was about the best part of my day, because as soon as the first race went off, I was out of the running for the $1 million payout. In the Sprint, Sheikh Albadou, a 26–1 shot and a horse I didn't have, won. Still, I thought, if I hit six of seven there should be a pretty fair consolation payoff.

That delusion lasted only an additional forty minutes: Pleasant Stage, another horse I had neglected, won the Juvenile Fillies. And on it went, defeat after defeat after defeat after defeat. Finally, I was down to the final race, the Classic.

It was the only race, frankly, I had a strong opinion on. It was grounded in solid handicapping, but it also was a hunch play for me. Black Tie Affair was a gray Irish-bred that had won four in a row in the Midwest, which was a step below the California, Kentucky, and New York circuits. My mother was half Irish, always fell in love with gray horses, and championed anything Midwestern or thought to be second-tier. She would have bet this horse. When Black Tie Affair came in, I took some comfort though I had fallen $999,900 short of my betting goal. There was no grand memorial for my mother, no hundred-dollar bills up in flames. I did, however, cross the street to light another candle before I went home.

Subsequently, I have attended Breeders' Cup day with an ineffable sense of loss. If I needed any further evidence that this is a cursed event for me, I was given it some eight years later in Florida when I lost my wallet on the morning of the races.

Picking horses, like all potentially profitable endeavors, takes money to make money. I had a few bucks in my pocket, but without a bank card I had no way of getting more. There's nothing worse than being undercapitalized when you believe you have a vision of how a day at the races will unfold. It's also terrible karma to borrow money at the track.

The act reeks of desperation and gives credence to the observation made by Damon Runyon that "all horseplayers die broke." I had reluctantly decided to make do with the little finances I had when I crossed paths with a terrible temptation: my soon to be ex-wife.

As fate would have it, she, too, is in the sports journalism profession and as a television producer was assigned to horse racing. We had been estranged for more than a year but were as amicable, I guess, as a couple could be when a marriage is dissolving. Maybe because we had spent seven not altogether unpleasant years together, or because we knew we'd have to see each other in professional settings, we had kept our hurt private and treated each other warmly whenever we saw each other.

Now I had a dilemma. On one hand, she was the single person in Gulfstream Park who'd be sympathetic to my situation and discreet about floating me a loan. Her father had taken her to the races as a little girl and she subsequently became an often and enthusiastic partner in my trips to the track. On the other hand, we hadn't reached a final settlement, and did I really want to hit her up for cash?

No Solomon am I, so I asked to borrow $100; she graciously offered $200 and my spirits rose. Then they actually soared after a victory in the second Breeders' Cup race of the day, the Juvenile Fillies. It didn't have much to do with my prowess as a handicapper. It was a good old-fashioned hunch.

Baffert's Chilukki was the well-deserved favorite. She had won all six of her races, beaten the boys once, and had earned $562,723. Lukas's Surfside was her most formidable challenger, having won three of four and possessing the ability to "rate" or run off the pace and close ground late.

But I had my heart and money set on an old acquaintance: Cash Run, the filly who had made Lukas forget momentarily that Charismatic was in surgery the day after the Belmont and had launched me on to the Triple Crown trail. Unfortunately, after that Belmont debut, Cash Run hadn't come close to repeating her monster maiden victory. She was beaten by 11¼ lengths in her next race, followed that with a victory, and then got crushed by 6½ lengths in a stakes race.

Like Chilukki, so far she had shown just one dimension as a runner—speed. Unlike the Baffert filly, she seemed to get discouraged when rivals ran early with her. She would quit. Lukas offered excuses for her. He said she was "horsing," or in heat, for her first loss. In the losing stakes effort, jockey Craig Perret was put on her at the last minute when bad weather prevented Jerry Bailey from getting to Kentucky on time for the race. The filly was also entering the race with a sore hoof caused by a stone bruise or a too-close shaving by the blacksmith in the week leading up to the race.

Lukas was never quite clear on what happened, but Cash Run was wearing the more comfortable and forgiving glued-on shoes for the race. Still, the trainer had faith in the filly and claimed that he had turned down up to $4 million from rival owners interested in Cash Run.

At odds of 30–1 and Bailey back aboard, I was willing to put some money across the board—a win, place, and show ticket all in one—on Cash Run for old times' sake. When the gates popped, she broke from the No. 1 post full of that early run I had witnessed at Belmont Park. The difference, though, was Chilukki was right on her flank and matching her every stride. At the ⅝ pole, David Flores turned Chilukki lose and the undefeated filly pushed her head in front of Cash Run. I thought, OK, now my filly quits and I'm on to the next race. But something extraordinary happened: Cash Run didn't quit.

With Bailey working the whip in his left hand, she fought back and, at the top of the stretch, got her slim head back in front of Chilukki. Bailey grabbed the reins with both hands near her jaw and urged her to give him one final burst. Cash Run drew away by a length and a quarter for the victory.

When the prices flashed on the tote board, there was a roar from the Gulfstream crowd. For a $2 bet, Cash Run paid $67 to win, $17.60 to place, and $6.40 to show. Immediately, my conscience was clear. I found my soon-to-be ex, thanked her, and paid back the money she had staked me. Maybe this wasn't going to be an awful day after all.

For Baffert, however, it was the beginning of a long afternoon. It was the second straight race in which he had sent out a favorite who had been beaten. In the prior race, the Distaff, Pegram's Silverbulletday ran a desultory sixth. And on it went.

In the Sprint, Forestry, the cofavorite, was a well-beaten fourth. In the Juvenile, Forest Camp was the top choice and finished sixth. In the Classic, General Challenge finished tenth, four lengths in front of his stablemate River Keen. Worst perhaps was that the $4 million Classic was won by the Lukas-trained Cat Thief, who had one victory in eleven starts in 1999, and was sent off at 19–1 with Day aboard.

The final score for the afternoon? Lukas with two victories; Baffert zero. Afterward, Baffert tried to summon a smile and shrug off the oh-for Breeders' Cup performance as the vagaries of racing. The racing gods were against him this day. While Lukas and Day celebrated their record fifteenth and eleventh Breeders' Cup victories in the winner's circle with Cat Thief, Baffert strode quickly from the track to the barns.

"There's too much emphasis on me," the trainer said glumly.

Fortunately for the trainer, a pickup truck appeared and offered an escape from the crowd and the questions. No wins. No smiles. No wit. Baffert climbed on the back and was unceremoniously carted to the backside.

The mood was more jubilant at the Lukas barn the following morning as the trainer and Pat Day carried on like an old couple who had just renewed their marriage vows and returned from a second honeymoon. The jockey's winning ride on Cat Thief had overshadowed the troubled trip he'd had on Lukas's prized filly Surfside. They managed to finish a fast-closing third behind Cash Run and Chilukki after being fanned wide the entire trip around the track. Of his two fillies, Lukas decided Surfside was tough enough to take on the colts and try the Triple Crown.

Of his 2-year-old colts, Lukas now knew High Yield was his top prospect for the spring classics. He wasn't worried about the colt's third-place finish. Lukas had sent a horse to the Derby for a record nineteen consecutive years. He had the horses; he knew how to get them there.

"When you get to the paddock there's an air of peace about him," Day was now saying of his partner. "He communicates everything between the horse's ears. He can take the shank and walk horses around in a circle and they calm down and respond to him. It's really something."

Lukas listened. Two Breeders' Cup victories. Two legs of the Triple Crown. Induction into the Hall of Fame. It had been a pretty good year for the trainer. He tried to resist gloating and even fended off the notion that he may have just wrested trainer of the year honors away from Baffert. He had tried to downplay the pair's feud for most of the week.

He thought it was too public already, but he couldn't resist having the last word.

"I didn't read his book, didn't read Charlie Whittingham's and Woody Stephens's books, either," he said, referring to two Hall of Fame trainers. "The only books that matter are the ones with the records in them. You'll find my name in them a lot, too."

Chapter 8

OUT TO PASTURE: TRIPLE CROWN DREAMS DERAILED

NOVEMBER 23, 1999

OCALA, FLORIDA

"I think horses get to the point that they're like, 'Why do I have to go out and run my ass off? It hurts—I'm sore for three days afterwards.'"
— *J. J. Pletcher*

More Than Ready was off the Triple Crown trail.

The closest the colt got to the Breeders' Cup Juvenile race was this farm near Ocala in central Florida about a mile from the Don Garlits Museum of Drag Racing. It was J. J. Pletcher's place, the Payton Training Center, on eighty acres with 248 stalls filled mostly with 2-year-olds who had yet to begin their racing careers. Jim Scatuorchio and Eddie Rosen made it to the Breeders' Cup at Gulfstream Park, sporting black ball caps with the lettering "More Than Ready 2000."

It was all they had left—hope that somehow the colt could bounce back from a mystifying fall season.

The colt that was a superstar in Saratoga Springs was forgotten now. The Kentucky Derby, Preakness, and Belmont Stakes were five months away, but Scatuorchio was no longer certain he had a Triple Crown horse. First, the owner would have to get More Than Ready back to the track in Florida in January. Then the colt would have to win, or at least run well enough, to show he belonged in the starting gate of the Kentucky Derby.

Scatuorchio. His trainer, Todd Pletcher. Nobody knew for sure what had happened.

On September 19, fifty-two days after missing the Hopeful Stakes in Saratoga Springs with that spiked fever, the colt returned in the Grade I Futurity at Belmont Park. He ran third, beaten just a half length by a pair of horses named Bevo and Greenwood Lake. It was a loss that Scatuorchio and Pletcher could live with because More Than Ready was coming off a long layoff and stretching out to one mile for the first time in his brief and brilliant career.

Three weeks later, on October 9, in another Grade I race at Belmont Park, the Champagne, the colt barely lifted his feet and finished fifth. Team Scatuorchio was mortified when More Than Ready uncharacteristically quit halfway through the race. Something had to be wrong. When they returned to the barn, however, the colt appeared to be fine—there was no limp or hitch or any other physical sign of an injury. He had trained well coming into the race and had finished up his oats afterward as if nothing was wrong.

It was a disconcerting development on a night that was supposed to be joyous. Jim was turning fifty-three and had reserved the wine cellar at "21" in Manhattan for a birthday celebration with more than a dozen friends. He was a distracted host throughout the evening, barely able to muster a smile. The evening ended early. In his head, Scatuorchio knew no horse wins every race. In his heart, however, he believed More Than Ready was going to take him to the winner's circle every time he showed up on the track. In the Futurity and Champagne, the colt's first two tries at the Grade 1 level or against the best of his generation, More Than Ready gave some evidence that he may not belong on the Triple Crown trail.

Two days after the race, Jim and Todd decided to send More Than Ready to Lexington, Kentucky, and veterinarian Larry Bramlage at the Rood and Riddle Equine Clinic, which was the Mayo Clinic for horses. They believed something had to be wrong internally, something they couldn't see. In Kentucky, the colt was scoped, x-rayed, and blood work was taken and examined. But Bramlage and his colleagues found nothing wrong. Not a cold, a virus, a hairline fracture, or a pulled muscle.

So More Than Ready was sent here to J. J. Pletcher, where he'd first learned the basics of being a racehorse almost a year ago. Then the colt was just like the hundred or so at the farm now—unproven babies seeing their first starting gate and learning how to change leads on the five eighths of a mile training track, or learning to lead with the left leg heading into a turn and switching to the right coming out. Now More Than Ready was ordered to do little or nothing. For an a hour a day, the colt circled a walking pen that was piled with six inches of rubber-foam shaving and paced by hydraulic gates that moved him in circles automatically. J. J. Pletcher had two of the state-of-the-art exercise machines, which cost $65,000 each.

But mostly what the colt did was what he was doing now, as the sun was coming up and evaporating the morning dew. He was frolicking in a large, grassy pen—up to six hours a day.

Watching More Than Ready rolling in the dirt until his black coat was dappled with beige mud, I could hardly believe that seven times he had been led onto a racetrack with a rider on his back. And five times he returned tired, sweaty, and the fastest horse in the race.

Here he acted like the adolescent he was. The colt scrambled to his feet and then burst to one end of the pen and back to the other like he was playing tag with an invisible playmate. He trotted to see J.J. and me, nodding his head up and down, asking to be nuzzled. Then, defiantly, he pulled away. The old trainer leaned over the fence, smiled, and began talking to the colt.

"You get to thinking you're invincible when you should know better. The best trainers, the best jockeys in the world, win 20 percent of the time. The best vets in the world took a look at you and couldn't find anything. Could they?" J.J. asked the colt, the smile still on his face. "You may have pulled a muscle somewhere down deep that didn't show up. Or maybe you got a hairline fracture somewhere. But you're trying to tell us something, aren't you?"

Then J.J. turned to me.

"I think horses get to the point that they're like, 'Why do I have to go out and run my ass off? It hurts—I'm sore for three days afterwards,'" he said.

There was no absence of theories to what had derailed More Than Ready. The one most often offered by racetrack sorts was the one More Than Ready's team members detested. He was just a sprinter meant for shorter distances, a precocious one to be sure, but now his peers had finally caught up with him. Eddie Rosen insisted the pedigree suggested the opposite. Todd Pletcher swore the colt's turn of foot and stride begged for more ground, and that More Than Ready was still learning, still improving as a racehorse. The trainer had had sprinters that had come to hand early and then flattened out. None of them had been as smart or tried as hard as More Than Ready.

The explanation they believed was the one that was the toughest for them to admit—that they had run the colt too much, too early, and had gotten caught up in how effortlessly he performed. That maybe they had missed the signs that they were wearing him out.

J. J. Pletcher could say that's what happened because he wasn't in charge. He also had forty-plus years of training experience and many mistakes behind him. His son was in charge, and no matter how accomplished Todd already was, no matter how in control he appeared, this was his first genuine Triple Crown prospect. Perhaps he had been too eager.

Scatuorchio, too, was second-guessing himself. Had he gotten too caught up in the winning? In the stud deals, which not surprisingly were now off? The balance sheet?

He was paying a $250,000 premium for an $8 million insurance policy for More Than Ready; the training, veterinarian, and transportation bills totaled an additional $75,000 a year. It was $100 a pop alone for a pill that treated the colt's ulcers.

Maybe he had pushed too hard.

Scatuorchio decided there was no sense in pointing fingers at himself or at anybody else. They had hoped for a medical reason as to why the colt stopped running. They didn't get it.

So they moved More Than Ready to J. J. Pletcher's and regrouped. Come spring they'd have a plan to get the colt back to the racetrack. They told one another, they told themselves, that this time they'd pay better attention.

Chapter 9

THE WEST COAST: THE BEST HORSES?

JANUARY 2000

ARCADIA, CALIFORNIA

"Horse sense is what keeps horses from betting on what people will do."
——*Damon Runyon*

The West Coast versus East Coast, Los Angeles versus New York, debate dominates everything from food and fashion to lifestyle and culture. It's no different in horse racing. The perceptions, too, are in the same vein. New York is home to old- money owners and taciturn trainers. They are caretakers of a grand and important heritage, which is embodied by its premier meet: in bucolic Saratoga Springs, at a racetrack that was founded in the 1860s and nurtured by the velvet touch of people named Travers and Vanderbilt. California racing, on the other hand, is a stop for the nouveaux riches who are enchanted with glib celebrity trainers. They are dilettantes who it is said don't know horses, which is embodied by their premier meet: in an overbuilt beach town named Del Mar at a racetrack that was founded in 1937 by Bing Crosby and became the play-ground of the likes of W. C. Fields, Red Skelton, and Burt Bacharach.

The pros and cons of each vary, but what brought me to Arcadia, California, and Santa Anita Park were a couple of indisputable facts. One, West Coast trainers had won the last five Kentucky Derbys, and their horses of late had become the most dependable competitors on the Triple Crown trail. Too, they appeared to be loaded once again with live contenders.

The winter base for most trainers and horses was here at Santa Anita Park, 320 acres of perfect Hollywood backdrop about forty miles northeast of Los Angeles. The track is rimmed by the San Gabriel Mountains, which, more often than not, are bathed in sun-shine and form a rouge halo above these foothills.

The weather and aesthetics were why the track seemed more crowded during the morning workouts—not only with horses but with people—than any other track in the nation. All gathered at the corner of the grandstand near the top of the stretch. This was Clock-ers' Corner, which was the nexus for trainers and touts, jockey agents

toting thick daybooks, their riders in flak jackets and helmets, owners with binoculars, and nearly all of them with a *Racing Form* tucked
under their arm. It was partly an office—agents buttonholed trainers and tried to hustle rides for their jocks as the conditioners clicked
their stopwatches and watched their horses stride around the track.
It was partly a watercooler—rumors and gossip were passed back and
forth as quickly as the horsemen darted from their barns to the break-
fast counter, which, in quintessentially California style, sold everything from cappuccino and lattes to bagels and omelettes.

One trainer, however, tried to recede into the background by sitting
at a table far back from the bustle. Jenine Sahadi had a steaming cup of
coffee and a brimming ashtray before her. She was thirty-seven and ar-
guably on her way to becoming the most successful female trainer in
the history of horse racing. She wore jeans and a sweatshirt under a
windbreaker, though it failed to camouflage the fact that she was a
woman, an attractive woman. She is tall with thick, brown hair that
falls on her shoulders. Sahadi possesses a direct, authoritative manner
perfect for television, which is the career a journalism degree from the
University of Southern California had prepared her for. Sahadi certainly
wasn't intimidated by the men's-club nature of her profession. She was
just weary of trying to prove she belonged.

She knew the game's highs: She became the first female trainer to
win a $1 million race when Lit de Justice took the Breeders' Cup
Sprint in 1996, then won it again with Elmhurst in 1997. She knew
its lows. In 1998, she suffered through a seventy-race losing streak and
finished the year without a stakes victory. Now she was somewhere
in between. Among the horses she had sent to the track today was
The Deputy, the obscure Irish-bred that Team Valor had purchased
in England. The colt was just out for a gallop, having already made
Barry Irwin, and the pitch letter he'd sent to potential Team Valor
partners back in September, look clairvoyant.

Less than two weeks ago, The Deputy had demonstrated the late
kick that the syndicate's president saw on videotape to win a $76,000

stakes race here in his American debut. Even though it was on turf, it was a fine prep race and an encouraging start to a Triple Crown campaign.

Getting The Deputy in her barn was a break for Sahadi. She had some good older horses and was winning prominent races, but none of them with the potential to attract the national spotlight like a good 3-year-old can. Even though Gary Barber, the South African movie producer, was her client and a 50 percent owner of The Deputy, it wasn't a given that she'd get the opportunity to train the colt. There were some members of the Team Valor syndicate—including Irwin's cofounder, Jeff Siegel—who wanted the horse to go elsewhere. Sahadi was too young, too inexperienced, and, of course, she was a woman.

Still, Irwin had known and come to like Sahadi from the seven years she had spent in the publicity and marketing department at Hollywood Park. She was bright, outgoing, and had a deft touch with grumpy media types. He knew she could also be headstrong, edgy, and not the most popular trainer on the California tracks. In fact, it was a strong-willed decision that had led her from the front side of horse racing to the backside in 1991. When she did not get a promotion in the track's administration that she felt she deserved, Sahadi quit and decided to train horses. It was hardly a stretch—her father, Fred, founded one of California's largest breeding operations, Cardiff Stud Farm, and owned the 1983 Kentucky Derby runner-up, Desert Wine.

"I understood this was a commonsense business," she said, "that you're a caretaker and the trick is to find the right spot for your horses to run."

She followed the traditional path and became an assistant trainer to a respected horseman named Julio Canani. That path got slippery and made her a topic of conversation at Clockers' Corner, however, when she became romantically involved with him as he was going through a divorce. When she took out her trainer's license in 1993, Canani became a bloodstock agent and left her three horses. Friends of her family sent her a dozen more and Sahadi persuaded a sorority sister, Mary Louise Sloan, and her husband, Mike, to increase their stock. Pretty soon she had a successful stable of twenty horses and showed skill with a variety of horses. Lit de Justice was so unruly he had to be blindfolded to enter the starting gate; Elmhurst was a 5-year-old maiden that Sahadi had gelded and turned into a sprint champion; and Megan's Interco won three Cal Cup Classics, and a stakes race at the age of ten, despite hoof problems that limited him to four races a year.

These accomplishments, however, were diminished by rumors that Canani was training the horses. The whispers on the backsides of tracks soon found their way onto radio shows and wore on Sahadi. "There are very few activities that are so male-oriented. They aren't excited about a woman entering the business and doing so well so fast," explained Mike Sloan.

Three years ago, Sahadi split with Canani, who has since returned to training, and the talk about who trained the horses disappeared, but only briefly. Even though she had the two Breeders' Cup victories, Sahadi's stable did not grow.

Shortly after marrying another trainer, Ben Cecil, Sahadi went into her seventy-race slump. It got so bad that her brother told her to drop one of his horses into a $32,000 claiming race and try to get a victory. She warned him they were going to lose a good horse.

"We got beat by a nose and the horse got claimed and went on to win three races for the new owners," she said. "I couldn't do anything right."

She was ready to quit and auditioned for TVG, a racing network available to 4.5 million subscribers in three states at the time and with ambitious plans for expanding. She spoke with track officials here about doing on-site television work. Then a good horse appeared and led to what may be a great horse. In both cases, Irwin was responsible.

In the mid-1990s, the Team Valor president admired how Sahadi had handled a claiming horse for his syndicate. When he purchased a filly in Italy named Sweet Ludy in late 1998, Irwin decided to try her again. It paid off when Sweet Ludy won a couple of important stakes races.

"She had done well with European horses, and is good at sizing horses up and running them where they belong," Irwin said. "Jenine lets them tell her what to do."

He was certain that The Deputy and Sahadi fit together and that the coupling was in keeping with Team Valor's Triple Crown strategy. The syndicate had chosen little-known trainers in the past and been successful. Irwin knew that The Deputy would be the best horse in Sahadi's barn and would receive more individual attention. Finally, Irwin got the partners to agree to let Sahadi train the horse.

But even Irwin wondered if he'd screwed up when he received a phone call from Sahadi soon after. It was November 14 and he was at Aqueduct in New York to watch another promising 2-year-old, named Uncommon Valor, work out.

"Where the hell are you?" she asked.

"I'm in New York getting ready to watch the winner of the 2000 Kentucky Derby," Irwin answered.

"That's impossible. I just worked him a half in forty-seven flat," she said.

The Deputy had been out of quarantine after arriving from Europe for only sixteen days. Irwin didn't understand what the hurry was to get him on the track. He also was irritated that the colt's time was so fast. He called Siegel and told him to keep an eye on Sahadi and to watch the next workouts of The Deputy.

Three weeks later, with Siegel watching, Hall of Fame jockey Chris McCarron was aboard for what was supposed to be an easy six-furlong drill. The colt tossed that one off in a very fast 1:11 and galloped out seven furlongs in 1:24. Siegel was excited when he reached Irwin.

"He is not being asked, believe me. He is just so good and does it so easily, it's a little hard to believe he is going that fast," he told Irwin.

The crowd at Clockers' Corner began to notice. They got more interested after The Deputy easily won a turf race, the Hill Rise Handicap. The plan now was to try out the colt on the dirt. Sahadi had little doubt The Deputy was going to take her a long way into the spring, perhaps as far as Louisville and the Derby. As fast as he was, what impressed the trainer most was the horse's maturity—he was as poised and patient as some of the older horses in her barn.

Sahadi needed to summon those same attributes herself. The old questions had been resurrected and were making the rounds. Her husband, Cecil, was the nephew of famed English trainer Henry Cecil. He'd been seen at his wife's barn an awful lot, hadn't he? He knows a thing or two about European horses, doesn't he? Maybe Cecil was training the Deputy? Sahadi was back in the uncomfortable position of proving that she could train a horse.

"No one else would have to put up with it, and it's frustrating," Sahadi said. "'I didn't hear anything for a couple years because I didn't have a horse of consequence. The minute I pop up with something good, everyone says I'm not responsible."

"He doth nothing but talk of his horse."
—The Merchant of Venice, *William Shakespeare*

It was 10 A.M. and Wayne Lukas's horses already had been worked, cooled out, bathed, fed, and returned to their stalls at his headquarters barn at Santa Anita Park. The only sound was that of a rake sculpting the dirt around his barn into a herringbone pattern. It didn't matter that the symmetry would be disturbed as soon as the trainer walked down the shed row to check on a horse, Lukas wanted this done twice a day. The old coach in him believed that good habits repeated over and over brought success. Lukas had many rules for his staff. There was no talking, no radio, no TV, no coffee, no headphones, no smoking, and definitely no alcohol in sight. His staff was not allowed to swear, and if his Hispanic employees wanted to talk to the boss, they did so in English. Twenty years ago, there also were no women on his barn staff, a ban that was lifted for practical reasons—a shortage of good help—not because of personal enlightenment.

This was Wayne's World. It was a sanctuary, as much for him as for his horses. He had a small office, a closet really, with a standard-issue desk whose top had room for one task at a time. On it now was a report faxed from his thirteen-person corporate office in Ocala, Florida, on what each of the 200 horses in his care were doing today. Who was shipping to Belmont. Who was racing in Kentucky. Who had worked how fast in each of his three horse racing divisions across the country.

On the wall, there was a board charting the horses training at Santa Anita; blue marker meant they were racing, yellow for those working. Lukas and his longtime assistant Randy Bradshaw had already taken four sets of horses to the track for training this morning, the first set in the dark. They were out there before anyone else. With Lukas on horseback riding point, the mist of his breath hitting the brim of his cowboy hat, and Bradshaw leading the stagger of four other horses and exercise riders, they looked like a posse returning home empty-handed.

Lukas had been here, as he is every morning, since 3:30 A.M. Between 4 and 5 A.M., he took the calls that are required from his assistants who head his divisions across the country: Mike Marlowe from New York, Mike Maker from Kentucky, and Barry Knight from New Jersey. This was an intercontinental office meeting that served two purposes. First, Lukas wanted to make sure his people showed up and the horses were all right; second, this was the time to give progress reports and discuss any problems encountered in training. Lukas still had a lot of teacher left in him. Not only did his assistants have to pose the problem, they had to offer two potential solutions to solve it.

"I have smart people. I pay them well. But I'm the boss. I don't want them to think for themselves. I want them to think like me. The enemy of good is better," he said, falling back on one of his many dog-eared maxims. "I want them to tell me what they would do. Then I tell them what we're going to do. They get five minutes of democracy. The rest is a dictatorship."

Between 11 A.M. and 1 P.M., the assistants would call again to talk about the afternoon's races and to review the performances of the horses who had been on the track that morning. They were required to call him again at home that night—it didn't matter when, because he was an insomniac who slept as little as two hours a night. Lukas was perhaps the only trainer in the sport who didn't own a cell phone. He said it made him too accessible, but really it was another way to enforce his regimen on those around him. All the rules were unbreakable, but the one that was sacred, that carried the threat of termination, was not notifying him immediately after a mishap.

"No damn surprises. I won't have them. The worst thing that could happen is if a client calls and says, 'I hear my colt got caught in the stall and took a chunk of skin out,' and I don't know anything about it. I better be able to say 'Yes, sir, we had a vet over there in ten minutes. He cleaned it, wrapped it, he's coming back in the morning, and I'll call you as soon as I know something.' I never want to be blind-sided. I won't accept one of my guys saying, 'I didn't want to bother you.' This is my life."

There were plenty of sticks for his assistants, but the carrots were in place, too. They got experience training expensive horseflesh. Lukas brought them into the office to listen to phone calls he had with owners, told them to listen to his tone and how he controlled the conversation. He made each of them give weekly briefings to the owners whose stock they supervised. To work for him, you needed more than talent with horses. You needed humility and a thick skin. You had to want to learn how to communicate. You had to develop some nerve, for better or worse.

Lukas has been a detail and image man ever since his days as a high school basketball coach and in the backwaters of quarter horse racing. At Logan High School in La Crosse, Wisconsin, his team wore matching sport coats provided by a local clothier and were given etiquette lessons by a hostess from the local Holiday Inn. He even built his own barn at Park Jefferson in South Dakota to contribute some grandeur to his operation on the bush track's run-down backside. He liked hearing himself talk about the Lukas way.

Both qualities led to his big break. In 1979, John Nerud, at the time the president of Tartan Farm, was in California scouting for a trainer to take over what he believed were quality stakes horses. He had never met Lukas, but he kept being drawn back to the trainer's pristine barn. One morning he saw Lukas on the track on horseback with that signature hat and decided to introduce himself. Lukas had no idea who he was.

"What can I help you with, old man?" he asked of Nerud, the trainer of 1957 Belmont winner Gallant Man and a member of racing's Hall of Fame since 1972.

Nerud is an irreverent sort himself and was amused by Lukas's nonchalance. They got to talking and Nerud became even more taken with Lukas's theories and bombast. He decided to turn over eight horses to Lukas. One of them was Codex, who gave Lukas his first victory in a Triple Crown race when he won the 1980 Preakness.

"A shed row is a hospital, and Wayne had the best of everything—feed, hay, wraps. Even when he didn't have much, he always acted like the first-class horseman," said Nerud. "He's an arrogant man. He's got his opinions and they come out quick. He wants you to hear them and listen to them. But I believe he has shown that he's earned that right for all he's done."

Lukas had created a national racing stable the same way McDonald's created a burger empire. He understood his assistants were the key component of the franchise expansion. Before he came along, New York trainers stayed in New York and California trainers in California. He recognized that by doing so, the one-barn trainers were missing large purses everywhere else. They were missing opportunities to spot their horses where they were able to win, to keep the good horses in their own barn from running against one another, which ultimately kept more owners winning and happy. They were missing an opportunity to grow and maximize earnings.

"It's about quality control. We don't ship people, we ship horses. It doesn't matter where they get off the plane. They're going to walk in the same stall, eat the same feed, get bathed with the same soap at the same time, and keep the same training routine. Our horses don't have to adjust when they get to a new place because everything is the same. It is the McDonald's principle, because wherever you go, you're going to get the same thing."

There was more than ego and accomplishments on his résumé at stake for the Lukas program. He needed to win races to make money. Lukas claimed that his day rate, the cost of keeping and training a horse, didn't cover his overhead. He started in the hole, he said, losing $1.06 per day for each horse he had in training. For his operation to break even, his horses had to win $10 million annually in purses. He said the only certain money he had, his pension fund, was the forty-three breeding rights that he was given by owners of horses he had trained.

It was customary for an owner of a horse who performed well enough to become a stallion prospect to award his trainer a lifetime breeding right. Bob Lewis, for example, gave Lukas two for Charismatic, who in his first season at stud commanded a $30,000 fee.

Like most trainers, Lukas sold them, which meant theoretically, on Charismatic alone, he could collect $60,000 a year. If Charismatic proved a quality sire, his stud fee would increase. If he was blessed with stamina, like Mr. Prospector, who died at the age of twenty-nine, Lukas could be collecting dividends on Charismatic for a long time. With breeding rights to horses like Thunder Gulch ($25,000) and more than a dozen others, Lukas had better pension than most.

But horses—buying, training, talking, and thinking about them— was all Lukas had. He was more relaxed here at his California base, but not because he had other outlets for his interests. Unlike Drysdale, the gourmand, reader, and theater-goer, Lukas had no other outside activities. From here, he'd go to his home in nearby Glendora and change into a suit before returning to the track. Even on days he didn't have horses running, Lukas was there to scout the competition and to roam the owners' boxes—either touching base with his current clients or wooing future ones. Leisure time for Lukas was sitting in front of his big-screen television with basketball games pulled down from the satellite, often watching two games at a time in the picture-within-picture feature.

He counted former Indiana University coach Bobby Knight as a close friend, as well as former California coach and legend Pete Newell. They not only shared a passion for the game, but were consumed with their single-minded visions of how things should be done. Like him, they were zealous about taking something with raw talent and enforcing their will on it, to make it a winner. Even watching a basketball game, however, wasn't a passive pastime for Lukas. He was too competitive. He liked picking teams against the betting lines and playing pools. It was another area where he needed to be right.

"I'm getting a reputation for being a guru around here for picking basketball games," he boasted. "I still know plenty about the game. I've just been killing them with how right I am."

Many—Bob Lewis for one—believed the combination of age and his new wife had mellowed Lukas of late. Lukas married Laura Pinelli on June 15, 1998. She was wife number four, thirty-one years old and a trainer herself. In fact, she had lured Lukas back into quarter horses and was conditioning a string of twenty-nine of them he had bought. Lukas wanted to fool around with them, but he also looked at them as another pension.

"We're building a band of quality brood mares so if I drop dead she'll have something to live off of," he said.

The quarters ran at night at Los Alamitos in Orange County, and Lukas often would change back into his jeans after the Thoroughbred races and make the trek across town to watch. Afterward, he helped his wife get the horses settled in the barn. That meant a long day of horses—3 A.M. to midnight—and the trainer loved every minute of it. Lukas didn't exactly go soft when talking about his new wife, but he agreed she had brought him some peace. He told stories about her. Like how at last year's Kentucky Derby she told him not to bet on Charismatic, even at 31–1. That no matter how much he liked the colt's chances, a bet would jinx Charismatic. Lukas sometimes makes a bet or two on his horses. So as soon as she headed to the bathroom, he made a beeline for the window and plunked $2,000 down on the colt's nose. Not until long after they'd left the winner's circle did she know her husband had a ticket worth $64,400 in his pocket.

"She's a little old cowgirl. She'd get in there and muck out the stall herself," he said with a fond smile. "We were racing in Kentucky recently and she came down, but her plane was late and she had to come straight to the track. She's wearing jeans and a work shirt, and bless her heart, she was embarrassed about not being able to change. I wouldn't have her any other way. The thing is, she understands this business and she understands me. I'm sure a marriage counselor will tell you I'm not a very good risk. I don't do anything but train horses.

"I know it's a very unbalanced life, but that's the way it is. It's almost a sickness. I don't recommend it to anybody, but I know that it works for me."

Still, his new wife provided some balance that Lukas had been missing since December 1993, when he nearly lost the only thing that meant more to him than horses: his son. Jeff Lukas had been his father's top assistant since 1978, when Wayne pulled him from the University of Wisconsin after a single semester. Jeff was as immersed in the horses as his father and, according to Todd Pletcher and other former assistants, was equally adept with them. One morning, however, a high-strung horse named Tabasco Cat got loose on the back stretch of Santa Anita and nearly trampled Jeff to death. He suffered multiple skull fractures, lapsed into a coma, and almost died when his brain swelled and nearly herniated his brain stem.

It had been Jeff, seven months earlier following Union City's breakdown in the Preakness, who had organized an intervention for his father. Lukas had become isolated and depressed as the ridicule of his methods mounted and his financial woes continued. Jeff Lukas gathered friends of his father to his home in California: Clyde Rice, the boyhood buddy from Wisconsin who had bought horses from the knacker's truck with Wayne; Bob French, a longtime client and Texas oil man; Lee Eaton, a Kentucky bloodstock agent. Ten people in all.

For seven hours, they took turns telling Lukas what he had meant to them. And Lukas told them his mistakes. It was a weeping, cathartic day that Lukas is uncomfortable speaking about.

"I really didn't think I was down or anything, but it meant a lot to have these people say they cared about me. They dropped everything and came to support me," Lukas said. "And Jeff was the guy who put it together. I mean, we drank coffee every morning together, worked side by side seven days a week. I've bounced back from a few things, but when that happened to Jeff it was the hardest thing I've ever gone through."

Jeff spent months in the hospital and years in rehabilitation. He has returned to his father's stable in an administrative role but is no longer Lukas's daily companion. He has good days and bad days, and both father and son have had a difficult time reforming their close relationship. Remarkably, perhaps, Lukas told his staff immediately after the accident that they were not to blame or to penalize Tabasco Cat. He told them the colt was a frightened animal and was not responsible for Jeff's injuries.

"I told them we were going to turn him around and make him special," Lukas said.

The following spring, with Lukas's attentions divided between his rehabilitating son and his stable, Tabasco Cat won the 1994 Preakness and Belmont.

"I think I was able to get into his head," Lukas said.

Now, with four months left till the first Saturday in May 2000, Lukas had three horses whose heads he needed to inhabit in order to get to the Triple Crown.

He thought his best chance was with High Yield. The colt followed his third place in the Breeders' Cup with a sixth-place finish and two seconds. Twice, however, he had finished behind Captain Steve, the Baffert-trained colt owned by Pegram.

On the same day, The Deputy had made his American debut, and Drysdale had sent out Fusaichi Pegasus in a maiden sprint race. Fusaichi Pegasus won easily and, at odds of 1–5, was developing a formidable reputation.

Lukas had decided to send High Yield to the East Coast. He'd run the colt one more time here in a stakes race and then send him to Florida with Pat Day on his back. Yes, Lukas was ducking competition, but it made more sense to go win races elsewhere. He was betting that High Yield would be a different and better horse when he showed up in Kentucky. It had worked before with Thunder Gulch in 1995.

Lukas honestly believed that Surfside, the filly, might be the best 3-year-old in his barn. She had huge feet—8½ plates—a sweet temperament, and a body that was more developed than most colts'. W. T. Young owned her and, at eighty-four, was looking for another Derby victory to go with the one Grindstone notched for him in 1996. Surfside was the daughter of 1994 Juvenile Fillies champion, Flanders, a horse Young also owned and adored.

"She had already shown dimensions that Winning Colors did not have. This filly can lay last, be second, be third, whatever. Winning Colors would not have done that that easily. I haven't considered the Kentucky Derby this early in the year with any other filly," he said.

Lukas had one other colt that he was intrigued with but was uncertain he could have ready: Commendable. Lewis owned this son of Gone West, who had looked like he was special when he won his maiden outing by four lengths in August 1999. In his next race, he finished fourth and came up with sore shins that had kept him from the races ever since. He just now was back on the track and looked like what Lukas called a "run-for-fun" type. His times were so fast in the morning that the trainer had gotten on his assistant Bradshaw for working him too hard.

Last week, however, Lukas had hoped to slow Commendable down by sending him on a long gallop, 2¼ miles. It didn't work. The rider fought him the whole way because Commendable wanted to skip down that marathon distance like it was a race.

"I've never, ever had a horse like that. Ever. He loves to work," Lukas said, an admiring smile splitting his face. "The son of a bitch is just like me."

"No ride is ever the last one. No horse is ever the last one you will have. Somehow there will always be other horses, other places to ride them."
                                        —*Monica Dickens*

Mike Pegram was in town to see his grandson, Gator, whose real name was Jacob, though Pegram really had hoped his first grandchild would be named Elwood.

"I've always loved that name. The best single handicapper I ever knew was a guy named Elwood Leggs from my hometown of Princeton. This is a true story. He died with a winning ticket in his pocket," said Pegram, who knew this because he had booked Elwood's bet. "His son came around the pool hall one day and wanted to know if Elwood owed anybody money. It was the other way around, we owed him. What a great way to go."

Until he picked up the seven-year-old Gator the following morning, he was at Santa Anita Park for an afternoon of racing and to find a "few smiles." We had worked our way up from the paddock to the clubhouse slowly, as Pegram stopped to exchange greetings with a colorful cross section of Santa Anita's horseplayers. There was Fat Eddie and Phil the Usher and a wisecracking old swell who said he had worked in the Truman administration before becoming a dedicated horseplayer.

We had barely stepped into a dark wood-paneled bar lit mainly by the big screens flickering races from around the nation when two beers appeared before us along with a tall, blond, attractive bartender.

"How's our filly doing, Mike?" she asked. The owner reached over for a hug.

"This is Holy Nola—the inspiration, not the horse, of course," he said, introducing me to her. "She's heading to New Orleans to see if we can pick up another stakes win. Then we're turning her out. Let's just see if she can throw some foals as pretty and fast as you."

Nola blushed. She was another in Pegram's world whom he honored by naming a horse after her. They had known each other for years, long before he had won the Derby and she had found peace and happiness as a born-again Christian. Pegram couldn't help but tease her about the bits of Gospel she served with the beers. He believed in omens and waited until he found the perfect horse for her.

"Tell him who she's out of, Nola," he said with the smile of a man who knows the punch line.

"Wicked Shrew," she said. They both laughed.

Despite Pegram's laid-back demeanor, he was restless and liked being on the move. There was a cocktail party for horsemen and owners upstairs in the track's new restaurant, the FrontRunner, and though it wasn't his scene, he wanted to make an appearance.

Upstairs, Pegram looked out of place in the glass-enclosed, dimly lit, sleek L.A.-styled nightclub. So did all the horsemen. This was supposed to be a casual affair, but it couldn't shake the tension that often hangs over a trade-association event where half the crowd views it as an opportunity to network, and the other is afraid they will be outhustled if they don't. Like anything else, horse racing is a business built on relationships, and Pegram's success had made him someone trainers wanted to have a relationship with. They knew that Baffert was his only trainer, and that they were also the best of friends.

Still, the trainers were compelled to take their shots. The most persistent was an amiable and successful trainer named Wally Dollase. Gently, he probed Pegram about his recent purchases, complimented him about his history of astute buys, then mentioned that he had been picking up some excellent prospects at bargain-basement prices in Europe. Had he ever thought about buying European horses?

After Dollase moved on, Pegram bumped into the jockey Kent Desormeaux. This time, the owner was the one who needed to demonstrate finesse. Desormeaux had ridden Real Quiet in the Triple Crown, but was no longer on any of Pegram's horses. He wasn't on any of Baffert's other horses, either.

Just twenty-nine, the Louisiana native's career had already swung from brilliant to baffling. Desormeaux looked like the next great rider from Cajun country when he set a succession of records beginning in 1987 after he won 450 races to lead all riders in the nation, which was startling because he was only an apprentice, or rookie rider. He earned $5.1 million in purses that year and won his first Eclipse Award as the champion apprentice rider. In 1989, he set a still-standing record by winning 598 races to earn his second Eclipse Award as the nation's outstanding jockey. In 1995, he became the youngest rider in history to win 3,000 races, and in 1997, he became the youngest to earn more than $100 million in purses.

The more Desormeaux won, however, the more arrogant he became. He was well spoken and enthusiastic, but no one could tell him anything. This was partly the old story of getting too much too soon, but it also had to do with the jockey's roots in the Louisiana bush tracks. The Cajuns were talented, fearless riders.

The dean of this group, Hall of Famer Eddie Delahoussaye, once told me that they all grew up with "horses or fighting roosters in the front yard. Usually both." There were about twenty of them with more than 1,500 career victories each across the nation, Delahoussaye, Desormeaux, and Shane Sellers among the most recognizable. They all started as boys riding horses for their fathers or uncles in match races at tracks in Carencro, Abbeville, and Breaux Bridge—all within a forty-mile radius of Lafayette in the heart of Acadia.

The tracks were unlicensed and the racing secretaries were imaginative. I had gone to a couple of them over the years and talked to the riders who came through them. Each told a better story than the next about their time on the bush tracks. Ronald Ardoin, one of the most successful riders in the history of the Louisiana circuit, estimated that he'd won 500 races in the bushes from age seven to sixteen.

"They'd tie you on the saddle in your underwear to keep you light as possible," said Ardoin. "They'd race you against a horse with a fighting rooster, or a bag of rocks. I've raced against horses ridden by monkeys. The only thing you could do was hold on and whip that son of a gun."

On his first bush mount, Ardoin's horse refused to stop at the finish line and had headed out into a field with the jock whimpering, "Help me, Daddy." When the horse finally ran out of gas, a friend of his father's lifted young Ronald from the saddle and felt the back of his pants. "He said: 'Ain't nothing back there. I guess your boy's going to make a rider,'" Ardoin recalled. The only thing more prevalent than the pungent smell of boudin sausage, Delahoussaye told me, was the horsemen's appetite for a betting coup. Sharpies would van over classier stock from Fair Grounds Racetrack in New Orleans.

"No one was checking papers, and they'd try to take those old country farmers' money," Delahoussaye said. "There would be us fifty-five-pound kids riding in a $10,000 match race put up by whole towns. Everybody would chip in because we were poor people."

The local legends, too, were numerous.

There was Black Mama, the pride of the Creole population of Breaux Bridge. Before each race, up to fifty men and women would march behind their champion as the old mare was walked up and down her running lane. They'd chant and sing and act like they were summoning up a mystical spell when what they were really doing was smoothing the mare's running lane and trying to get that edge.

There was Jerome Hernandez, a trainer who often sat behind the starting gate with a pearl-handled .45 to make sure his horses got a clean break.

So it was a macho culture and Desormeaux had been slow to put polish over it. He was more daring than reckless on the track, but had a reputation for riding everyone else's horse except his own. He wasn't afraid of fanning other horses wide or muscling into a seam to stop another's charge. While he was winning, trainers ignored his swagger and dismissive responses to their instructions. But in the mid-1990s, he began to lose mounts after a series of costly errors; the biggest, perhaps, was in one of the world's richest races, the Japan Cup in Tokyo. There, he misjudged the finish line aboard horse of the year Kotashaan and lost.

In 1997, Baffert offered him a second chance and began riding him on his better horses. The following year he was aboard Real Quiet when the colt followed his Kentucky Derby victory with the Preakness win and came a nose from capturing the Triple Crown.

On that afternoon at Belmont, he stalked the leaders as he did the previous two races, then launched a bold run on the far turn. Real Quiet was four lengths ahead in the stretch and Desormeaux whipped desperately as the colt drifted down the lane. He had moved too early and Victory Gallop was making his lead disappear. Desormeaux knew it and, right before the finish line, pulled Real Quiet's head up to bump into Victory Gallop. It was too late—the colt had caught him by a nose at the wire.

Even if somehow Real Quiet could have kept that nose in front, he probably would have been placed second as punishment for

Desormeaux's late foul. Neither Baffert nor Pegram blamed the
rider publicly, but Desormeaux never rode Real Quiet again. Soon
after, he was off all the trainer's horses.

Now, elbow to elbow with each other, the owner and rider tried
for a cordial tone. Pegram asked about Desormeaux's children, his
nine-year-old, Joshua, and an infant named Jacob. "My baby is seven
inches longer than Josh was at this age. He's going to be tall, dark,
and handsome like his old man. Maybe he'll reach five-five," the
jockey said.

They made small talk for a few minutes more, but it was awkward
for both men. Desormeaux said good-bye first and slipped out of the
party altogether. The rider knew he had alienated some trainers. Desormeaux confessed he'd "gotten too big for my britches" and attributed
it to immaturity. He was truly hurt when he was taken off Real Quiet;
the colt had given him his first taste of winning Triple Crown races.
He was riding mainly for Drysdale now, and together the two won
twenty-one stakes races in 1998. But the following year, Desormeaux
slipped back into his old habits of not adhering to instructions and losing concentration. The trainer gave him a wake-up call by offering other
riders an opportunity on his horses. It worked. Now a more attentive
and focused Desormeaux was rebuilding his relationship with Drysdale
and recently had ridden Fusaichi Pegasus in his maiden victory.

The encounter seemed to drain Pegram as well. He decided this
room was out of smiles. As soon as he was out the door, the owner
was revived. We had picked up another companion, a trainer named
Al May. He was a Canadian pushing sixty who had six inexpensive
horses he was racing here. He had trained in Washington, where he
had become friends with the owner. He wasn't looking for anything
but a good time and some Mexican food.

We found it on the main drag of Arcadia in a small storefront with
ripped booths. We also found Baffert, who had decided to escape his
room in the nearby Embassy Suites. It had been his home for a
couple of months now as he tried to settle his divorce and refurbish

a condominium in which he intended to live. He was more relaxed than he was at the Breeders' Cup, though his run of tough luck had continued. He got on Pegram for his restaurant selection, noting that it looked out on a Popeye's Chicken franchise.

"I guess we got to keep our eye out for guys in ski masks coming out of there," he said.

But that was about as light as it got. Baffert was in a funk after a trying week. Sheik Mohammed had just bought Chief Seattle, the Seattle Slew colt that had finished second in the Breeders' Cup Juvenile, for $4.5 million. Not long after that race, Baffert had offered $3.5 million for the colt and was willing to go up to $4 million. It was the second time in the last six weeks the trainer had lost out to Godolphin. Sheik Mohammed's stable had hired Baffert's trusted top assistant, Eoin Harty, to handle a 2–year-old division, which meant the Sheik was intent as ever to conquer the Triple Crown races. Harty, a thirty-seven-year-old native of Ireland, had helped bring Silver Charm and Real Quiet along the Triple Crown campaign.

The Sheik's plan was for Harty to train the 2-year-olds in Dubai from January to April, then return to the United States with them for some American-race seasoning. Baffert couldn't blame his assistant for taking a major pay raise. He also liked the Sheik, respected his horsemanship, and thought that sooner rather than later he was going to win a Derby. If not with Chief Seattle in May, then with one of the prospects Harty would shape in the next couple of years.

Chief Seattle was on Baffert's mind because his Triple Crown prospects had just taken a major hit. As did his barn. Four days earlier, Aaron Jones, the owner Baffert had hoped would put him on level footing with Lukas at the sales, had fired him after Forest Camp finished second at odds of 7–10 in the San Miguel Stakes. It was the colt's third loss in a row. Jones took six very nice horses from Baffert's barn and denied him the opportunity to condition another nine promising 2-year-olds that were still on the farm—including a Mr. Prospector colt that Baffert had picked out at the cost of $3 million.

Baffert had seen it coming as early as the previous May, when Jones's Prime Timber finished fourth in the Kentucky Derby. So did Pegram. The previous summer after a sale, he had accepted a ride back West with Jones on the timber baron's Lear jet. It was a friendly ride for the most part, with the exception of one testy exchange.

"How much did you pay last year?" Pegram remembered Jones asking him, referring to money he had spent at the sales.

"A couple hundred thousand," Pegram answered.

"How much did you earn?" Jones asked.

"A couple million," he replied.

"You're lucky," Jones fired back.

Jones didn't like how close Pegram and Baffert were and had groused about what he perceived as special treatment the other owner received. In fact, he was irritated the month before when Baffert held Forest Camp out of the Hollywood Futurity on December 18.

"He thought I held him out because I was running Captain Steve for Mike. The horse wasn't ready," Baffert said. "I never could keep him happy. If you think you're going to get fired, you can't train the horses."

What the trainer was most upset about, however, was what he believed was Jones's mean-spirited swipe at his integrity. He was due a breeding right to Forestry, who had just been retired to stud after winning four stakes races under Baffert. Jones told him he'd give it to him, but the owner wanted to put it in the name of one of Baffert's children. The implication was that the trainer was either too irresponsible or untrustworthy to look after his four kids. They exchanged heated words before Baffert refused the arrangement.

Baffert's stable had just concluded one of the most successful years in racing history: His horses had earned $16,934,607 in purses and won twenty Grade I stakes in 1999. Sill, the trainer looked like a man whose world was caving in on him. There was too much turmoil in his life.

"If I'd known this was going to happen, I wouldn't have had an Aaron Jones chapter in my book," he said, trying to find his smile.

He looked across the table at Pegram. "Looks like it's just me and you," he said. "Whatever happens, at least I know we'll have fun."

Baffert and Pegram were once more Triple Crown–bound, this time with Captain Steve. The colt had rebounded from his poor Breeders' Cup race to win two in a row. In the Grade I Hollywood Futurity, the colt looked superb in trouncing High Yield by four lengths.

"Yes, we will," Pegram answered, tilting his long neck beer in salute.

"When you take the back roads to run with the big dogs," said Pegram, "you know it ain't going to last forever."

Chapter 10

PREP RACES: THE TRIPLE CROWN CUT

FEBRUARY 2000

THE SCATUORCHIO HOME
RUMSON, NEW JERSEY

"Owners still believe that anything with a leg on each corner has a chance in Louisville."

—New York Times *columnist Red Smith*

More Than Ready was off the farm in Florida and back in Triple Crown contention. Jim Scatuorchio had the videotape to prove it.

"Look right there. Johnny hit him with his left hand and he stopped," said Scatuorchio, hitting the pause button on his video-cassette recorder. "I went back and did some research, and he did the same thing in the Futurity. Look, he swishes his tail and stops."

We were in the den of Scatuorchio's house in Rumson, New Jersey, watching More Than Ready in the stretch run of the Hutcheson Stakes two weeks before, on January 29. The owner paused, rewound, and played the tape over and over. Terry Scatuorchio stood next to us, shaking her head at her husband's manic behavior, but he had a reason to be encouraged.

More Than Ready had returned to the track at Gulfstream Park in Florida after a four-month layoff and shared first place in a rare dead heat with a colt named Summer Note. The colt showed the early speed of old and led by a length in mid-stretch. When Summer Note hooked him, he had fought back to finish on dead-even terms—the photo showed the pair's nostrils hitting the wire at the same time. Did this mean the colt had overcome the mysterious illness or malaise of the fall? Did the convalescence at J. J. Pletcher's farm rejuvenate him?

Scatuorchio thought so. More Than Ready carried ten pounds more than Summer Note in the race and still managed to go a blazing 1:21 ⅗ for seven furlongs, or seven eighths of a mile.

The bottom line was that More Than Ready had taken an encouraging first step toward the Triple Crown at a time when it mattered most. Nominations to the Triple Crown races were in: Owners of 387 horses believed they had some kind of shot at making it to the Kentucky Derby, Preakness, or Belmont Stakes. Scatuorchio was among them and had paid the $600 fee; he believed again, and once more he was looking forward to the spring.

Over the next eight weeks, the Triple Crown contenders would identify themselves in more than forty prep races at tracks from Florida to New York, Kentucky to California, and Arkansas to Louisiana. Their owners and trainers would select a series of races, anywhere from three to six, that they believed would best prepare the horse for the Kentucky Derby. The horses did not have to win any of the races they selected, but they had to run well and earn purses.

The starting gate at Churchill Downs for the Kentucky Derby had room for only twenty horses. Of those 387 horses, injuries would knock a few out, but the majority wouldn't make it to Louisville because they simply weren't good enough. If owners of more than twenty horses wanted to pay the $30,000 entry fee to race in the Derby, the field would be ranked by purse earnings in graded events. The top twenty earners were in; the rest out.

Knowing that More Than Ready did not respond to a left-handed whip, Scatuorchio believed, was a crucial piece of knowledge. It may be the difference between a first- or second-place finish, or a third- or fourth-place check. It may be the difference between winning enough purses to earn a spot in the starting gate.

"Johnny came back and told us about the left hand. Maybe it's an old injury, I don't know, we're still learning about this horse. Horses are like people. They got all kinds of strange tendencies," the owner said.

Scatuorchio and his trainer, Todd Pletcher, talked by phone every day, and each conversation brought more anxiety. This is what they knew: They wanted More Than Ready to run three races before the first Saturday in May, at least one of them at the distance of 1⅛ miles. What Scatuorchio and Pletcher didn't know was more daunting: Could More Than Ready win at a distance of more than a mile? Could he rate, or relax behind horses and then pass them? The Hutcheson was his first prep race; which two prep races should More Than Ready run next?

As for the question of distance, of course, they didn't know. More Than Ready had finished third and fifth in the only two times he'd tried to go a mile or beyond.

"Right now, it's blind faith. We'll see," Scatuorchio admitted.

Could he rate, or run behind horses and pass them in the stretch? He was learning to in the morning workouts. Pletcher now worked More Than Ready in the company of another horse. His exercise rider, Cindy Hutter, was instructed to keep More Than Ready behind and off the shoulder of his workmate and lay back anywhere from one to six lengths. In the final furlong, or at whatever point they had preordained, she was told to turn the colt loose.

In the morning, it was obvious More Than Ready preferred the front. Hutter often looked like a water-skier with a tense hold on the rope as the colt dragged her around the track. She was a skilled rider, though, and always won the tug-of-war, and day by day the colt was developing the extra gear that allowed him to pass horses late in a race.

The decision of which two races to run in the future was up in the air. The night before, Scatuorchio and Pletcher had decided against the Fountain of Youth, which was to be run in a week, on February 19, at Gulfstream. Pletcher had called from his winter base at Hialeah, Florida, and the two had hemmed and hawed for more than an hour. Scatuorchio didn't want to run in the Fountain of Youth, but he ceded final decision-making to Pletcher.

The trainer wasn't so sure he wanted to pass. He believed the field was soft and More Than Ready was sitting on a big race. Lukas's horse, High Yield, was the likely favorite, but that colt had gotten slapped around a lot out west. Pletcher believed More Than Ready was better than High Yield.

"It's tempting. I'm thinking I have a horse who can go out there and win. It's only a fifteen-minute van ride. I'm not sure why I'm not taking him over there," Pletcher told Scatuorchio.

Scatuorchio reminded Pletcher that to run More Than Ready in the Fountain of Youth defied their plan, their promise to each other, to bring the colt up to the Derby slowly. If the colt won or even ran well in the Fountain of Youth, logic dictated they run him in the Florida Derby three weeks later, on March 11. That meant More Than Ready would have run three races in six weeks and still have two months left until the Derby.

That was too long a layoff without another race. More Than Ready would have to race again before the Derby, and Team Scatuorchio didn't want to stress their colt. They didn't want him to quit running like he had the previous year.

"Where do you want to run the horse?" Scatuorchio asked.

"I don't know. Let's call the psychic," said Pletcher.

This made them both laugh.

One of Jim's friends had visited a psychic the week before the Hutcheson. The clairvoyant said she saw a small black horse somewhere in her future. Jim's buddy was heading to Gulfstream for the race, but the psychic did not know this.

With the door into the cosmos now cracked, he asked the inevitable question: Would More Than Ready win? The psychic couldn't tell because she said the vision was too crowded. So Scatuorchio gave her the benefit of the doubt for calling the dead heat with Summer Note.

By passing on the Fountain of Youth, Scatuorchio and Pletcher acknowledged that the future of More Than Ready was predicated on the colt's past. They were still haunted by his surrender the previous fall. If More Than Ready hadn't been hurt and was just tired, then they had to space his races properly and conserve his strength. Scatuorchio and Pletcher wanted the colt to run himself into the Derby. They didn't want to be the ones to run him out of it.

"I know the Derby is only a few months away, but it seems like forever," Scatuorchio told his trainer. "This waiting and worrying is going to kill me."

"We've established a beachhead on all three fronts and now it's time to dig in the trenches."

—*D. Wayne Lukas*

This was the time of year Lukas threw away the sports metaphors in favor of something more forceful, and he had good reason after the weekend of February 19, 2000. On that Saturday, High Yield did win the Fountain of Youth, leading every step of the way for a 3¼-length victory. The move to Florida had paid off and now the colt was the big horse in the East.

High Yield would stay in Florida before heading to Kentucky. The next afternoon at the Fairgrounds in New Orleans, Exchange Rate was an easy winner in the Risen Star Stakes. He would stay there for the Louisiana Derby, then ship to New York for the Wood Memorial at Aqueduct.

Lukas had nominated twenty-one horses to the Triple Crown and now had potent ground forces in the East and Midwest. His beachhead in the West was less secure.

The week before, on February 12, Surfside won the Las Virgenes Stakes at Santa Anita but hardly looked dominating in a narrow ¾-length victory in the stretch. Weeks of heavy rains in southern California had upset the training routines of all the circuit's best horses, as their trainers chose to keep them off a muddy track. Just as he did with the filly, Winning Colors, Lukas had Surfside pointed for one more race against the fillies in the Santa Anita Oaks, and then he would run her against the colts in the Santa Anita Derby.

"Those big feet of hers do not like slipping around the mud. I think she's gotten a little complacent by beating up on these other fillies so much. When she got looked in the eye, she fought back, though, and that was what she needed to do. She needs to understand that this time of year is when you go to war. We're taking care of that in the mornings," Lukas said.

That same afternoon Commendable returned to racing for the first time since September 1999, and finished a sluggish fifth in an allowance race. Lukas wasn't worried about that, either.

"He just needed a lap around the track, a little field exercise. I haven't really bore down on Commendable yet," he said. "Right now it's about outflanking the competition. These are baby steps on the road to Kentucky."

"When you see a horse who makes you feel as if you've just walked out of a movie theater having seen The Black Stallion *and* Phar Lap *at the same time, then it's hard not to stumble into fool's paradise, where so many lost souls have ended up."*
　　—*Steve Haskin, of* The Blood-Horse, *on Fusaichi Pegasus*

It was only his third race, but Fusaichi Pegasus had established himself as the horse to watch for in the Kentucky Derby. On February 19, 2000, he bested a field of six in an allowance race of 1 1/16 miles at Santa Anita. The 3½-length victory in the time of 1:42⅗ wasn't particularly startling. It was more that horse racing, like every other facet of American culture, likes its stars larger than life and mysterious.

The colt fit the bill with his $4 million price tag, the absentee Japanese owner, Fusao Sekiguchi, and Neil Drysdale, his fussy English trainer. He was now being called simply Pegasus because that afternoon he seemed to glide over a track still heavy with moisture.

Kent Desormeaux never had to put the whip to him as he steered him outside in the stretch past two Bob Baffert–trained colts.

"My horses didn't run bad, but they weren't in the same class as Pegasus. That horse hardly looked like he was trying," Baffert admitted. "He didn't look like he was running the third race of his life. He looked like he'd been doing this for a long time."

Drysdale sent Fusaichi Pegasus out with wraps around his front ankles. The trainer insisted this was a precautionary measure due to the colt's size and strength. Besides adding extra support, Drysdale wanted to minimize the small cuts and scrapes horses often accumulate as they stride out in flying dirt. But front wraps are rarely seen on young horses, especially on top-level 3-year-olds. When they are, it often signals an injury.

Though Drysdale had spoken about the minor veterinary work done on the colt's ankle, rumors abounded that perhaps there had been a more severe injury.

The rumors didn't jibe with Drysdale's reputation for caution, but this was the colt everyone out west was talking about. This was the season bettors and horsemen picked over every aspect of a horse's appearance and performance to divine a Kentucky Derby, Preakness, or Belmont winner. Before the race, when Fusaichi Pegasus was warming up, the public also got its first look at the colt's eccentric behavior. He was galloping along with Desormeaux when he caught a glimpse of the starting gate. Fusaichi Pegasus came to a dead stop, pitching the jockey forward in the saddle. The colt stared at the iron contraption for a moment as Desormeaux tugged very gently to move him along. Eventually Fusaichi Pegasus did move on, but he tossed his head back a few times toward the gate as if he wanted to make sure it wasn't following him. Drysdale shrugged this off, too.

"He's just curious," Drysdale said. "He's an ebullient sort."

MARCH 11–12, 2000

NEW YORK CITY OFFTRACK BETTING PARLOR

"The first favourite was never heard of, the second favourite was never seen after the distance post, all the ten-to-oners were in the rear, and a dark horse which had never been thought of, and which the careless St. James had never even observed in the list, rushed past the grand stand in sweeping triumph."

—*Benjamin Disraeli (Earl Beaconsfield)*

I was in New York for a pivotal weekend of prep races, which meant I had to spend back-to-back afternoons at an offtrack betting parlor not too far from Times Square. I was doing my job, which, on the weekend of March 11 and 12, meant covering the Big East basketball tournament. The games were at night at Madison Square Garden, so I watched the Florida Derby on Saturday and the Louisiana Derby on Sunday afternoon.

Granted, New York's OTB parlors are not the most glamorous rooms in Manhattan, and the clientele runs the gamut from middle-aged guys in overcoats with ringing cell phones to really old guys in ripped boat shoes chewing on frayed cigars.

In between these two extremes, the majority of folks were guys like me—there aren't many women. We were there because we had an interest in a particular race and we wanted to compete and relax.

Like golfers, our passion could be gauged by the tools we brought. The *Daily Racing Form* was like carrying a light bag with the basics: a driver, a few irons, a sand wedge, and a putter. The more accomplished handicappers toted laptops or thumbed through reams of computer sheets.

In short, the OTB was an eccentric place where you could watch a horseplayer camp in front of a television set after he got shut out at the betting window and declare: "I have a mind bet on the number four in this race" and then root him home like he had bet his house on the horse.

It was my country club and I truly enjoyed going there.

On the afternoon of the Florida Derby, in my OTB at least, there was a strong rooting interest for a colt named Hal's Hope who was trained by eighty-eight-year-old Harold Rose. Horse and conditioner were a long-shot player's dream and the parlor was filled with them.

In January, Hal's Hope had won the Holy Bull Stakes at Gulfstream as a 40–1 shot. He returned to run a solid second to High Yield—today's favorite—in the Fountain of Youth at odds of 10–1. So there were quite a few players in the parlor who had already cashed nice bets on the underappreciated colt. Why get off him now with generous odds of 7–1 for the Florida Derby?

The reason for the betting public's skepticism had more to do with Hal's Hope's connections than it did with the colt's ability. Harold Rose was primarily a claiming trainer in Florida who came to the backside late in life—in 1968 at the age of fifty-six—after selling his printing and publishing business in New Jersey and moving to Florida.

Rose bred, owned, and trained his horses—all of modest pedi-gree—and they were solid bets in the everyday races on the Florida circuit. But in the Grade I Florida Derby, could he really beat a $1.05 million horse trained by D. Wayne Lukas?

The old trainer thought so. He had named the colt he bred Hal's Hope for a reason: It was the one that was going to return him to the Kentucky Derby, where he had finished tenth in 1984 with a horse named Rexson's Hope. In August 1999, after a stroke and quadruple-bypass surgery, he told his doctors that he had to get better fast. Hal's Hope needed him.

Earlier that week, in a story for *The New York Times* by my col-league Joseph Durso, Rose summed up what drives every owner and trainer's compulsion this time of year.

"If you're not an optimist, you shouldn't be in racing," Rose said. "If you don't have the dream, you don't want to be in racing. The dream is the basis for everything."

This certainly resonated with the OTB parlor crowd. As did the story of Hal's Hope's jockey, Roger Velez, who'd suffered a stroke ten years ago and was a recovering alcoholic.

It was a two-horse race as soon as the gates opened, with Velez gunning Hal's Hope to the front and High Yield inside on his flank. Day didn't believe that Hal's Hope was the horse he needed to worry about. At the 5/16 pole, the jockey wrangled High Yield back and moved to the outside of Velez. Day's body language was loud: He thought Hal's Hope would fade.

The two colts came out of the turn with Hal's Hope a head in front.
Day asked High Yield for some run. The colt drew even with Hal's
Hope, but Velez spanked him vigorously with his left hand. For the
length of the stretch, the two colts and two riders were the only thing
on the screen because they were ten lengths ahead of the field.

"Get up. Get up for the old man," yelled a guy next to me.

"Hold him together, Roger," cried another before a television
monitor.

Roger Velez aboard Hal's Hope and Pat Day atop High Yield
moved in tandem, their whips crashing down on the colts like shad-
ows of each other. High Yield got to within a nose of Hal's Hope and
seemed to hang there for an eternity. Not inching forward. Not bob-
bing back.

"Get there wire," came a shout that sounded as plaintive as a prayer.

The nose lead of Hal's Hope grew ever so slightly. One jump, two
jumps, three jumps—still no wire. The air was gone from the room.
We were frozen. Our nervous tics were cured; the finger-snapping,
the program-slapping, the absentminded mutterings—all gone.

Until Velez pumped his fist in the air when he crossed the finish
line first. There was applause, as well as a chorus of yeses. This was
a rare communal moment in the OTB.

"Looks like the old man is going to the Derby," said one gentleman, an old-timer himself.

From the lines forming at the windows, however, it was clear that
there weren't many "mind bets" wasted on Hal's Hope and Harold
Rose.

The following afternoon for the Louisiana Derby, the OTB parlor was back to its erratic self. This was the toughest field so far of
any prep race. More Than Ready, Mighty, Captain Steve, and Exchange Rate all had won important stakes races.

The colt with the most to prove, of course, was More Than Ready.
The others had run this far before and done well. The track at

the Fairgrounds was a deep, heavy surface and had one of the longest stretch runs in the nation. It favored closers; early speed, or front runners, such as More Than Ready, often died in the final straightaway.

This was step two of Jim Scatuorchio and Todd Pletcher's plan. They weren't masochists, though Scatuorchio felt like one when he saw how salty the field came up. The owner and trainer believed this was the right race, 1 1/16 miles, at the right point on the calendar to prepare the colt for the Kentucky Derby.

If he could handle the distance, More Than Ready would be sent to Keeneland for the 1 1/8-mile Blue Grass Stakes on April 15. It meant the colt would arrive at the Derby three weeks later with races of increasing lengths spaced one month apart. The plan was sound but nerve-racking. Scatuorchio and Pletcher knew each race could be More Than Ready's last on the Triple Crown trail. Scatuorchio often wrestled aloud with that possibility.

"If he can't get the distance, we'll run him back in sprints. It won't kill me," he said.

Pletcher never wavered: "We're committed to the Triple Crown."

The tote board reflected how tight a race this was: Baffert's Captain Steve was the favorite at 2–1; Lukas's Exchange Rate was at 3–1; More Than Ready was 5–1; and Mighty, trained by Frank Brothers, was 7–1.

When the gates opened, whatever More Than Ready had learned about relaxing was forgotten as the colt shot for the lead and looked like the sprinter everyone accused him of being. More Than Ready set fractions of :23 for a quarter mile and 46.1 for the half mile, which were too quick and especially dangerous because a long shot named Peninsula was pressing him every step of the way. Heading around the far turn, Peninsula surged toward him.

I wasn't sure More Than Ready had anything left. But he did, and he opened a three-length lead on Peninsula at the top of the Fairground's endless stretch. More Than Ready had a different sort of running style than most colts. His head always remained upright and his legs rolled beneath him in the smooth action of a paddle wheel. It never looked like he was lunging or striding out. Like human sprinters, he managed to maintain an efficient form within himself. More Than Ready had a two-length lead and was perhaps sixty yards from the finish line when his form began to loosen. Still, he looked like the winner.

Then out of nowhere a colt rushed by on the outside and beat him to the finish line by two lengths. It was Mighty, the same colt that More Than Ready had beaten by nearly ten lengths the previous July in the Sanford Stakes at Saratoga Springs.

Mighty had broken from the gate second to last but started picking off horses on the rail in the backstretch while More Than Ready and Peninsula were fighting it out seven lengths ahead. The colt then angled to the middle of the track in the stretch. He blasted past More Than Ready like a rocket; Captain Steve closed quickly along the rail to finish third.

It was a solid second-place finish for More Than Ready, especially after the wicked pace he had set under pressure. But those final yards and broken form indicated that going beyond a mile might indeed be too far for More Than Ready, and the Kentucky Derby was 1¼ miles.

What did Scatuorchio think? He was hoarse and a little disappointed. He hadn't seen Mighty coming. In fact, he barely saw the end of the race. Eddie Rosen got so excited in the stretch that he knocked Scatuorchio off his chair in their box. By the time the owner regained his vantage point, More Than Ready was finishing second.

Still, Scatuorchio viewed the race as a step forward and not a setback.

"It wasn't our kind of racetrack. He was under pressure the whole way and still had fight in him at the end," he said. "We're moving on until someone shows us we don't belong."

APRIL 2000

"A horse gallops with his lungs, perseveres with his heart, and wins with his character."

—*Tesio*

The Santa Anita Derby figured to be a battle of the sexes with Surfside signed on to challenge the colts. The filly had won four stakes in a row and Wayne Lukas believed he had her primed to run down the likes of The Deputy, Captain Steve, and Neil Drysdale's second big horse, War Chant, a late starter on the Triple Crown trail who so far had won all three of his races.

Two days before the race, however, on April 6, gender lines were indeed established at the post position draw, but they had nothing to do with Surfside. What is usually an innocuous affair turned nasty when Bob Baffert popped off with a comment he thought was witty and irreverent. Jenine Sahadi disagreed.

She was sitting next to Chris McCarron, the jockey for The Deputy, and Baffert was at the other end of a long table. They both were taking questions about the race when Baffert leaned in and looked toward McCarron and asked, "Who's training The Deputy? You or Jenine?"

Baffert was friendly with Sahadi's old boyfriend, Julio Canani, and was aware she was weary of having her skills questioned. Sahadi seethed at the other end of the table. Her face turned red, as if she had been slapped. When, after a few moments had passed, she was asked what instructions for riding The Deputy she might give McCarron on race day, Sahadi snatched up the microphone and said, "I won't give him instructions. Thank God my horse has class, because there are a lot of people who don't."

She then pounded the microphone to the table and bolted out of the room.

Baffert immediately went on the defensive, saying he was just joking: "People have no sense of humor around this place."

No one bought it—especially the 41,222 people who showed up at the track on April 8, 2000, to see the Santa Anita Derby. It was the most prestigious 3-year-old race on the West Coast, with a $1 million purse, and Baffert had won it in three of the previous four years.

This year the white-haired trainer was fitted with a black hat and Sahadi was a new heroine. In the paddock before the race, she was applauded and encouraged while Baffert was taunted.

"It was amazing. I felt sort of like Julia Roberts—not that I look like her—but I felt like somebody walking out of the paddock next to my horse," Sahadi said.

She was indeed somebody when the 1⅛-mile race concluded: the first female trainer to win the sixty-three-year-old race. The Deputy made sure of it by running down War Chant in the stretch for a one-length victory. The woman-trainer-scorned received an ovation as she bounced down to the winner's circle to meet that bargain-basement Irish-bred horse.

Surfside's day was not nearly as satisfying—after leading for three quarters of a mile, the filly finished fifth. Sahadi and The Deputy were Kentucky Derby–bound; Surfside would not be.

Baffert was stone-faced as he made his way through the crowd to collect Captain Steve, who had finished three lengths back in third place. The crowd let him have it the whole way: "Who trains your horse, Bob?" they asked.

APRIL 15, 2000

AQUEDUCT RACETRACK

JAMAICA, NEW YORK

> *Horse, thou art truly a creature without equal, for thou fliest without wings and conquerest without sword.*
>
> *—The Koran*

Neil Drysdale didn't exactly sneak into town for the Wood Memorial. Nor did he try to downplay his supreme confidence in Fusaichi Pegasus. But he certainly was low-key.

Drysdale treated his time in New York like a vacation, hitting the restaurants and catching a couple of plays on Broadway. Strange as it sounds, New York is a good place to hide in plain sight at this time of year on the Triple Crown calendar.

The big race on the same afternoon was the Blue Grass at Keeneland, which had attracted High Yield, Hal's Hope, Mighty, and More Than Ready. The Wood was an important prep with a $750,000 purse, but it carried a Grade II designation, which usually meant a lesser field; a win in the Grade I Blue Grass was worth more in the breeding shed. The recent history demonstrated this: No Wood winner had captured the Kentucky Derby since Pleasant Colony in 1981, though fourteen of them had tried since then.

Drysdale, though, wasn't looking for an easy victory. He also wasn't looking to duck a strong Blue Grass field. He had always intended to come to New York. The race was at Aqueduct in Jamaica, Queens, which after being rebuilt in 1959 was thought to be a state-of-the-art facility that would lead horse racing into the future. What was uber-modern then—concrete, glass, and sweeping angles—was sterile and soulless now.

Its meeting ran November to May, and in those brutal winter months, it was more like a television studio because, unlike the jockeys and trainers, horseplayers could bet and watch the races on television in the city. Often on those days, the track felt like an abandoned bus terminal for the most lost of travelers. Still, Aqueduct's races were beamed across the country because horseplayers would rather bet on bad races than no races at all.

What remained state of the art about the track, however, was its surface, which was kind and forgiving and mostly immune to the elements. It was considered a safe track, and what appealed to Drysdale as well was its urban isolation.

Just as in California, where the trainers with big stables preferred the bucolic surroundings of Santa Anita, most high-profile New Yorkers kept their horses at Belmont Park. In Los Angeles, Drysdale was based at Hollywood Park, which was in Inglewood, not far from LAX. He was used to finding peace in the white noise of forgotten parts of a city.

He borrowed a couple of stalls in the corner of the backside and most mornings sat quietly with the *Racing Form* or a newspaper on a chair overlooking the stall that held Fusaichi Pegasus. When it was time for the colt to gallop or work, Drysdale pulled the collar of his barn jacket up around his neck and tugged his touring cap over his eyes. It was cold for April, and a stiff morning wind tossed hot dog wrappers and betting tickets like tumbleweeds in a ghost town. As Fusaichi Pegasus was taken to the track by his exercise rider, Drysdale climbed an embankment, cut through a gap in some shrubs, then leaned on the rail in the backstretch. His colt usually was the only one on the track, and the trainer locked on him like an air traffic controller absorbed by the dots on his radar screen.

Up close, Fusaichi Pegasus was a vision. The colt's bay coat stretched like velvet over the contours of a couch stuffed more for art than comfort. He had a long forelock that bobbed between his eyes. His neck was long and furrowed with muscle. Only his eyes told of his high-strung nature. They weren't frightened or distrustful. They were vigilant, like those of a traffic cop taking in all four corners and two lanes of traffic.

It was this alert quality that, in the moments before and after the Wood, transfixed many of the 15,684 people who came to Aqueduct on April 15, 2000, to see the horse everyone was talking about. His competitors were nearing the starting gate when Fusaichi Pegasus stopped and decided to look around. His reticence caused a five-minute delay and necessitated an escort with a lip chain to pull him to the gate.

"Maybe he figured they wouldn't start the race without him," Drysdale said later.

Then there was the matter of getting to the winner's circle. After running a 1:47.92 for the 1⅛-mile race—the fourth-fastest Wood in history—the headstrong colt again refused an escort from the out-rider and stood defiantly at the clubhouse turn for another five-minute delay. "It's like he's saying, 'I'll come when I'm ready,'" Drysdale said.

In between the petulant displays, the colt—spoiled or not—showed why Sekiguchi was willing to spend $4 million for him. Fusaichi Pegasus broke leisurely from the gate and settled in fifth place as the front-runner, Country Only, and the second favorite, Red Bullet, battled around the first turn and into the backstretch. He allowed his jockey, Kent Desormeaux, to slow him when the pace quickened ahead. "I was really taking hold of him," Desormeaux said. "I gathered a little rein on him to slow him down."

With three furlongs left heading into the final turn, and tracking the front-runners, Desormeaux kicked him into gear again. This time the colt got to work.

"He didn't go out and do anything silly," the rider said. "He continued to canter, and he's so fluid that I was fearful that I had put him to sleep. I kind of nibbled at him in the apex of the turn, and he just reached forward and went after the targets."

First he gobbled up a retreating Country Only, then he rolled by Red Bullet. Desormeaux only waved his whip at him for an easy win and the $465,000 first prize. The effortless 4¼-length victory was Fusaichi Pegasus' fourth in a row.

"I liked seeing him relax behind horses," Drysdale said. "When he was asked to go, he went, and that's very encouraging. The whole thing unfolded like a little fairy story."

The pricey and particular Fusaichi Pegasus was heading to Louisville as the likely favorite for the Kentucky Derby, which may have been a curse—the last favorite to win the race was Spectacular Bid in 1979.

"Is that good or bad?" Drysdale asked. "Maybe we shouldn't mention that."

Chapter 11

THE KENTUCKY DERBY: THE
GREATEST TWO MINUTES IN SPORTS

APRIL 25–MAY 5, 2000

LOUISVILLE, KENTUCKY

"Who's your Derby horse?"
> —*Horseplayers on the days leading up to*
> *the Run for the Roses*

Their horses had gotten here. They had survived bruised hooves, pulled muscles, ulcers, fevers—a medical dictionary worth of ailments—as well their own bad races in weekend after weekend of prep races. They were Kentucky Derby horses.

They had earned their yellow workout saddle clothes with their names embroidered on them and a stall beneath the famous twin spires of Churchill Downs. They had a place in the starting gate of what has come to be known as the greatest two minutes in sport.

Their owners and trainers had survived, too. The best and worst, however, were still in front of them as they counted down the days to the May 6 race.

Their dream was still alive—maybe they did have a potential Kentucky Derby or even a Triple Crown winner in their barn. The owners and trainers were asked the question repeatedly by crowds that swarmed the forty-eight barns on the backside of Churchill Downs. It was the one time a year here that people threatened to overwhelm the horses. In the days leading up to the race, reporters and camera crews, Rotary Clubs and Girl Scout troops, picnic baskets and T-shirt stands turned the barn area into a mall and these racehorses into bystanders.

It was part of the Kentucky Derby experience and often spooked the trainers and owners more than it did their horses. Each morning the biggest crowds gathered around stall 12 in Barn 41 where The Deputy was stabled, and Jenine Sahadi had no choice but to hold court.

In a full field of twenty horses, there were plenty of stories for everyone. The eccentric superhorse Fusaichi Pegasus, Harold Rose and Hal's Hope, and D. Wayne Lukas trying for his second consecutive Derby victory and fifth overall. But Sahadi was the one who resonated beyond horseplayers because she was only the tenth woman to saddle a Derby horse and she was trying to become the first to win the 125-year-old race. Off the Santa Anita Derby victory, The

Deputy was regarded as a contender and was likely to go off as the second or third favorite in the race. But Sahadi's appeal was broader than that. She treated her horses to peppermint candies, shampooed them with the same brand she used on her own hair, and mixed a cup of Zinfandel in their oats. This made Sahadi, well, feminine. By now the country already knew, or was about to know, that she'd told Bob Baffert to go to hell and then beaten him on the racetrack. That made her a heroine.

The media queue outside her barn formed at dawn and was more than the usual suspects of turf and national newspaper writers. Two cable channels targeting women—the Oxygen and Lifetime networks—wanted to do segments, as did the *Martha Stewart Living* show. Sahadi appeared on ABC's *World News Tonight*—a request she was happy to fill due to an admitted crush on anchorman Peter Jennings. Then there were the visits from the public. Miss America stopped by, as did numerous little girls with their parents or pony clubs.

Sahadi tried to accommodate every request for an interview or autograph. She demonstrated more grace under this siege than most would have. In Lukas, whom she approached for advice on her first Derby, she had found an unlikely ally.

"He's been great," she said. "The main thing he told me was to stick to my routine, stay in control, and not worry about what anybody else is doing. There are guys out there who are secure enough to help. Charlie Whittingham was like that for me."

Sahadi was trying to follow Lukas's advice. Still, it was difficult to stay focused. She certainly was the only trainer asked how many carats there were in her diamond ring, what she was going to wear to her first Derby, and how did it feel to be a role model. The answers: five carats; she hadn't decided between three outfits, though if she had her druthers it would be the black pants and black cashmere sweater she wore at the Santa Anita Derby for good luck; and Sahadi didn't mind being a role model, but she said she tried not to encourage the notion that she was an icon in the gender wars.

"I'm not trying to make a political statement. I'm doing this because I love to train horses. I was not put on this earth to justify myself," Sahadi said.

The Deputy, on the other hand, appeared unaware, even laconic, about the spectacle greeting him each day. What he lacked in pedigree, the Irish-bred made up in cool.

Sahadi preferred to work the horse after the track was reharrowed at 8:30 A.M. By 8:10 A.M., the colt was led from his stall, and even before he was saddled, The Deputy would stretch his front legs and take a deep breath. He knew he was going to work. Once Chris McCarron climbed on, the pair parted the crowd and walked to the gap leading to the track.

There, The Deputy stood stone-still for fifteen minutes, like he was waiting for a bus, until the track reopened. The whir of cameras, the titter of hundreds of people, the approach of other horses—nothing ruffled him.

On the morning of April 26, I hopped in a truck with Sahadi and Barry Irwin, who had put together the syndicate that owned The Deputy, to go to the grandstand of Churchill Downs and watch him work out. As we got to the second level, Sahadi saw Baffert in front of her in the center of the grandstand.

"I'm not going down there. I'll watch it here," she said.

Baffert had publicly apologized for his remark at the Santa Anita Derby, but Sahadi had refused to meet with him for a personal one. As seasoned as the Team Valor president was about cultivating and satisfying the interest of the media, Irwin was taken aback by how much attention his trainer was attracting.

Sahadi and Irwin quieted as The Deputy came out of the turn. He was striding easily even though McCarron had a firm hold of him. This workout was for fitness; Sahadi didn't intend to turn the colt loose for a blowout until the following week.

"Oh Barry, he looks good," Sahadi said softly. "I think he's ready."

Irwin watched The Deputy gallop out. He absently reached out and patted his trainer on the shoulder. "Are you?" he asked.

"He's a long shot, but he's a bettable long shot."
  —*Bob Baffert on Captain Steve's Kentucky Derby prospects*

The previous two years, Bob Baffert's barn had been circus central. This time around, no one much was looking for Baffert. If they were, it was to ask about Sahadi. He had lowered his profile, and the nicest thing to happen to the trainer was the doing of Mike Pegram. Instead of a track-issued courtesy car, the owner arranged for Baffert to have a Jaguar to drive while he was here.

"Everybody has turned on me except Mike," Baffert said with a faint smile that failed to hide how hurt he really was.

Baffert brought Captain Steve here not sure if he really belonged. The colt had yet to rediscover his 2-year-old form, and after the third-place finish in the Santa Anita Derby, the trainer figured that currently Captain Steve was three lengths slower than the best horses running in the Derby. Still, the colt had won the Kentucky Jockey Club Cup the previous November and had shown an affinity for this surface. His previous two workouts were fast and visually impressive. He was going out again this morning.

"I've been bearing down on him, and he's shown that old enthusiasm—that want-to—and that may be worth a length. He loves this track so let's give him another length," Baffert reasoned. "This is a make-or-break workout. It will tell if we belong. It's not any fun to have a horse here that doesn't have a chance."

Baffert was tight. He headed to the track with all the joy of a man awaiting test results from his cardiologist. Twenty minutes later he was back with a smile sprayed across his face. He would live. The stopwatch cradled in his palm said so. Captain Steve had ticked off seven furlongs in 1:12 2/5 and had inhaled his workmate, a 4-year-old named Boundless, in the stretch.

"We're in the show," he said. "The Captain loves it here."

Baffert's preworkout tension was real enough that neither he nor his assistants remembered to fit Captain Steve with blinkers, the piece of equipment that limits a horse's peripheral vision and is intended to focus the animal on what it's doing. The colt had worn them in all twelve of his races.

"You try to be cool and calm, but I'm telling you I wasn't sure we were doing the right thing," Baffert explained. "I forgot to put the damn things on. I guess he doesn't need them anymore. We're taking them off, I guess, for the Derby."

A couple of nights later, I found Pegram at Furlongs, a Louisville tavern. He displayed none of the angst that Baffert had. He had Captain Steve Thompson with him and was there to support Robby Albarado, his colt's rider. The jockey was working as a bartender for a fund-raising event, though at the time he was on the wrong side of the bar.

Pegram sent Albarado a beer. Captain Steve, however, went over and tapped the rider on the shoulder and, in the interrogative tone he usually employed on suspects, asked:

"Do you really think you should be drinking, Robby?"

The rider hesitated and a look of concern washed his face. Captain Steve flashed a smile and motioned for the bartender to get Albarado another when he was done.

Captain Steve had taken the Derby week off and was alternately having the time of his life and worrying himself sick. Twenty-nine years ago, one of his first duties as Louisville police officer was guarding the roses at Churchill that were designated for the winning jockey. He had worked every Derby day since. His colleagues already had held a potluck dinner for him at the station house, and the colt was a source of pride for the local cops.

"I'm nervous about him staying healthy until the race. Mike's letting me halter him and walk him," Thompson said.

"Hell, Captain, it's a damn horse race," Pegram interrupted. "So much shit can happen, you can't worry about it. The best you can hope for is that our horse is in the race when they come to the quarter pole. It's a thrill you'll never forget. And if we're alive at the quarter pole, buddy, then I like our chances."

"There are three things nobody can guess the outcome of: a ball game, a love affair, and a horse race."

—*Wayne Lukas*

No one was more comfortable as the Derby approached than Wayne Lukas, who was starting a horse in this famous race for the twentieth consecutive year. In fact he was starting three: High Yield, Commendable, and Exchange Rate. In the 125-year history of the race, Lukas held the record for most starters—thirty-five; most starters in a single race—five, in 1996; and was tied for second with most victories—four. This was Lukas's show and he acted every bit the headliner.

He raced the dawn to be among the first on the track to work his horses and then spent the rest of the morning working the media with a Don Rickles–meets–J. Edgar Hoover act. When a crowd or reporters pressed him with questions about High Yield, Lukas grimaced. They wanted to know if the colt would be compromised with so many front-running horses in the field.

"He's run four times this year, won twice and finished second twice. He ran from the front because that is where we figured he could win from. You take what you have to to get in the winner's circle," he said. "I don't understand you guys. You're wrong 99 percent of the time and still keep your credibility. You never see a lawyer or doctor stay in business with that sorry a rate of success. Or a horse trainer."

When he saw Elliott Walden, the young trainer who had finished second in the two previous Derbies but who didn't have an entry this year, Lukas shouted out to him.

"Don't worry, Elliott, you're still a young man. You'll get back again someday."

When Marlon St. Julien, a twenty-eight-year-old jockey, stopped by the barn, Lukas good-naturedly roughed him up. St. Julien, who was black and one of the most promising riders in the nation, was looking for his first Kentucky Derby ride, perhaps on Commendable or Exchange Rate.

"You're still on probation. I rode you on three straight a while ago, then sat there in front of the television out in California and watched as each race got worse," Lukas said.

The trainer offered intrigue whenever he saw an opportunity. Despite his advice to Sahadi, Lukas kept close tabs on what the competition was doing. He enjoyed the gamesmanship and tried to get in the heads of rival trainers. Lukas believed his competitors were doing the same. Or worse. He refused to put the Kentucky Derby saddle clothes on his horses so they'd be indistinguishable from the scores of everyday horses based at Churchill. In the mornings, the track filled up with them and turned the racing oval into a chaotic autobahn. Lukas hoped to make it difficult for his rivals, as well as for the official clockers, to track his horses' training. He also was a bit paranoid.

"What's to stop someone from running out in front of my horses one morning and trying to take one of my horses out of the race," Lukas reasoned.

Lukas had a sly way, too, of turning up the heat on the rumors that had already been simmering—namely about the rowdy antics and light workout schedule of Fusaichi Pegasus. In the mornings, the colt was interrupting his light gallops with bouts of bucking animated enough for a rodeo horse. He was crazy, he was hurt, or he was both, was the word swirling around the backside.

Lukas had loaned Neil Drysdale the sandpit he had built near his barn so Fusaichi Pegasus could expend some energy rolling around. Lukas had used it often in his training of the erratic Tabasco Cat and said that no one should read too much into the spectacle Drysdale's horse was providing before the race. But at the same time, he professed to be in no hurry to name jockeys for Commendable and Exchange Rate.

"I got a feeling some good riders are going to be available sooner than you think," he said, implying that Fusaichi Pegasus might be scratched and Kent Desormeaux would be available.

Lukas didn't believe Commendable was ready for a big effort and had little hope for Exchange Rate after the colt finished a distant ninth behind Fusaichi Pegasus in the Wood Memorial. Satish and Anne Sanan, who owned Exchange Rate, had nominated fourteen horses to the Triple Crown races. They had bought those horses for $14.4 million at auctions in 1998.

What did it get them? Half of the horses had never won, four of them had never raced, and the combined earnings of the fourteen horses so far was $1.4 million. Exchange Rate had earned $226,000 of that, and Cash Run, who was running in the Kentucky Oaks—held the day before the Derby for fillies—accounted for another $862,000. So what $14.4 million had gotten the Sanans was one impossibly long shot to win in the Kentucky Derby.

One Lukas horse not here was the filly Surfside. She was recovering from surgery to remove a chip from her right front ankle, which was discovered after her poor finish in the Santa Anita Derby. She would race again but not until the late summer or fall. Surfside was another Lukas casualty on the road to the Triple Crown.

So that left High Yield, who three weeks earlier had held off More Than Ready in the stretch drive to win the Blue Grass Stakes. Lukas knew he was a player in the Kentucky Derby, and that had to be enough. The trainer figured ten horses actually had a chance to win while the rest of the field were paying a $30,000 entry fee for the chance to sing "My Old Kentucky Home" before the race.

"Not us," said Lukas, pinning his hopes on High Yield. "We're one of the ones with a chance to win."

"Everywhere we go, people are rooting for us. Everyone feels like they have a piece of this horse."
                    —*Elsie Rose, wife for sixty-five years of Harold Rose*

The white Nissan Maxima was the meeting place for the Rose party, which included four children, nine grandchildren, five great-grand-children, Roger and Patti Velez, and cousins and friends totaling sixty people and commanding thirty hotel rooms. The car belonged to Harold Rose and was parked around the corner of the barn, not far from the lawn chair where he conducted interview after interview. Every-one wanted to know about the breeder-owner-trainer of Hal's Hope, about his heart bypass, about his family, about being old.

The car was where he hid to avoid this tiring exercise. It was where Elsie, eighty-five herself and the author of three family-circulated books about the couple's adventures at the racetrack, directed the family traffic. She kept tabs on who was riding with whom. She made sure everyone was getting enough to eat.

Rose had a narrow, craggy face set off by wide wireless glasses. He stooped and spoke in the soft cadence of a storyteller in rhythm with a rocking chair. Rose pushed himself from a leaning position on the car when he saw Velez cantering Hal's Hope back from the track.

"You tell me that good-looking horse couldn't get you out of a hospital bed and make you want to get well. He was the one I had been waiting for," he said as Hal's Hope passed by. "He was the one who was going to bring me here. To bring all of us here."

The jockey walked Hal's Hope in long, looping circles. He barely had a grip of the lead shank as he smooched and hummed and cooed to the colt. On the next pass, Rose handed Velez a baggie full of thin oatmeal cookies. The jockey led Hal's Hope underneath a tree and fed him one. He handed the shank and baggie back to Rose and unhooked the colt's saddle. Velez disappeared for a moment and returned with a bucket and sponge. Nothing was beneath Velez when it came to Hal's

Hope. He was the colt's groom. He was Harold and Elsie's chauffeur. He was the couple's dining companion at nearly every meal.

Velez could have remained in Florida and kept riding and earning money. Instead, he went to Lexington with Hal's Hope at the beginning of April for the Blue Grass Stakes and had remained in Kentucky ever since. The race went badly, as Hal's Hope ran with High Yield and More Than Ready early before fading to last place. It didn't matter to Velez.

"Without Papa and Mama Rose, I'd just be a guy exercising horses in the morning and trying to stay sober the rest of the day," Velez said as he stroked a sponge over the colt's hip. "They gave me a chance when nobody else would. They made me remember how to be a rider. There's no amount of money that can pay for that."

Rose acted as if he didn't hear Velez. Soon, there were camera crews circling the trainer and jockey, and questions were flying. I backed out of the pack, but before I got away Rose had one more thing to say.

"You be sure to tell our friends in New York we got a contender," he said.

I assured the trainer that they already knew.

"In the immortal words of Mr. Charlie Whittingham, 'Being the favorite and bus fare will only get you downtown.'"
—*Neil Drysdale*

Lukas wasn't the only trainer engaged in gamesmanship in the days before the Kentucky Derby. Drysdale had appropriated the role of a British Intelligence agent for his first Derby appearance and employed misinformation and spin to deflect unnecessary attention from the skittish Fusaichi Pegasus. He did it in a perfectly patient and charming manner.

Unlike Sahadi and Rose, who were at the mercy of the media and well-wishers, Drysdale was making the rules. On April 20, he claimed to have worked Fusaichi Pegasus three furlongs on the

Churchill Downs track. But no one saw it—not the track's official clockers, not any reporters or fellow trainers. A few days later, the trainer acknowledged that the colt had breezed easily in the company of other horses.

"It was dawn or before dawn. It was too dark to see my watch," he said blithely. Drysdale also wouldn't say when Fusaichi Pegasus might work again. He maintained that he didn't know, which was in keeping with his philosophy of letting his horses dictate their training, but Drysdale also was having a bit of fun.

"Who knows, maybe I won't work him again. I don't know, I really don't," he told one interviewer. "He'll ring me up in the middle of the night and tell me when he's ready to work."

Often it looked like the middle of the night when Drysdale turned Fusaichi Pegasus and his stablemate and fellow Kentucky Derby entrant War Chant loose in the morning for slow walks or trots around the track. By beating the sun up, Drysdale had the track clear of other horses and reduced the traffic at his barn of those asking about the colt's fitness or mental state.

The racing surface, too, was in top shape then: fresh, hard, and fast. It got too loose after hundreds of horses had trod on it. On Derby day, Drysdale knew Churchill Downs would make sure its premier race was run on a track just like it. His horse would know what a Kentucky Derby track felt like.

No one doubted that Drysdale was a consummate horseman; in the days prior to the Derby, he was elected to the Hall of Fame. But the light trots that were the staple of Fusaichi Pegasus' training were puzzling even to his fellow trainers. Drysdale was essentially putting Fusaichi Pegasus through trail rides. What he was doing, however, was not so much different than what swimmers or marathon runners do before top efforts. He was tapering Fusaichi Pegasus for a peak response. The colt had come out of the Wood Memorial wanting more. Drysdale decided to back him off so his muscles were refreshed, but without deflating the colt's desire to run.

Still, Fusaichi Pegasus was on edge. Late in the mornings, he stomped and tumbled in the rolling pen like he was stuck in the solitary confinement wing of a prison. In the afternoons, when the barns were quiet and clear of people, Drysdale saddled the colt, put an exercise rider on his back, and walked him back and forth to burn more energy.

On the morning of April 27, Fusaichi Pegasus was exiting the track when suddenly he reared on his hind legs and reached his front hooves so high that he collapsed on his hindquarters and rolled over on his side. His rider, Nunos Santos, was thrown as Fusaichi Pegasus flailed like a frightened child trying to pick himself up off the ice in a skating rink. Drysdale, waiting near the rail, bolted to the colt and captured the lead shank just as Fusaichi Pegasus found his feet. The colt hopped backwards and reared again as Drysdale clung to the shank.

Eventually, the colt calmed and Santos got back on him and returned to the barn. But it was a fascinating and frightening occurrence. It was fascinating because, as Fusaichi Pegasus climbed that ladder to the sky, he established himself as among the most willful horses ever to grace a racetrack, particularly in a race of this magnitude. It was frightening because it demonstrated how the best-laid plans could be shattered in an instant. The colt could have wrenched his knee, turned an ankle, and missed the race, or worse, injured himself badly enough to be retired.

For those who wanted to doubt the budding superhorse, which meant a majority of people because a favorite hadn't won the Derby since 1979, this was the final piece of evidence proving that Fusaichi Pegasus was indeed crazy. If he was this rowdy in the quiet of the morning, how would the colt deal with 150,000 people at Churchill Downs on the first Saturday in May?

Drysdale was prepared for the rush of reporters in his barn with questions about the display. He acknowledged that Fusaichi Pegasus had never fallen over as a result of rearing.

"He was doing superbly, and then he felt so good that he reared up and then sat down," Drysdale said. "So far he hasn't put on a real show. When he's in California, he can really do some tricks. We may be coming up to them this week. Some mornings he's a perfect gentleman, some mornings he's feeling so good he doesn't know what to do with himself."

What the trainer did the following morning, however, was more telling. Drysdale turned Fusaichi Pegasus out for a vigorous gallop. That wasn't all. He put a new exercise rider on the colt. His name was Andy Durnin, and he was a wisp of a man from Dublin, Ireland. Drysdale needed the right hands to keep the colt from hurting himself.

A former steeplechase and flats jockey in Ireland, Durnin now was a guru for difficult horses. He worked frequently for Drysdale, who credited him with coaxing decent behavior from Labeeb, an ornery stakes winner who was famous for tossing his rider at the quarter pole at Belmont Park. Before the Wood Memorial in New York, Durnin had climbed on Fusaichi Pegasus for the first time. The colt left a memorable impression.

"I've never been on a horse so powerful. It was like I was a fly on top of him and he could have swatted me off at any time. He isn't mean—more like a big kid who doesn't know his own strength," said Durnin. "I've been on thousands of horses but never one that has felt like this colt."

When Durnin rode Fusaichi Pegasus the following morning, the colt wanted to play "Fusaichi Says" during a first easy lap. Fusaichi Pegasus started, then stopped, then started and stopped again. Durnin sat still and waited for the colt to decide what the pair would do next. Eventually, Fusaichi Pegasus trotted a mile around the track in between a lead pony and his ever-present workmate, an older horse named, fittingly, Bodyguard.

As the horses rounded the far turn for the second time, Durnin lightened up his hold and Fusaichi Pegaus bolted ahead in a gallop.

The colt celebrated this freedom by kicking up his heels and, for a full thirty yards, seesawing back and forth like a child's rocking horse. Durnin barely stirred, and soon Fusaichi Pegasus was back in stride, moving like a locomotive for another mile.

As Durnin returned to the barn, Drysdale had a look of utter contentment. The rider hopped off the horse and in a lilting brogue declared, "We had fun today. The key with horses like this is to try and be quiet. They would rather be without a rider, so while you're on, you try to be as quiet a passenger as possible."

It was hardly Zen. It was common sense. A slave to detail, it was Drysdale's way. Two days before the Derby, the trainer had found one more "T" to cross.

He duplicated the race's saddling procedure. He walked Fusaichi Pegasus from his barn to the paddock, circled him without a saddle, circled him with one, then gave one of his exercise riders, Marcelino Olguin, a leg up and watched as his colt left the paddock just as he would on Derby Day. As the favorite.

> *"He was such a strong, big-boned colt, so well built and well boned that I talked to him. I'm a little funny that way. 'Buddy,' I told him, 'you may run for roses someday, buddy.' He look at me and say, 'Buddy, I might win it.'"*
> —*Handsome Sam Ransom , the foal man at Stone Farm, about the 1981 Kentucky Derby contender Tap Shoes, from a May 2, 1981, Red Smith column in* The New York Times

Todd Pletcher had his feet up on the desk, his hands clasped around his head, and his eyes fixed on the television set that hung in the corner of the small office in his barn at Churchill Downs. He had made it to his first Kentucky Derby. So did More Than Ready, as well as three other colts Pletcher had trained. One named Graeme Hall earned a trip to Louisville by winning the Arkansas Derby;

another named Impeachment was here because of a third-place finish in that race; and a speedster named Trippi had yet to be defeated
in four starts.

Besides the five horses Lukas entered in 1996, only one other trainer,
James Rowe Sr., had brought as many as four, and that was in 1923. It
was a hell of a Kentucky Derby debut. Just as Jenine Sahadi couldn't
escape the questions about female empowerment, Pletcher was asked
about learning under the great master Lukas.

At this moment, Pletcher was hiding out and the television was
tuned to TVG, the all-horses-all-the-time network's workout show.
The program had become a must-see for trainers because it showed
the morning workouts of every Derby horse on the grounds.

It let them know what the competition was up to beyond their
published times. The times really didn't matter; it was how the horse
ran. The simplest explanation of a good workout was that first, the
horse looked comfortable finding his stride. Second, he got faster as
the workout neared the end. Finally, he galloped out strongly, looking like he wanted more.

Above Pletcher, on the television, Captain Steve did just that.

"He looks scary," Pletcher said. "He looks like a different horse
than the one we saw in Louisiana. He looks like he's grown up."

More Than Ready, too, was being noticed in the mornings. His
black coat glimmered like onyx, his small frame rippled with muscle,
and in the mornings, he floated around the oval like an old soul who
had haunted this racetrack for generations. All of Pletcher's horses
here earned their spots in the starting gate but none more than More
Than Ready. The trainer knew that.

"I think all my owners know that More Than Ready has the best
shot of winning—that he is the best of the bunch," Pletcher conceded.

More Than Ready was like Pletcher's oldest child. The highs had
been higher and the lows lower that first go-round. Trainer and colt
had been stars last summer, winning five races in a row, and also-

rans together in the fall. Over ten races, they had won six of them, finished second twice, third once, and earned $670,229. All against the best horses in the nation.

Their journey had been difficult right down to their arrival at Churchill Downs. On the afternoon Pletcher had vanned the colt over from Lexington after the Blue Grass Stakes, he found More Than Ready rolling in his stall. Agitated. Nickering. A veterinarian examined the colt and gave him some antibiotics, but More Than Ready was still upset.

Worried, Pletcher decided to van the colt back to Lexington to the Rood and Riddle clinic. He called Jim Scatuorchio in the Bahamas where he was vacationing with his family.

"The first thing I said was 'Does this mean we aren't running in the Derby?' " Scatuorchio recalled. "And I hated myself as soon as it came out of my mouth. Here my horse was in trouble and I was thinking me, me, me. I couldn't believe it."

By the time More Than Ready arrived at the clinic, however, he was fine. He'd had a bowel movement in the van; More Than Ready had colic. The vets knew who the black colt was, but agreed with Pletcher that no one needed to know that More Than Ready had gotten sick. One of the most important responsibilities of being a trainer is protecting your horse's reputation. With the Kentucky Derby approaching, Pletcher did not believe anyone needed to know More Than Ready had suffered a stomachache.

The vets agreed to bill Scatuorchio for work on a fictitious horse named Jim's Prize. Twenty minutes later, More Than Ready was back on a van for Churchill Downs and Scatuorchio was back on the phone apologizing to Pletcher for his callous reaction.

Consider the odds More Than Ready had overcome to get here. Bevo, Greenwood Lake, Summer Note, and Mighty—all colts that beat or tied More Than Ready—never made it to Louisville for the Derby. After suffering one injury or another, they weren't even racing.

Scatuorchio and Pletcher believed they had a genuine chance to win the race. In the Blue Grass Stakes on April 15, More Than Ready had shown he could rate as he loomed in third place until the stretch before taking on High Yield. Pletcher's plan for the colt over the spring looked like it was working. As More Than Ready and High Yield hit the stretch neck and neck, they bumped each other again and again: More Than Ready got beaten by eight inches.

Normally stoic, Pletcher abandoned measured tones, unhooked his hands from the back of his head, and let his voice tighten and climb octaves as he described the colt's last race. "That much," Pletcher said with his hands spread the eight inches.

"That much cost Jim about $5 million. That's how much that Grade I win would have been worth in the breeding shed. I could tell you the inside part of the track where High Yield played like a conveyor belt. It was good for that eight inches. I could tell you I've lost plenty of close races, but none that have hurt as much. What I will tell you is that More Than Ready has done everything we've ever asked. He's never quit. He's the neatest horse I've ever been around. I don't know if he's going to win the Derby, but I know he's going to kill himself trying."

As soon as I left Pletcher's office, I began scribbling in my notepad. When I stopped, I looked up, and there I was in front of stall 7, with More Than Ready looking me in the eye. His ears were perked and he stared right at me.

To myself, really, I asked out loud, "You going to run a big one in the Derby?"

More Than Ready nodded his head twice emphatically. He then buried his nose in a bag of oats hanging on the door. Now, I'm no Dr. Dolittle, and have never had a conversation with a horse before, but I felt More Than Ready had heard my question and answered it. I waited a couple of minutes and watched him nibble on the oats.

I asked him again, this time clearly and directly.

"Are you going to win the Kentucky Derby?"

More Than Ready pulled his nose from the bag and nodded again, twice, this time blowing bubbles between his lips and stomping his front foot for emphasis.

I had found my Kentucky Derby horse.

"It was a choice of going in the gate first and waiting around, or loading next to a keg of dynamite. We went for staying in the gate."
—*Barry Irwin, after the May 3, 2000, Kentucky Derby Draw, explaining why he chose post 11*

On the Wednesday before the race, the owners and trainers of Derby horses were gathered together for the first time in the well of the Kentucky Derby Museum. They sat on stiff white lawn chairs and baked underneath hot television lights. They waited to draw post positions for a race that they had spent a lifetime dreaming about and a roller-coaster year to reach. The privilege of sitting here had cost them an entry fee of $15,000; they'd pay another $15,000 starting fee the day of the race. The entry fee was nonrefundable—if a horse suffered an injury and was scratched from the race tomorrow, an owner was out $15,000.

"I can barely breathe," said Jim Scatuorchio, beads of sweat trickling down from the top of his head. "I've wanted to be here so badly and now I'm scared shitless."

Terry Scatuorchio clutched a crumpled piece of paper with four post position numbers scratched on it: 8,9,10, and 11. Because ESPN televised the event and wanted to create some made-for-television suspense, a two-tier system had been implemented. The first was a blind draw to determine the order of selection, followed by the picking of the actual post positions.

So if More Than Ready drew the No. 1 pick, the Scatuorchios could decide between their preferred numbers. If they pulled No. 20, then they would have to take whatever gate remained.

There was strategy involved, because trainers knew where their horses preferred to break from the starting gate and how long they could stand comfortably as a big field was loaded. Horses are loaded two at a time and in a field of twenty, which meant that gates 1 and 11 would be loaded first, then 2 and 12, and so on, until 10 and 20 were led to the gate last.

No one generally wanted posts 1, 2, or 3 because they meant a colt would have a long wait until the rest of the field loaded. From the inside gates, the horses could get bumped or boxed in on the rail after the gates opened. Most wanted to avoid the last six stalls because that was a separate auxiliary gate used only in fields larger than fourteen; starting from way outside meant a long, potentially exhausting run for a horse to get proper position for the first turn.

As luck would have it, Mike Pegram drew the first selection, which as far as strategy goes was a wasted pick. He had no strategy. The owner asked his grandson, Gator, from what post should Captain Steve start. The seven-year-old looked up in the rafters and saw the number 8 painted on the wall as part of museum exhibit. So No. 8 it was.

Gator and Captain Steve Thompson walked up to a large board with a painting of Churchill Downs' starting gate. The little boy hung a placard bearing the likeness of the Pegrams' red and yellow silks beneath No. 8.

The Scatuorchios were in decent shape, too. They drew the fifth selection. The No. 10 hole was available, which meant More Than Ready would be one of the last pair to load in the starting gate. Jim took the placard bearing his peacock-blue and beige silks in his hand and staked out his starting spot.

Neil Drysdale had drawn the second selection for War Chant and the twelfth choice for Fusaichi Pegasus. He put War Chant in the No. 9 post. When it came his turn to choose Fusaichi Pegasus' gate, he surprised his rivals again. The first and second posts were still available, as were 11 and 12 and 16 through 20. Most assumed he would stay in the main gate in 11 or 12. Instead, Drysdale hung Fusao Sekiguchi's red jersey, yellow-yoked silks, in the auxiliary gate on No. 16.

"I picked it to keep him out of trouble," Drysdale said. "I didn't want him to stand in the gate too long in case something goes wrong."

This wasn't what Barry Irwin, Jenine Sahadi, and Chris McCarron had expected. They had drawn the fifteenth pick for The Deputy. They were already having a bad day. Their colt was dehydrated and receiving electrolytes back in the barn. Sahadi, who had been in Kentucky for most of three weeks, was tense and looked like she, too, could use some fluids.

Irwin believed his worries had come true: that his trainer had been pulled in too many directions and was run down. There was time yet to get The Deputy back in shape, but Irwin couldn't help but wonder if, between demands on her time and the pressure of the Derby, The Deputy's condition had escaped earlier notice by Sahadi.

Right now, however, they needed a gate. Before the draw, Sahadi had hoped for anywhere from 5 to 12. No. 11 was open, but McCarron was favoring No. 17. Sahadi stopped Irwin before he left his seat and, with a glance at the board, reminded him who was in post No. 16: Fusaichi Pegasus. She and McCarron had spoken about staying away from the unpredictable colt. McCarron, reminded, now agreed. The Deputy would break from post 11.

It was Wayne Lukas, however, who took the worst of the draw. He pulled the No. 18 selection for High Yield, and that's the post number the colt ended up in. Exchange Rate would break from No. 17 and Commendable from No. 13.

The trainer, however, didn't despair, because bad posts had been good to him in the past. He had won the Derby from the 17 hole with Charismatic; from the 15 with Grindstone; from the 16 with Thunder Gulch; and from the 11 with Winning Colors.

"Each time that we've won it, we had gone home and agonized a little bit about the post we had drawn," he reasoned. "And each time it turned out to be favorable for us."

THE EVE OF THE DERBY

MAY 5, 2000

"A few years ago you went to a horse sale
and ever since then it seems like a fairy tale
You brought along a team of the best
and they were all going to put their horse knowledge to the test . . ."
                    From "The Derby Poem," by Andrea Rosen

On the eve of the Kentucky Derby, there is nothing left to do but party. I began at a restaurant called John E's, where Jim and Terry Scatuorchio were hosting a cocktail party in honor of More Than Ready. Jim had learned not to plan a postrace party after the Champagne Stakes when the colt had finished fifth and his birthday party at "21" was ruined. If More Than Ready won the Derby, they'd find pizza and beer somewhere.

But tonight they had a room off the bar and about fifty people cruising a buffet of chicken wings and ribs and waiters with trays full of cocktails.

For Jim, the prerace nervousness had given way to exhaustion. Hotel rooms and tickets to the Kentucky Derby were at a premium, and the owner needed dozens of both. He pried two last-minute rooms out of his hotel by giving the general manager Derby tickets. Then he needed to replace those tickets and cut another deal with the concierge.

At the track that afternoon for the Kentucky Oaks, he and Eddie Rosen went from box to box making sure everyone was in good shape. Scatuorchio was especially tickled that two of Terry's cousins had ended up in a box on the finish line near former president George Bush.

"We're running on adrenaline. We've maybe slept three hours," said Terry Scatuorchio, who had taken over the host duties for the evening.

Earlier that morning, Terry had finally persuaded Jim to take her shopping for a Derby hat. The shop they found had only eight hats left, which was a good thing. "Jim was looking at his watch after five minutes. I just grabbed one to get him out of there," she said.

I started to tell Terry about my encounter with More Than Ready, how he'd told me he was going to win the Kentucky Derby, but before I could finish, she put her hand on my shoulder.

"He nodded his head twice, right, and blew bubbles and stamped his feet, right?" she asked with an amused smile. "I know, he does that sometimes when you look at him. Oh God, I hope you're right. But you didn't bet a lot of money on him, did you?"

I had—that afternoon when the advance wagering opened. It didn't matter, the colt was still my Derby horse. He figured on paper, especially at odds of 10–1. Fortunately, before I had to fess up, J. J. Pletcher joined us. He had inherited the edginess Jim Scatuorchio had shaken.

J.J. looked to the table where Todd was sitting. He tilted his beer bottle at him and shook his head. "Look at that son of a gun. He's got four horses running in the damn Kentucky Derby tomorrow and one of them might win the thing," J.J. said with a proud smile.

"And all he can do is concentrate on his chicken wings. That there is a sixty-eight-year-old man stuck inside a thirty-two-year-old's body. He damn sure doesn't take after me."

Soon, there was a clink of a glass and one of Eddie Rosen's daughters, Andrea, got everyone's attention. She had been to nearly all of More Than Ready's races. She understood how much it meant to Jim Scatuorchio, as well as her father, to get a horse to this race. Andrea read a poem she had written, which was a thank-you and good-luck toast all in one. When she finished, there was a smattering of applause from people with wet eyes.

"We made it here," Terry Scatuorchio said, "and really that's enough."

THE WALK

*"Horsemen, please bring your horses to the paddock for the eighth
race, the Kentucky Derby."*
        —*The backside announcer at 4:20 P.M. on May 6, 2000*

You could barely hear that announcement over the scratchy loud-
speaker. It was delivered in a monotone that failed to capture what
those words meant to the dozens of owners and trainers sweating
through their suits on a humid, unseasonably hot 86-degree day. The
barn area had been transformed into picnic grounds on Derby day as
many of the horsemen based at Churchill Downs rolled out barbe-
cue grills and coolers to entertain family, friends, and help.

There were maybe a thousand or so people milling between the
barns in shorts and flip-flops with beers in their hands, but most stayed
clear of where the Kentucky Derby horses were getting ready for the
quarter-mile walk across the track and maybe into history. Two days
before, the field had lost an entrant in the kind of mishap that had
every owner and trainer knocking on wood. A colt named Globalize
was on the track for an innocuous gallop when he was accidentally
kicked by his saddle pony. It caused a deep gash and he was scratched
from the race.

The announcement brought a moment of silence at Bob Baffert's
barn, followed by a roar and wave of hoisted beer cans. As usual, the
trainer and Mike Pegram had a full-blown hoedown going on in the
hours before the race. They were loose and bantered with anyone who
dropped by, which, this afternoon, was predominantly pretty girls.

The prerace mayhem that had surrounded Jenine Sahadi and The
Deputy had thinned out. She had chosen a blue Escada suit for her
Derby outfit. It didn't stop her from stomping around her colt's stall to
nuzzle and soothe The Deputy. A case of nerves had prompted Sahadi
to throw up earlier in the afternoon. Still, she looked radiant.

"I'm anxious, nervous, proud. I feel a lot of things. I just want it to be over," she said. "I've held up because I believe the racing gods have already decided who is going to win. I'm acting like it's not me."

Jim Scatuorchio stood underneath a tree by himself with his gray suit coat folded over his arms as Todd Pletcher and Cindy Hutter silently choreographed the parade of the trainer's four horses to the paddock. Scatuorchio had a pensive, faraway look as if he were getting ready to run the race himself.

Neil Dysdale was oblivious to everyone and everything except Fusaichi Pegasus and War Chant, and his intensity radiated a force field that kept the curious at a distance. Even the owner of Fusaichi Pegasus, Fusao Sekiguchi, and his small entourage kept fifty paces away as Drysdale pulled on a cigarette and eyed his colt.

Sekiguchi, too, had a face that matched his dark suit, quite a contrast from the figure he had cut since his arrival. Earlier in the week, he had shown up at a party in a mustard-yellow leather jacket with three geishas in tow. They were powdered and robed and had done everything from fixing his plate at the buffet line and tucking his napkin in his shirt to performing a traditional dance and mingling with the other guests. Now they waited in the paddock for Sekiguchi and his superhorse to arrive.

As the horses and owners left the barn area, they passed through a gauntlet of noisy well-wishers lined up five deep before a gap on the backstretch. They stood in the beds of pickup trucks and cheered the horses and owners as they took their first steps onto the racetrack. As spirited as this group was, they were nothing compared to the 153,204 people crammed a quarter mile away beneath the twin spires of Churchill Downs. Those were the lusty Romans waiting for the gladiators to enter the arena.

"Good luck, Sheik," someone yelled as Sheik Mohammed al-Maktoum walked alongside one of his colts, China Visit. The Sheik responded with a broad smile and a wave to the crowd.

Neither China Visit nor the Sheik's other colt, Curule, were given much of a chance at odds of 50–1. But they were in the race, unlike Chief Seattle, the colt the Sheik had paid $4.5 million for in January. He had gotten ill on the trip over from Dubai and was scratched.

The Walk, as this ritual is known, is an exhilarating experience for an owner, second only to winning the Kentucky Derby. It is like a commencement exercise. It meant you had bred or bought a winner and now had arrived at horse racing's grandest stage. The owners' first steps on the track often were wobbly because before them reverberated a wall of sound from a seemingly never-ending line of human bodies.

To the right, the infield was packed with more than 50,000 people and was a rowdy city in itself. This crowd was more concerned with the mint juleps than the fancy hats. The only time Sahadi had been to the Derby before was as a college student in the infield. All she said she remembered about that day was a naked guy climbing a flagpole.

Those on the edges of the infield began the roar that grew through the grandstand and was sustained as one horse after another began the promenade clockwise around the track's first turn, to the stretch, through to a tunnel, and finally to the paddock or saddling area. Horses and owners walked barely twenty yards to round the turn before they encountered fans close enough to touch them.

"You're a loser, Pegasus," screamed one red-faced man barely six feet from Sekiguchi when the colt stopped to relieve himself. Sekiguchi ignored him, leaned on his walking stick, and waited for Fusaichi Pegasus to finish.

"We love you, Jenine. Go get them, girl," they yelled at Sahadi. The trainer beamed a smile as tears brimmed beneath her sunglasses.

Captain Steve Thompson, too, was beloved by the local crowd. He bounced on the track as if he were a manager leading his boxer to the ring. He raised up his arms to the cheers and promised a victory "for the regular folks." Pegram, in his blue jeans and blazer, trailed with a tickled grin on his face.

Jim Scatuorchio walked the point with More Than Ready, Terry at his side. Last-minute hat purchase or not, she looked the part of a Derby fashion plate with cream hat, dark tailored suit, and black ankle-high boots. They both blinked back tears. Their kids, as well as Eddie and Barbara Rosen and J. J. Pletcher, followed.

"Man, look at this. I've never," said J.J. as they rounded the turn.

For as far as you could see, people were on their feet in the grandstand cheering. It was a painter's palette of various-colored hats accompanied by a numbing noise. There were shouts from those pressed on the rail and holding their mint julep glasses up.

Up ahead on the straightaway Fusaichi Pegasus was walking directly into this sensory assault. He was bearing up pretty well, too, until Drysdale tried to drape a mesh fly net over his sweating back. The colt stopped and bucked once, twice, and the crowd roared for more. Drysdale waited, as did the procession of owners and horses behind him. After a moment, they moved on.

Sixty or so yards later, in the tunnel beneath the grandstand, Fusaichi Pegasus stalled again. This time, Drysdale patted the colt, who turned his head to make sure he was not alone. Satisfied, Fusaichi Pegasus moved toward the light and into the paddock.

Every inch of the grass in the center of the saddling area was covered by owners and their friends. The dirt walking path was the moat that separated the horses and their handlers. They went about the business of saddling their horses as cameras snapped and camcorders were held up in the air. Todd Pletcher and D. Wayne Lukas were mirror images of each other as they moved from stall to stall readying their multiple runners. They moved purposefully and tugged on their horses' bridles. They assumed the same spread-legged, folded-arm stance when they talked to their riders.

Earlier in the week, Lukas had approached Pletcher on the training track and offered a handshake. "I'm proud of what you done," he told him. "If I can't win it, I want you to."

Drysdale was in his shirtsleeves as he saddled Fusaichi Pegasus. He wore a tie spotted with turtles, a nod to the nickname he had earned with his deliberate training. His big horse was taking in the crowd and inching forward from his stall as if he wanted a closer look.

Sahadi stood with Irwin, who wore an eye-catching pink sport coat. They hoped that they had gotten The Deputy back in shape after his bout with dehydration. The colt, however, was washed out. Irwin shook his head and walked away. He knew already The Deputy wasn't going to win.

The riders were on the scene now and huddled individually with each trainer. When the bugler belted out the Call to Post, the riders accepted a leg up on their colts. They circled once around the owners. "No matter what happens, I'm going to win like I'm used to it or lose like I enjoy it," said Pegram, as Captain Steve passed by.

The colts disappeared into the tunnel and, with Broadway stage timing, once the last one hit the track, "My Old Kentucky Home" echoed in one voice that probably could have been heard in all of Louisville.

The owners and trainers filed out of the paddock with surprising solemnity. They had done all they could do, and now all that was left was a horse race.

THE RACE

"The horse is God's gift to man."

—*Arabian proverb*

At 5:31 P.M., no one was sitting down in Churchill Downs as the field of nineteen walked those final yards to the starting gate for the 126th running of the Kentucky Derby. Lines shortened at the betting windows—more than $9.7 million in wagers were made at the track on this single race, and more than $65.6 million throughout North America.

So far, Fusaichi Pegasus had kept his neuroses in check. He walked the length of the stretch unperturbed after a very light warm-up. Drysdale had told Kent Desormeaux not to overdo it because of the heat and humidity. To make sure Fusaichi Pegasus remained calm, Drysdale had sent the colt to the track with his usual morning pony, Elvis, and barn foreman, Enrique Larios, aboard. Nothing was left to chance.

Two by two, the colts were led into the starting gate, with The Deputy and long shot Ronton the last to load. Starter Roger Nagle peered down the line. He stood eight feet above the ground atop a podium that was planted twenty feet ahead of the starting gate. Beneath his light-colored fedora, Nagle squinted to make sure the colts had all four feet on the ground and were quiet. He had a handset connected to a long cord cradled in his right hand.

When he was satisfied that all was well, Nagle pushed the button. The crowd sent the field off with a cannon shot of noise and the speed horses, Hal's Hope, Trippi, More Than Ready, and Graeme Hall, were out front first. They rushed to the rail as they headed into the first turn.

The only instruction Drysdale had given Desormeaux was to take his time moving Fusaichi Pegasus inside. The rider followed the advice, but perhaps he had little choice; the colt broke slow from the gate. Like a pony, Desormeaux thought. Maybe he was too far back? He gradually guided the 2–1 favorite to the rail as fourteen horses hit the first turn ahead of him.

Baffert believed that the race was won or lost on the first turn. Your horse had to get there with the minimum of contact and in a full, easy stride. Silver Charm and Real Quiet had. In 1999, General Challenge, Excellent Meeting, and Prime Timber hadn't. Baffert was relieved when he saw that Captain Steve was in seventh place and running freely three paths away from the rail. He had a chance.

Sahadi and The Deputy didn't. The colt was stuck on the outside in tenth place, and the other horses were pushing him wider. The race's 4–1 second favorite wasn't off to a good start. "I knew he wasn't going anywhere, and I couldn't do anything about it," she said.

Up front the same four horses led the field into a perilously fast half mile of 45.99 seconds. John Velazquez eased the throttle off More Than Ready and relaxed the colt on the rail into fourth place at the ⅝ pole. He knew Hal's Hope, Trippi, and Graeme Hall weren't going to be in front much longer.

Lukas believed the race started at the backside kitchen, or in other words around the three-quarter-mile point, heading into the far turn. When he looked through his binoculars, Lukas knew he'd have to wait another year for his fifth Derby triumph. High Yield was in fifth place after being bumped at the start and caught wide around the turn. His stride was getting shorter, and Pat Day knew he was out of horse. Exchange Rate was in twelfth place, Commendable in sixteenth.

Lukas, beaten, scanned the pack for Fusaichi Pegasus.

In the backstretch, Desormeaux kept his colt next to the rail and was riding high on the horse, not asking Fusaichi Pegasus to do anything but stay in stride. Desormeaux risked being boxed in or stopped by tired horses. But Fusaichi Pegasus sped up and slowed down like a Cadillac negotiating rush hour—measured and elegant. The rider thought it was eerie. The colt kept slowing down on his own when there was no place to go. He was just a passenger.

Fusaichi Pegasus entered the far turn in eleventh place, but ahead of him the early runners were backing up. Those horses had gone three quarters of a mile in a sizzling 1:09.99. Desormeaux moved the colt off the rail then tucked back in to avoid the faltering Graeme Hall and High Yield. Jerry Bailey, aboard War Chant, watched Fusaichi Pegasus pass and knew his horse wasn't going to win. "It was like *zzzzzzzooom* and he was gone," Bailey would say.

Coming out of the turn, Hal's Hope and Trippi were faltering on the inside while Captain Steve and Wheelaway were making bold

moves outside. More Than Ready was at the rail, and Velazquez remembered what Pletcher had told him: Don't get excited coming out
of the turn; some other jock is going to move too early.

It was Robby Albarado on Captain Steve and Richard Migliore on
Wheelaway who shot out. Captain Steve got to the top of the stretch
first. Pegram had gotten his wish; at odds of 10–1, he was feeling very
much alive. But Wheelaway bumped Captain Steve, and both stumbled
toward the rail.

Velazquez, meanwhile, cut the corner perfectly and now had the
lead. There was 1,234½ feet of stretch in front of More Than Ready.
Could he last?

The question was moot in an instant. Desormeaux angled
Fusaichi Pegasus out from the rail seven wide on the heels of Cap-
tain Steve and Wheelaway. When those two colts bumped each
other, he had a clear path and floated past, Desormeaux tapping
Fusaichi Pegasus with a right-hand whip. He smooched in his ear.
The colt took off like a rocket and was three lengths past More Than
Ready in seconds.

Once in the middle of the track in the stretch, there was no catching Fusaichi Pegasus. Desormeaux tucked his whip beneath his arm-
pit and moved his hands underneath the colt's chin. He hung on as
Fusaichi Pegasus gobbled up the final yards, becoming the first favorite to win the race since Spectacular Bid in 1979 in 2:01.12 to tie
the sixth-fastest time in Kentucky Derby history.

Alex Solis aboard a colt named Aptitude finished a length and a
half behind. Six more behind them, More Than Ready tried to hold
off his stablemate Impeachment. The late runner moved from thirteenth place in the last quarter mile and caught More Than Ready
by a neck at the wire.

It didn't take long for the riders to gallop their colts back to the
finish line and turn them back over to the trainers. One by one, the
jockeys, their faces spotted with dirt and sweat, hopped off their horses
and gave their trainers a rundown of the race.

Soon, Kent Desormeaux and Fusaichi Pegasus were the only rider and horse remaining on the track. They also were the only pair with a chance to sweep the Triple Crown. They made their way to the winner's circle and were joined by Sekiguchi's jubilant entourage. The geishas carried roses and unfurled paper parasols with the Fusaichi Pegasus name printed on top of them. They bowed repeatedly to the ponytailed owner.

Kentucky governor Paul Patton mangled Sekiguchi's name at the trophy presentation, but the Japanese owner didn't seem to mind. The colt he paid $4 million for had just become the most expensive horse ever to win the Kentucky Derby. Sekiguchi earned a first-place check worth $1,038,400; in addition, he collected a $150,000 bonus from the New York Racing Association for completing the Wood Memorial and Derby double. But Fusaichi Pegasus was now worth far more than that—at least $30 million as a Kentucky Derby–winning stud.

With the help of an interpreter, Sekiguchi promised that his colt would not be shipped to Japan to seek richer purses. He would remain in the United States.

"I want him to be an American treasure," Sekiguchi insisted.

Before the owner was hustled to the Derby Museum's postrace celebration, he had something to say about Drysdale, his trainer.

"He doesn't kiss anybody's ass," Sekiguchi said. "Whatever he did, I knew it was the right thing. He never talked to me about details, but I have 100 percent confidence in him. When I see his eyes, I know he has confidence in himself."

Drysdale slipped into the Derby Museum unnoticed as Sekiguchi told the audience what horse racing, what this colt, and what this victory meant to him. Drysdale kept a finger pressed to his lips. "It's his moment," he said, as he left the museum and headed back to his barn.

Not long after, Sekiguchi and company arrived there, too. Bystanders and barn help along the backside stopped what they were doing and applauded as he passed by. The reception was warmest when he made the shed row at Drysdale's barn. Sekiguchi strode to Fusaichi

Pegasus' stall, laid a kiss on the colt's snout, and pulled up a chair in front of him.

He wanted to admire his big horse.

THE MORNING AFTER

"They run this race every year and I guarantee we'll be back next year."

—D. Wayne Lukas, May 7, 2000

Wayne Lukas leaned over a sawhorse at the entrance of his barn and tried to explain that he had no explanation for why Exchange Rate finished twelfth, High Yield fifteenth, and Commendable seventeenth.

"Sometimes good horses run bad—all three ran flat. Especially High Yield. I felt awful good walking him over there. I was sure he was going to run a big one," Lukas said. "There's always an explanation, but we don't have it now. We've been there before. It's time to forget about this one and move on down the road."

Lukas intended to run High Yield in the Preakness, but Commendable was going to sit that one out and try the 1½-mile Belmont Stakes in five weeks.

"I'll try to pick up one down the road," he said. "Nobody should go and bronze Fusaichi Pegasus yet. He ran a great race, but there's a long way to go for the Triple Crown."

Mike Pegram, too, was moving Captain Steve on to Baltimore, Maryland, and the second leg of the Triple Crown. His colt had finished eighth, and that was the best thing that happened to the owner on a frustrating day. Everything that possibly could have gone wrong did. He had bet on two of Bob Baffert's horses on the undercard. They lost. A third that the trainer didn't think had much of a chance won. The owner had a long shot picked out for another race, but didn't get to the window. That horse came in and paid $38.

"Hell, I didn't even bet on Captain Steve. I let my own horse go off without any of my money because with the way things were going, I wasn't going to jinx the poor son of a bitch," Pegram said.

Pegram had studied the replay of the race and concluded that the hit Wheelaway put on Captain Steve in the stretch hadn't compromised his colt's chances.

"The Captain was done. I talked to Robby and he said the colt had nothing left," he said.

But the owner wasn't going to concede the Triple Crown to Fusaichi Pegasus, though he was as wowed as anybody by the colt's awesome showing.

"Maybe somebody will impede him before he takes off. He was real impressive," Pegram said. "But the thing about this business is that you can't be afraid to get beat. If you're not willing to reload and fire again, then get out."

The rest of the challengers, however, weren't so eager. Fusaichi Pegasus' contemporaries—most of them tired, a few bandaged—had had enough. The runner-up, Aptitude, was going to skip the Preakness and run in the Belmont Stakes. The colt's trainer, Bobby Frankel, was not overwhelmed by the winner's performance. He was more irritated with the ride Alex Solis had given Aptitude.

Over at Jenine Sahadi's barn, both trainer and colt were finished. After finishing fourteenth, The Deputy had come back from the race with a cough. Chris McCarron bemoaned the fact that The Deputy had picked a terrible day to run the worst race of his life.

"He was tired and kept spinning his wheels. He kept going backwards," McCarron said.

Sahadi had left the track in tears after the Derby. She was hoarse and now looked as if she were about ready to collapse.

"Both me and my horse are exhausted and want to go home," she said with a weak smile. "This has been fun and I don't regret a thing. I wish it could have worked out differently, but it didn't. I don't want to sound too philosophical, but that's the beauty of racing. One minute you're flying high and the next you're not."

I knew what to expect from the horses in Todd Pletcher's barn. Shortly after the Derby, I had watched the replay with him in a small office off the paddock tunnel. He was stone-faced until, at the top of the stretch, More Than Ready took the lead.

"My heart skipped a couple of beats right there," he said without taking his eyes away from the screen. "Look at Impeachment bulling his way through there," he said a few moments later as both colts hit the wire together.

Pletcher watched intently as Trippi staggered home in eleventh place and Graeme Hall finished dead last. They were cooked on the front end and would be laid up until summer. The trainer was inclined to run Impeachment back in the Preakness.

Not More Than Ready. The colt had run a near lightning-fast pace and was the only one of the speed horses not to collapse.

"It's too far for him, by about this much," Pletcher said, separating his fingers an inch. "He tries too hard and needs the rest. We'll wait until the summer. He has nothing left to prove."

Jim and Terry Scatuorchio and Eddie Rosen were in good spirits as they watched More Than Ready graze outside the barn. All four of the colt's legs were bandaged. He had small cuts and scrapes above his hooves from his effort. The More Than Ready supporters, indeed, had found a pizza place after the Derby and had shot pool and drunk beer late into the night.

Their Triple Crown campaign was over.

"No long faces. No anxiety," Jim Scatuorchio said. "We got a good trip. He tried as hard as he could. No excuses. We were beaten by a better horse. I ran fourth in the Kentucky Derby. I've got nothing to be ashamed of. This may be a once-in-a-lifetime horse. I wouldn't trade this experience for anything in the world."

Chapter 12

THE PREAKNESS:
THE CROWN'S MIDDLE JEWEL

MAY 13–20, 2000

PIMLICO RACE COURSE
BALTIMORE, MARYLAND

"His neigh is like the bidding of a monarch, and his countenance enforces homage."

—King Henry V, *William Shakespeare*

Not since 1979 had a favorite won the Kentucky Derby, and as soon as Fusaichi Pegasus crossed the finish line at Churchill Downs, the colt was hailed as "the next great horse," a certain Triple Crown winner, and certainly superior to the horses that had come close to sweeping the series in the previous three years.

In 1999, twelve other rivals showed up at the Preakness Stakes in Baltimore to take on Charismatic, and the Kentucky Derby winner was sent off by bettors as the fifth favorite. In 1998, Real Quiet was the second choice in a field of ten. In 1997, Silver Charm was the third choice in another field of ten. Those three colts were among the twenty-seven horses that had won the Preakness and moved on to Belmont to attempt a Triple Crown sweep.

Only eleven had completed that feat and the last to do so, Affirmed, accomplished it in 1978. Still, the "flying horse" or "FuPeg," as Fusao Sekiguchi's colt was now being called, was virtually being given a free pass to the history books.

Only seven rivals were at Pimlico Race Course to take on Fusaichi Pegasus. Of the eighteen other horses that ran in the Derby, only four wanted to try the colt again: Impeachment, High Yield, Captain Steve, and Hal's Hope. Even Bob Baffert said the only way that Fusaichi Pegasus would lose is "if they loaded him backwards." So the superhorse was made the prohibitive 3–5 favorite in the morning line.

The oddest thing of all was that Neil Drysdale didn't want Fusaichi Pegasus there at all. The trainer hadn't planned for his colt to mount an assault on the Triple Crown.

Drysdale's goal was to win the Kentucky Derby, then capture the Breeders' Cup Classic six months later in November. That's what he had told Sekiguchi the previous October; that's how he had trained the colt ever since. Drysdale was too diplomatic to say the notion of a Triple Crown was antiquated and that it was too trying on young,

developing horses—no matter how blessed with talent—to follow the
1¼ mile Derby with the 1³⁄₁₆-mile Preakness two weeks later, and then
the 1½-mile Belmont three weeks after that.

Drysdale knew the Kentucky Derby winner was expected to move
on to the Preakness and, if victorious, to try the Belmont.

"You follow a game plan to the Derby. You can tailor your training schedule and adjust to however your horse is feeling or what he
is doing," Drysdale explained. "But once he wins the Derby, the plans
are out the window. You have only two weeks to the next race and
you have to make it up as you go along."

That wasn't the Drysdale way, but he did his best to impose his
own sense of order on the second leg of the Triple Crown. The trainer
waited nearly a week after the Derby to confirm that Fusaichi Pegasus, indeed, would compete in the Preakness even though he had
already made a day trip to Pimlico to scout barn locations. He gave
Fusaichi Pegasus a single timed workout after the Derby, but he did
it at Churchill Downs on May 15.

When Drysdale and his colt finally arrived in Baltimore, he con-
founded Pimlico officials by choosing a barn in an isolated part of the
racetrack. Usually, the Kentucky Derby winner stays in Stall 40 of
Barn E, which is behind the grandstand and is home to all the other
competitors. Not Fusaichi Pegasus; Drysdale chose Barn 7, which was
nearly a half mile away on the east side of the track.

Pimlico, a 130-year-old relic, had little charm, and Drysdale's chosen headquarters looked like a bomb shelter. It was a cinder-block
structure with macadam floors and was guarded by an outside wall.
There wasn't a blade of grass to be found anywhere near it.

In the past two years, track officials had been plagued by mishaps,
which compounded the perception that the Preakness was a poor
cousin in the Triple Crown series. In 1998, a power outage on race
day left more than 91,000 people without air-conditioning or eleva-
tors, as well as downed betting machines and the track's electronic
timing system. In 1999, a drunk and disturbed man slipped through

security from the rowdy infield and onto the track, where he tried to take a swing at one of the horses barreling down the stretch during one of the races prior to the Preakness. The track had to refund more than $1.4 million in bets.

Now the trainer of the most talked-about horse in years had chosen a corner of the racetrack that looked like a tenement. Drysdale said he selected the barn because it was removed and quiet. When horse and trainer arrived at 2 P.M. on May 17, 2000, it seemed as if Drysdale wanted a place to hide Fusaichi Pegasus.

With a media scrum awaiting the superhorse's arrival, Drysdale hopped up on the running board of the large van that carried his star and told the driver to drive by the greeting party. The van edged up to the barn and Fusaichi Pegasus was let out into his enclosure where nobody could see him. The big horse was in town even if his trainer didn't want to be.

Drysdale was not the only one distracted. His jockey, Kent Desormeaux, was balancing the high of his second Derby triumph with some tough news at home. In April, a couple of days before he won the Wood Memorial with Fusaichi Pegasus, Desormeaux learned that his fourteen-month-old son, Jacob, was deaf and needed surgery if he was ever to hear. Desormeaux tried to remain upbeat, but his high-pitched voice choked slightly as he tried to explain the past month.

"It's heartbreaking for me and his mother. We just sat down and cried. It's terrible to think what your child is going to miss," he said one morning.

"I love the sounds of the Derby, the way the gates rattle as the horses go in. The buzz of the crowd that becomes a roar when they open. All those hooves pounding into the first turn. I'm going to find another way to share that with him."

The colt's owner, Fusao Sekiguchi, was not coming to Baltimore for the second leg of the Triple Crown. Back in Tokyo, he was busy with offers to buy Fusaichi Pegasus for stud from the world's leading stallion operations.

At the Derby, the owner had been intent on putting on a good show. He had done so by bringing the two geishas and their *oka-san,* or "mother," to Louisville. In Japan, spending a couple of hours with a sole geisha can routinely cost $500 and extend as high as $3,000. Sekiguchi said he didn't care about money. But there was more to know about how he came to own Fusaichi Pegasus, and the owner admitted that he'd had financial backing from partners when he bought the horse at Keeneland in 1998. Sekiguchi had repaid them within ten days of the sale. "I own it entirely now," he said.

He was vague, too, about his personal finances. Sekiguchi said he owed his entire fortune to a "major capital gain" when he sold the 38 percent of the former company—Meitec—he owned for 18 billion yen, or about $166 million at today's exchange rates. He declined to say how much he was worth. "That might create tax problems," he said.

But he did concede that the company he started in 1997, Venture-Safenet—in the same outsourcing niche he'd pioneered in Japan—was badly extended and losing money.

"We have no profits," he said of his 1,200-employee operation. "This company lives off of my own capital. I am spending my own money."

Now Sekiguchi was already missing Fusaichi Pegasus and the glory it had brought him back in America. "In the U.S., when I won, everyone congratulated me," he said. "Here, in Japan, people just turned their heads and looked away."

"I didn't bring my horse here to run for second-place money."
—*Joe Orseno, trainer of Red Bullet*

Not since 1983 and a colt named Deputed Testamony had a horse that skipped the Kentucky Derby won the Preakness Stakes. Since then, seventy-one had tried. Now three very focused men were in Baltimore intent on bucking history with a colt named Red Bullet.

The son of Unbridled was owned by Frank Stronach, an Austrian-born industrialist who had the horse racing industry on edge with his recent purchases of the premier racetracks Gulfstream in Florida and Santa Anita in California. He and Churchill Downs Inc. were competing to purchase other racetracks as well as gain control of the industry.

He was a breeder as well as an owner, and had an antiauthoritarian streak that was often satisfied by doing things differently. One of them was skipping the Derby. He had done so in 1997 with a colt named Touch Gold and had finished fourth here before thwarting Silver Charm's Triple Crown bid with a come-from-behind victory in the Belmont Stakes.

Red Bullet was trained by Joe Orseno, a Philadelphia native who grafted European training methods onto his conditioning regimen. The colt's rider was Jerry Bailey, the Hall of Fame jockey who had led the national jockey standings in five of the past six years.

They, too, were tough guys who did things their own way.

Red Bullet had finished second to Fusaichi Pegasus four weeks ago in the Wood Memorial. It was the colt's first loss in three starts and, though Stronach had never had a horse in the Kentucky Derby, owner and trainer met immediately after the race and decided to skip it. "When a horse doesn't finish well, it takes more out of him than you think," Stronach said. "I knew then we weren't going. My heart said it would be nice; my head said not to go."

Orseno agreed. Red Bullet had lost sixteen pounds on the day of the Wood. The fighter in Orseno wanted a rematch; but he knew the colt needed five weeks to grow into his still-maturing frame. When he watched Fusaichi Pegasus win the Derby on television, two things occurred to him.

"I thought I'd be disappointed when they broke from the gate without us. I wasn't," Orseno said. "I also knew we had a very talented horse and we weren't going to duck the winner."

The trainer's fitness theory was simple: If a horse couldn't complete three, four, five easy gallops of two miles a week at say two minutes, then how was he going to run as fast as he was able at race time? "It's just like conditioning a human athlete," he said. "They have to have a foundation or they will come up with nicks and pains."

Seven years ago, the trainer had ten second-rate horses trying to clump their way around the track on the New Jersey circuit and no audience interested enough to hear his training theories. After becoming Stronach's private trainer in 1998, Orseno now had more than forty of the best-bred horses in the nation. He was a square-built forty-four-year-old who had won big races before, but never had saddled a horse in a Triple Crown race. He patrolled the stakes barn at Pimlico and told anyone who would listen that it was a mistake to overlook Red Bullet. His colt had gained back the sixteen pounds, as well as added another ten, and was ready.

"There's a lot of ways to lose and one way to win. These are race-horses, not machines. You can't say Fusaichi Pegasus is an iron horse. Not yet. He had a perfect trip in the Kentucky Derby," he said. "I can't make my horse have more talent than he has. But I can tell you Red Bullet has enough talent and I have him at his very best."

Stronach and Orseno had more reason to be confident when Jerry Bailey accepted the mount on Red Bullet. The jockey looked every bit like the dentist's son that he was, with his benign smile and receding hairline that pulled back into a widow's peak. But coiled in a wiry five-foot-five and 112-pound frame was one of the fiercest competitors ever to get on a horse.

Like Pat Day, Bailey, forty-two, was a recovering alcoholic. He grew up in El Paso, Texas, wanting to play football and basketball but never made it beyond team manager in each sport because of his size. His father owned a few cheap racehorses, but Bailey had no real affinity for them. He never really thought about becoming a race rider until he tasted success as a high school wrestler. Bailey discovered that what he liked better than competing was winning.

He immersed himself in riding and won his first race with his very first mount, a horse named Fetch, in 1974 at Sunland Park in New Mexico. Still, Bailey was ambivalent enough about the sport that when his mother, who was dying of cancer, asked him to attend college, he interrupted his career and enrolled at the University of Texas-El Paso. He lasted a semester before returning to the racetrack. Like Day, the more he won and the more money he made, the more he drank. Bailey worked his way to the New York circuit in 1982 and distinguished himself as a midpack rider in the nation's toughest jockey colony. He got married. He continued to make a good living. He continued to drink.

By the time he was thirty-one, Bailey's drinking had him slurring words by mid-afternoon, and he had become injury-prone—a broken jaw, three cracked vertebrae, a broken collarbone, a foot broken in three places, fifteen broken ribs. Soon, he began losing mounts.

"The drinking had taken over every part of my life," Bailey said. "My reaction time was slow on horses. I had poor judgment."

At home, his wife was weary of her husband's stormy mood swings. The Baileys were at their home in Florida, awaiting the opening of Gulfsteam's winter meet, when Suzee Bailey called a friend with experience in the substance-abuse field. Together they confronted her husband about his addiction and got him into an outpatient program. On January 1, 1989, Bailey quit drinking. The jockey's sobriety rekindled his need to win.

"Look at my career before 1989. I was mediocre," Bailey admitted.

In the 1990s, however, Bailey won three riding titles, two Kentucky Derbys, on Sea Hero ('93) and Grindstone ('96), and guided Cigar to all but the first of sixteen consecutive victories. He is considered the best jockey in the world and rarely did any trainer take him off a horse. But that did not mean Bailey was the most popular jockey in racing.

Some trainers disliked his mercenary approach. They believed Bailey had little loyalty and often threw them over for a hotter horse.

Of the nineteen colts that started the Kentucky Derby, for example, Bailey had ridden seven of them before choosing to ride War Chant for Drysdale. Many of his fellow riders thought he was aloof and arrogant.

Bailey, more or less, pleaded guilty. He understood he was at the peak of his skills and wanted to ride only the best horses in the biggest races.

"I'm not going to be able to ride at this level forever, so I have to do what's best for me and my family. This is my business," Bailey said.

He was friendly but not too familiar with rival jockeys because part of his preparation was identifying their weaknesses and exploiting them. The horses change from race to race, but Bailey understood that the riders didn't. Like a football coach, Bailey devoured videotapes of races and spent hours with the *Racing Form.* He studied the tendencies of both rider and horse to visualize how a race might be run.

If Bailey knew a rider was stronger with a left-hand whip, he would crowd him until that rider had to switch hands. If he knew another got spooked on the rail, he'd force him there. While Day's approach was to become one with the horse, Bailey was more cerebral.

He knew where he wanted his horse at every stage of the race and made sure the horse got him there. Then he would wait. Nine out of ten times, Bailey figured, if he positioned his horse where he thought there was supposed to be an opening, one would materialize. Horses got tired, jockeys made wrong decisions—all he needed was a slice of daylight and he'd be the first one to the finish line. Nine out of ten times Bailey was right. He'd push his horses through the slimmest of openings and, if necessary, thump them with a punishing left-handed whip.

"Whatever it takes," he said. "The point of this game is to win. Isn't it?"

"It may be that the race is not always to the swift, nor the battle to the strong—but that is the way to bet."

—*Damon Runyon*

What kind of shoes to put on your horse was not the kind of decision a trainer wanted to make on race day. But on the morning of May 20, 2000, that's what the trainers of the eight horses competing in the Preakness were trying to decide. It had rained all night and the Pimlico track was a bog. At the stakes barn, Bob Baffert fitted Captain Steve with mud caulks, or stickers, in the hope that his colt might grab the ground better.

"When you're running for a million bucks with a long shot, you need every edge you can find," Baffert reasoned.

Across the racetrack at Barn 7, Drysdale considered putting mud caulks on Fusaichi Pegasus. He even flew in his farrier from California, but ultimately he decided against the change. Fusaichi Pegasus had handled a wet track at Aqueduct in the Wood Memorial. His pedigree suggested he could handle mud. Drysdale believed the colt was too valuable to risk an equipment change and possible injury.

The morning showers gave way to mist and a cool, gray day in the 60s. It didn't stop more than 98,000 people from filing into Pimlico for the 125th running of the Preakness Stakes, but as the races continued through the afternoon, the racing oval appeared to get slower, especially along the rail. As post time approached, Drysdale knew the conditions were not ideal for Fusaichi Pegasus to capture the second leg of the Triple Crown.

When the eight horses stepped on the track for the post parade, Fusaichi Pegasus was a daunting 1 to 5 favorite. The second choice, Red Bullet, was 6 to 1; High Yield was 7 to 1; Captain Steve 11 to 1; Impeachment and a Triple Crown newcomer named Snuck In were 19 to 1; and then Hal's Hope and another newcomer, Hugh Hefner, rounded out the board at 35 to 1 and 50 to 1.

In the paddock before the race, Frank Stronach had intended to give Bailey riding instructions. He and Orseno had watched race after race on the card trying to determine how the track was playing. They couldn't. Finally, the trainer turned to his owner and said, "We're outthinking ourselves. We're only going to confuse him."

Stronach agreed.

"The less we tell Jerry, the better," Stronach said, his Austrian accent turning Bailey's first name to "Cherry." I would have loved to have told him to stay back and watch Pegasus, then race by him. Instead, I told him good luck.

As the horses moved to the starting gate, Stronach and Orseno moved to their seats on the finish line. Two rows behind them was Yukari Sekiguchi, the daughter-in-law of Fusaichi Pegasus' owner. Baffert, Mike Pegram, and Captain Steve Thompson sat a couple of rows behind her. Drysdale found a small monitor for himself in the breezeway of the paddock. He lit a cigarette.

When the gates opened, the trainer winced—Fusaichi Pegasus was squeezed by Captain Steve on the inside and Hal's Hope on the outside. Kent Desormeaux gathered the big colt and angled him outside to the middle of the track. Red Bullet bolted cleanly from the gate, but Bailey pulled up on the reins and settled him inside in seventh place, two lengths behind Fusaichi Pegasus.

Bailey had ridden Red Bullet to victory once before and knew the colt possessed sudden acceleration when asked. The rider also knew exactly how he was going to try to beat Fusaichi Pegasus: by firing those jets in a bold move. But he wasn't sure when.

Bailey didn't know exactly how he was going to ride the race until the break. He wanted to be off the pace, but the jockey wasn't sure if Fusaichi Pegasus would be behind or ahead of him. Bailey first needed to determine how hard Red Bullet was going to run the first third of the mile. As far as the jockey was concerned, this was a match race between his colt and Fusaichi Pegasus.

As expected, the front-runners Hugh Hefner and Hal's Hope shot to the lead, but in between them was High Yield. By the way Pat Day was pulling back on him, it was clear he didn't want the colt that close. It was too late—those three led the charge around the first turn and into the backstretch. Bailey loped Red Bullet along inside, then asked the colt for a little oomph before the far turn; Red Bullet catapulted forward three lengths in between Captain Steve and Fusaichi Pegasus, who was still racing three wide. Desormeaux glanced left and saw Red Bullet floating toward him as Bailey guided his colt a length ahead of Fusaichi Pegasus.

Bailey had wanted Desormeaux to see that Red Bullet was barely trying. He also wanted to force Fusaichi Pegasus wide. He did. The field had run a half mile in 46:62 and mud was flying. Soon Hugh Hefner, High Yield, and Hal's Hope were leg-weary and coming back. It was time for Bailey to make the move he had visualized before the race.

Around the far turn, Bailey moved Red Bullet inside Hal's Hope and blew past Snuck In. Desormeaux was moving Fusaichi Pegasus wide. The two colts were briefly in stride, but then Bailey dropped the hammer on Red Bullet.

"He just exploded on the turn, and as he was striding out he, just left the other horse behind. I'm surprised he didn't stay up with us at least until the middle of the stretch," Bailey said.

Red Bullet's move stunned Desormeaux and stalled Fusaichi Pegasus. Bailey cut the corner while Desormeaux was stuck in the middle of the track. He thumped Red Bullet with that left-handed whip once, twice, four times, then switched to his right for two lighter passes. Desormeaux crossed the reins of Fusaichi Pegasus to shake him up, but the colt looked confused and ducked his head in. Then Fusaichi Pegasus jerked his head outside.

"We pushed the button at the same time, but Red Bullet had a bigger button," Desormeaux would say later.

The late-running Impeachment was hustling inside Fusaichi Pegasus and Captain Steve was zigzagging, looking for running room. Not only were Red Bullet and Bailey gone and not coming back, Fusaichi Pegasus was having to fight to finish in second. Desormeaux popped him once. Nothing. The powerful stride that had swallowed Churchill Downs two weeks earlier had been reduced to a back-and-forth pogo hop.

While Bailey was pumping his fist in the air 3¾ lengths ahead at the finish line, Fusaichi Pegasus was gutting out a second-place finish by a head over Impeachment.

The superhorse was human. For the first time in four years, there would be no Triple Crown at stake when the 3-year-olds pulled into New York for the Belmont Stakes.

While Stronach and Orseno pushed their way through the crowd and to the winner's circle arm in arm, Drysdale walked to the middle of the track and waited for Fusaichi Pegasus. He had rubber wader shoes on and he studied his own steps, trying to understand the mud his horse had contended with. He waited with his arms crossed for Desormeaux to bring Fusaichi Pegasus back. Thirty yards away, Stronach pulled a black-eyed Susan from the winner's blanket and put it in the pocket of his gray suit. He grabbed the lead shank away from Orseno and led Red Bullet with Bailey still aboard through a crowd of photographers and into the winner's circle.

When Fusaichi Pegasus arrived, Drysdale shot Desormeaux a quizzical look.

"He was slipping and sliding, Neil. It was greasy out there. He couldn't get ahold of the track," said Desormeaux.

Drysdale nodded in assent and patted his big colt on the withers.

"That's the way I saw it. I think on a fast track it would have been different," he said.

A half hour later, Bailey was showered, dressed, and ready to catch a flight back to New York. His work here was done. He had a satisfied grin and a pinpoint explanation for what he and Red Bullet had accomplished in the 1:56:04 it took him to get around the track.

"We've all seen over the years horses coming off the Derby who looked like they were invincible," Bailey said. "And two weeks later, at 5:45 P.M., we see that they're not."

Chapter 13

THE BELMONT STAKES:
TEST OF THE CHAMPION

JUNE 1999

BELMONT PARK, NEW YORK

"There is no secret so close such as that between a man and his horse."
—Robert Smith Surtees, nineteenth-century author

Neil Drysdale had returned to Aqueduct with Fusaichi Pegasus to prepare for the Belmont Stakes. The trainer put his colt in the same barn and same stall he had inhabited two months earlier for the Wood Memorial. Fusaichi Pegasus had rebounded from his defeat at the Preakness. So, it appeared, had Drysdale. He was planning his restaurant and theater schedule for the upcoming week, soliciting reviews for Pastis, a hot new bistro in Manhattan's meatpacking district, and for the award-winning revival of Sam Shepard's play *True West*.

Of course, Drysdale had not confirmed that Fusaichi Pegasus would run in the 1½-mile Belmont Stakes a week from now on June 10. Drysdale wanted to see the colt work the following morning before reaching a final decision. If he liked what he saw, he'd move Fusaichi Pegasus from Aqueduct in Queens to Belmont Park in Elmont, Long Island, a couple of days before the race.

"But we're here, aren't we?" Drysdale asked with a smile. "I've always said this longer distance was better suited to my horse. I'm more comfortable with having three weeks between races than the two weeks between the Derby and the Preakness."

The race needed Fusaichi Pegasus because Red Bullet was not going to run here. What many had hoped might be a rematch and ongoing rivalry on par with Affirmed and Alydar, Sunday Silence and Easy Goer, was not going to materialize. A week earlier, Frank Stronach and Joe Orseno decided their colt was not ready to come back in three weeks for the Belmont. They believed the race had taken too much out of Red Bullet, but promised they would renew the battle later in the summer.

"They're doing what they believe is best for the horse. It doesn't concern me." Drysdale shrugged. "But it does show how tough these contests are on horses. I'm not sure if I ever have another Kentucky

Derby winner that I'd run him in the Preakness. It is too much. Let's wait and see how my horse does tomorrow and we'll make a decision."

Fusaichi Pegasus never worked out the following morning. Later that afternoon, at 2 P.M. on June 3, the colt was asleep in his stall. Nearby, a blacksmith was working on another horse in Barn 1. When he dropped a tool, Fusaichi Pegasus startled. The colt jumped forward, lost his footing, and slid into the door. He caught a sharp corner and sustained a cut about the size of a dime in his right front hoof wall. A veterinarian treated and bandaged him and assured Drysdale the colt was not sore. The trainer checked the doors of every stall in the barn, wondering if a crucial detail may have slipped by him. All of the doors had sharp corners.

Drysdale scratched his horse from the 132nd running of the Belmont Stakes.

Fusaichi Pegasus would be fine in five or six days, but the trainer feared if the colt raced, the cut might turn into a larger crack on the hoof wall. Just like that, Drysdale's Triple Crown campaign was over, and the trainer looked relieved as he stood outside his barn.

"Maybe this is a blessing in disguise," he said. "The decision whether or not to run him hadn't been made. Well, he made the decision himself."

"I am still under the impression there is nothing alive quite so beautiful as a Thoroughbred horse."

—John Galsworthy

In the previous three years, Silver Charm, Real Quiet, and Charismatic had all come to New York as Derby and Preakness winners for a try at sweeping the Triple Crown. Now, for the first time in thirty years, the third jewel in the series did not have either the Kentucky Derby winner or the Preakness winner in the starting gate.

They still were going to run the $1 million race, but without Fusaichi Pegasus and Red Bullet, the Belmont Stakes lacked star power. The race was called a "Test of the Champion" because it was the final leg of the Triple Crown and contested at the longest distance of 1½ miles. But none of the eleven horses in New York had ever won a Grade I race, had ever been victorious at the highest level of the sport.

Five of them had skipped both the Kentucky Derby and the Preakness. Four of them had skipped the middle leg, the Preakness. Four of them boasted only a single career victory, including the favorite and Kentucky Derby runner-up, Aptitude. There were no past champions in this field and little evidence that there was a future champ to come.

Of the nineteen horses that started in the Kentucky Derby on May 6, 2000, only one was going to make it to all three races: Impeachment. The late-running colt had finished third in both the Derby and Preakness for Todd Pletcher. With only one victory in eight races, Impeachment wasn't even the trainer's best 3-year-old. This wasn't lost on Pletcher as he leaned over the stall to eye his chestnut colt and reflect on the lessons he had learned in his first Triple Crown campaign.

"Did I ever believe that this was the horse who was going to hit the board in the first two legs and make it all the way through the series? No way. Just look at him," said Pletcher with a smile.

Impeachment was a restless and nervous horse who always lurked in the front of his stall. He bobbed. He weaved. He remained in motion. Now Impeachment was playing with a ball that Pletcher's staff had hung from his door to quiet the colt.

"More Than Ready, Graeme Hall, and Trippi are more talented. So what does that tell me? Impeachment is a big horse, he's more durable. He drops way behind and comes on with one closing run, so it's fair to say he doesn't get bounced around a lot. It shows that we've been lucky. I don't think you can make it through these three races without luck. Maybe the difference between a very good horse and a great one is as simple as a couple of breaks."

The backside of Belmont on the days leading up to the race indeed had taken on a philosophical bent with the defection of Fusaichi

Pegasus and Red Bullet. Would there ever be another Triple Crown winner? Another Sir Barton, who was the first to sweep the series in 1919? A Gallant Fox—1930? Omaha—1935? War Admiral—1937? Whirlaway—1941? Count Fleet—1943? Assault—1946? Citation—1948? Secretariat—1973? Seattle Slew—1977? Affirmed—1978?

No one was more thoughtful about the future of the series than Bobby Frankel, who trained Aptitude. The fifty-eight-year-old Brooklyn native had never won a Triple Crown or Breeders' Cup race. He was a Californian now who had earned his way into the Hall of Fame with a stable primarily made up of older horses and grass runners.

He didn't expect to be here. In the summer of 1999, a Juddmonte Farms manager named Garrett O'Rourke delivered a 2-year-old dark brown son of A. P. Indy to Frankel and predicted he'd be a Kentucky Derby horse. Frankel didn't think so. He debuted Aptitude in a turf race in October at the distance of a mile where he finished a decent sixth. In November, Aptitude launched a late-closing run for a second-place finish, again on the grass. Better, but hardly a ticket to Churchill Downs.

On New Year's Day at Santa Anita in a 1¹⁄₁₆-mile race on the dirt, however, Frankel discovered what O'Rourke had been certain of: Aptitude was meant to go longer. The colt won that day and finished second in the Gotham Stakes and third in the Wood Memorial and showed he was good enough to run in the Kentucky Derby.

"He was right," Frankel said. "It's nice to be right. You ever been to the racetrack and heard somebody yelling, 'I told you that horse would win'? It's not even about the money. They just want to be right."

And that to the trainer was the essence of the sport. In the Derby, Aptitude closed strongly to finish second by a length and a half to Fusaichi Pegasus. Frankel knew the colt was going to be formidable in the longer Belmont. His father, A. P. Indy, had won the race in 1992.

So Frankel skipped the Preakness and now, with Aptitude, was trying to do what no other horse had done in the 132-year history of the Belmont: win the third leg of the Triple Crown without a race of any kind between the Kentucky Derby and the Belmont.

"It's not something you can train into a horse. It's in a horse's pedigree and the way he runs," he insisted. "I know I'm right about that."

Frankel often acted like the guy in the OTB parlor who wanted to be right. He was emotional, combative, and a straight talker. Earlier in the spring, he lambasted jockey Corey Nakatani for reneging on a riding commitment and said Nakatani would never ride for him again. After a two-month ban, however, Nakatani was back on some of Frankel's horses.

And moments after the Derby, when the racing world was just beginning to canonize Fusaichi Pegasus as a superhorse, a forlorn Frankel said his horse should have won. His jockey, Alex Solis, moved off the rail too soon and ceded the ground-saving inside trip to Kent Desormeaux and Fusaichi Pegasus, he reasoned.

"It would have at least been a photo," he said.

Besides the physical toll the series took on a horse, the trainer believed that the Triple Crown was endangered because there were an increasing number of wealthier races now available to owners, especially for older horses. The eight races on Breeders' Cup day, for instance, offered purses ranging from $1 million to $4 million. What was once called the Arlington Million at Arlington Park in Chicago was now actually worth $2 million.

Now being right for an owner was as much about unearthing a runner at the sales and turning him into a multimillion-dollar stud. They ran their horses less. They mapped out a one-, two-, or three-year plan targeting the right races, the Grade I's. They built value.

"The Kentucky Derby is the one race everyone wants to run. If you don't win the Kentucky Derby, there's no reason to push a horse into the Preakness. Only the Derby winner has a chance to win the Triple

Crown—for everybody else, the Preakness is just another $1 million race. Why not wait five weeks when your horse is rested and try the Belmont," Frankel reasoned. "It's a question of longevity. Do you want your horse to make money as a 4-year-old, 5-year-old, or 8-year-old? If you do, you're not going to beat them up when they are young."

"You have to have an undying confidence in what you're doing and your horse's ability. You can't waver. You can't come over here and say, maybe we'll go, we should go, I don't know. You've got to believe in what you're doing and let it all hang out."

—D. Wayne Lukas

Lukas had switched horses for the third leg of the Triple Crown. After High Yield finished seventh at the Preakness, Lukas sent the colt back to California to rest until summer. In his place, Lukas was running Commendable, which many believed was another display of the legendary trainer's hubris. The colt had a sprinter's pedigree, had finished no better than fourth in his last six starts, and ran a dismal seventeenth in the Kentucky Derby.

Lukas lost a horse, too. His saddle pony, a $750,000 Thoroughbred named Sudden Impact, had disappeared in transport somewhere before their arrival in New York. Not since the sale at Keeneland the previous September, when he was without any of his deep-pocketed owners, had Lukas looked so ordinary. He walked back and forth to the track just like every other trainer and was virtually ignored on the backside.

The trainer was distraught about his horses' performances so far in the Triple Crown, especially High Yield, who had failed to be a factor in either of the races. He honestly believed that High Yield was one of the best horses he had ever brought to the Kentucky Derby. But Lukas wasn't going to sit out the Belmont. With his track record, why should he?

From 1994 to 1996, Lukas had won an unprecedented six consecutive Triple Crown races with four different horses. His training program was geared to these races; his reputation was built by dominating them. In some forty years of training horses, Lukas had amassed the most staggering numbers in the game and earned his place in the Hall of Fame by honing to this basic tenet:

"When a horse is good and he's doing well, lead him over there and give him a chance to perform. You take what's in front of you. The sport gets too shaky and you just can't predict. They're not wind-up toys; when they're good, run them, when they're not, rest them."

But Commendable? He had won once in his very first start at the pedestrian distance of six furlongs. The colt finished a binoculars-challenged twenty-six lengths behind Fusaichi Pegasus in the Derby. Even the colt's owners, Bob and Beverly Lewis, doubted his ability. As co-owners of High Yield, the couple also weren't having a successful Triple Crown. On the night before the draw, Lewis called Lukas from California and asked, "Wayne, are you sure we're doing the right thing?"

It was a valid question, considering how cruel the last leg of the Triple Crown had been to the Lewises. In 1997, Silver Charm won the Kentucky Derby and the Preakness only to see a Triple Crown sweep vanish when Touch Gold caught the gray colt in the last fifty yards to win the race by three quarters of a length. Last year was even more heartbreaking when Charismatic came to this grand old track on the verge of Triple Crown history only to fracture his foreleg at the top of the turn and gamely hold on for third place.

"Get on a plane, Bob, and get on out here. I'm not going to embarrass you. We belong," Lukas told him.

The previous fall, Lukas had told the owner that Commendable was their Belmont entry. The trainer didn't believe the colt was limited to sprinting. This, after all, was a horse who reminded Lukas of himself—who loved being up in the morning and hard at work.

But it was only a week earlier that Lukas had become convinced Commendable could have a say in the race. He sat down with a legal pad and listed the ten other horses in the field of the Belmont with columns marked "Pro" and "Con" to gauge their chances.

"Sometimes it's more important when you're training horses to know what the other guy can do and can't do," Lukas said.

The upside of the long shot Hugh Hefner, for example, was that the colt was the lone speed in the race. The downside: He could not carry it 1½ miles. The favorite, Aptitude? Lukas figured he would be too far back and have too much ground to make up in the long stretch. It was the same for the other closers: Unshaded, Impeachment, Wheelaway, and Curule. Two horses, Globalize and Postponed, would stalk the pace, but Lukas simply didn't believe they were good enough.

When the columns were examined, Lukas believed Commendable had a shot at winning for a single reason: "He could run his natural race with his tactical speed and have a say in the outcome," Lukas said. "Everyone else had to change their running styles. Not us. Commendable could run from the front of the pack and carry the distance. No matter how bad our record looks, there's no world beaters in that field. There's some good horses, but I think we're one of them."

All week, Lukas acted the part of overmatched Triple Crown trainer, telling anyone who asked that he didn't have any "grandiose ideas" about Commendable winning the Belmont. But he did have that idea. Lukas believed he had the puzzle of the race solved if only he got Pat Day.

"It is paramount that we get him," Lukas said one morning. "He is the one guy who can execute the plan to perfection."

The jockey had ridden Commendable in three of his losses and blamed himself for getting the colt beaten in April at the Lexington Stakes. Frankly, Day was afraid of hopping on anything other than a Lukas horse. Commendable wasn't the trainer's best horse, but Day had a hunch.

"You can't count Wayne out of the classic races. He has the courage to put his horses in the big races and take a shot with them," he said.

Still, not everyone believed in Lukas's strategy, and one of them was very close to home. On the morning of the race, his wife, Laura, called him from California and asked if he really believed he could win. "Absolutely," he told her.

"What will it take?" she asked.

"If I can get the same thing I get in the morning this afternoon, we're going to be a factor in this," Lukas told his wife. "When he's moving, he's very fluid. I'll leave it up to Pat to back me up on that."

"Why do I love the racetrack? It's the only place left you can drink, smoke, cuss, and gamble at the same time. And no matter what happens, when you leave, you feel better than when you got there."
—Tommy Jacomo, general manager of the Palm restaurant
in Washington, D.C., and a devoted horseplayer

The superhorse, Fusaichi Pegasus, was across town at a racetrack with no races, waiting to catch a plane back to California. His conqueror, Red Bullet, was trying to stay cool in his home barn behind Belmont Park on a sweltering 95-degree day. Still, 67,810 people had come to this racetrack that hovered above the Cross Island Parkway in Long Island to watch eleven unproven horses complete the final leg of the Triple Crown 2000.

When the horses entered the paddock for the ninth race of the day, the 132nd running of the Belmont Stakes, I discovered that I had a very live ticket in the Pick Six. Winning a Pick Six ticket for a horse player is what capturing the Kentucky Derby is for a horse owner: a noble but quixotic pursuit. It entailed picking the winner of six consecutive races. You could play the ticket for as little as $2, but that meant picking one horse to win in each of the six races. Nobody is that perfect a handicapper. So most of the time you play combinations of horses in each race, which increases the price of your ticket. To pick two horses to win each of the six races, for example, cost $128. Some bettors form syndicates to raise thousands of dollars and spread out dozens of horses on a ticket.

Not me. I hardly ever played them, but with a $1 million pool guaranteed, I put together a small ticket that cost $64. I kept the cost down because I "singled," or picked one horse to win in a single race. I singled a horse in the first leg of the Pick Six and I was correct. I've never hit a Pick Six before. I've collected a couple of consolation payouts for hitting five of six, but on each I had suffered my lone loss early in the six races. Now I had picked four races of four. Never had I been so perfect with two races left.

Maybe it was because of New York's oppressive June heat, but I was thinking about parlaying my winnings into a flight on the Concorde to Paris for a weekend of racing at Longchamps. I picked two horses to win the Belmont Stakes; I needed one of them to win.

In the paddock, the horses seemed to be bearing up to the scorching temperatures better than the humans who were saddling them. Between the fans hovering on the rail and the towering grandstand, the air was still and appeared to suck the energy from the owners and trainers. Lukas looked particularly uncomfortable, wrapped as he was in $3,000 of tailored fabric.

Commendable had lost his left front shoe in the saddling area. The colt had scuffed his foot on the rubber-brick walkway and pulled it off so cleanly that the eight nails pointed straight up, just as they had originally gone in. It was a first for Lukas, but it failed to rattle him. He tried to kid a very nervous blacksmith who was scrambling to reshoe Commendable.

Now sweat ran down the side of Lukas's face as he went over with Day one more time how he wanted the jockey to ride Commendable. Lukas wanted him on or near the front. Day agreed. In the Lexington Stakes, the rider discovered that the colt didn't like running in traffic, that he got anxious when he was covered by other horses.

"If you can get clear by the first turn, then do it, but I believe Hugh Hefner may get there first. If he does, just sit behind him and wait. He's not going to last. We're looking for slow fractions and to save energy. I'm telling you, our horse can run all day," Lukas told him.

"It sounds like a plan." Day nodded.

Lukas catapulted the rider on the back of Commendable. While horse and rider headed for the track, Lukas told Bob and Beverly Lewis that he'd meet them in their box later. He glanced up at the tote board to see that the bettors judged Commendable an 18–1 long shot.

Lukas didn't break stride—right now he needed some air-conditioning.

He found it in the trustees' room, a private dining area on the clubhouse level above the finish line. Lukas stood beneath the vent and let the cool air wash over him. The room was emptying as post time approached, and Lukas found himself alone with an elderly couple. Through the glass below him, he saw the Lewises waving for him to come to their seats. He was still too hot and decided to watch the race from inside.

Just as Lukas had called it, Hugh Hefner angled inside from the No. 10 post, intent on leading into the first turn. Day let him go and parked Commendable in second place two lengths behind. Behind him another couple of lengths Wheelaway, Postponed, and Tahkoda Hills were fighting for position; far behind them, the closers, Aptitude and Unshaded, loped along.

When the board flashed the half-mile split of 49.29 seconds, Lukas broke the silence in the trustees' room with a matter-of-fact declaration. The race was unfolding in slow motion.

"Commendable is going to win this," he said.

There was still a mile of running left, but the trainer recognized his chestnut was just coasting along, and Day was frozen on top of him in the Lewises' green-and-yellow-striped silks. Heading into the far turn, Day nudged Commendable, and the colt inhaled Hugh Hefner. Aptitude, the 8–5 favorite, picked it up in midpack and Unshaded geared up on the far outside, but they were a dozen or so lengths back. Impeachment, too, was trying to rally.

And Day had yet to ask his horse to really run. He looked beneath his arm and saw he was pulling away from the field. At the eighth pole, Commendable had 2 ½ lengths on Aptitude and Unshaded, and Day was merely shoving on the colt's neck and smooching in his ear. The rider knew then that no one was going to catch Commendable.

"They were going to have to come on really hard. Even then I knew I would have more in the tank," Day said later.

The rider never even brandished his whip as the colt was a 1½-length winner over Aptitude, followed by Unshaded as Impeachment finished fifth. The theft was complete—by slowing the race to a comfortable pace, Lukas and Day sneaked off with the Belmont Stakes in a final time of 2:31.19, nearly a full four seconds slower than the previous year's race.

"Give Lukas credit," Frankel said. "I don't know how he did it."

In the trustees' room, a woman standing next to Lukas was perplexed.

"How did you know he was going to win?" she asked.

"I trained that horse," Lukas replied.

"No, you didn't. You didn't yell, you didn't scream, you didn't act like you even had a bet on that horse," she said.

"Ma'am, I'm Wayne Lukas, and I trained that horse. You see that trophy down in the winner's circle?" the trainer asked with a grin large enough to swallow his wraparound sunglasses. "You keep a good eye on it, because in a few minutes, I'm going to go down there and I'm going to hoist it over my head."

Then Lukas bounded down the steps to meet the Lewises, whose second-string horse had just given them a first-rate victory, repairing some of the heartbreak the couple had suffered with Silver Charm and Charismatic. It was the trainer's fourth Belmont win and thirteenth in Triple Crown races. It meant more history: Lukas now was tied with Sunny Jim Fitzsimmons as the winningest trainer in the famous series.

When it was time for him to meet the press, the trainer started off his remarks with a simple sentence: "My name is Wayne Lukas, and I ran a horse in the Belmont today, for those of you who didn't notice."

Believe it or not, I hadn't. Commendable was not one of the two horses on my Pick Six ticket. It looked as if Paris was not to be.

JUNE 7, 2000

BELMONT PARK

It was a year nearly to the day since Lukas had readied Cash Run for the filly race in the paddock here and waited for Charismatic to get out of surgery after the colt's Belmont accident. I found the trainer in the same place at exactly the same time. He was saddling another 2-year-old for a first race, a colt named Drumcliff. Lukas pulled his stable's signature white bridle over Drumcliff and sent him to the track.

It already had been a good day for Lukas to plan for the Triple Crown in 2001. Just moments before, he watched on television as one of his 2-year-olds, a filly named Tricky Elaine, ran away from the field in a 5½-furlong race at Churchill Downs. Just like the previous year, a crowd of barely 11,000 people were left at the track, most of them hardened horseplayers. Still, as Lukas made his way through them, they reached to shake his hand, to congratulate him on the Belmont victory the day before, to tell him that there was no one else like him. As he waited for Drumcliff to load in the gate, Lukas ticked off the names of six colts that he could envision wearing the blanket of roses next May.

"I've got some big boats for next year's assault," he promised. "I can hardly wait. I think about these Triple Crown races every minute of every day."

EPILOGUE

NOVEMBER 4, 2000

THE BREEDERS' CUP CHAMPIONSHIPS

LOUISVILLE, KENTUCKY

"There is something about the outside of a horse that is good for the inside of a man."

—*Sir Winston Churchill*

There is life after the Triple Crown for the horses and owners.

Some of the class of 2000 horses improved in the ensuing summer and made their owners a little wealthier, and all but one of them were eager to pump more money back in the game to take another shot at those three famous races in the spring. There is always next year.

More Than Ready finally grabbed his Grade I victory, the designation worth the most money at the breeding shed, and Jim Scatuorchio landed an offer to turn the colt out to stud. After a couple of near misses at 1$\frac{1}{16}$ and 1$\frac{1}{8}$ miles, Scatuorchio and Todd Pletcher ran him in a sprint, the seven-furlong King's Bishop Stakes on August 28 at the colt's favorite track, Saratoga Springs. He had come full circle.

When More Than Ready ran in the Kentucky Derby, he was a speed horse on the front end of a 1$\frac{1}{4}$-mile race. Now, running shorter distances, the colt came from behind; he had learned to relax and pounce just like Todd Pletcher had hoped. With Pat Day aboard, the colt kicked past five horses in the stretch for the victory, but for the Scatuorchios, it was a bittersweet victory. The previous month, Jim had sold the breeding rights to the horse for $8 million; the victory in the King's Bishop gave him a $1 million bonus.

But it also ensured that More Than Ready would be retired at the end of the year. With son Kevin and daughter Courtney away at college, the Scatuorchios were sad about losing another member of the family. In fact, after the colt ran fifth on November 4, 2000, in the Breeders' Cup Sprint, Jim was considering restructuring the deal and, if necessary, returning some money so that More Than Ready could race another year.

It didn't appear that the horses Team Scatuorchio had bought at the 1999 Keeneland Sale were going to follow in the fast footsteps of

More Than Ready. So far, they had one victory among them. But at the 2000 sale, Scatuorchio spent $1.3 million to buy five yearlings. They were at J. J. Pletcher's farm in Florida, and the old trainer assured Jim there wasn't a J.A.H.—"just another horse"—in the bunch.

When I last saw Mike Pegram in the spring, it was at a crab-cake joint outside Baltimore after Captain Steve had finished fourth in the Preakness. He was at a big table, beer in hand, acting like he enjoyed losing. When I asked him if he was going on to the Belmont, he roared.

"Hell, no. I'm taking my horse to the Iowa Derby."

Captain Steve, indeed, won that race, as he did two other important stakes races. Over a strong summer campaign, Captain Steve earned Pegram more than $1.2 million in purses.

So the owner brought him to Louisville to run in the $4 million Breeders' Cup Classic at Churchill Downs. Pegram had to pay a $240,000 supplemental, or late fee, to get a spot in the starting gate in the toughest field of the year, which included Fusaichi Pegasus. It was a gamble, but one that paid off: Captain Steve ran third and earned a $562,800 purse.

The Deputy never recovered from his successful spring and disappointing Kentucky Derby. Veterinarians put the colt through a full battery of tests and found nothing wrong. Jenine Sahadi and Team Valor president Barry Irwin gave the colt a thirty-day break and there was still no improvement. The Deputy underwent a nuclear scan. It discovered some stress on his ankles but no fractures. The Deputy rested for another ninety days and was back at work by the fall, but never raced again and was retired to stud.

Sahadi enjoyed a successful summer in California and now trains seven horses for Team Valor—more than any other trainer the syndicate employs.

Bob Baffert and D. Wayne Lukas remain number 1 and number 2 nationally in purses won. Each have had their ups and downs. Baffert brought three colts to the Breeders' Cup Juvenile race—all of whom are strong contenders for the 2001 Triple Crown. One of them, Point Given, lost by a nose, while the other two, Arabian Light and Flame Thrower, finished fifth and eighth. Baffert appeared ready to shake his yearlong blues.

"We've restocked, reloaded, and we're ready to have some fun," he said.

Lukas never did get High Yield back to the racetrack. In mid-June, the colt fractured a sesamoid while training at Churchill Downs and was retired to stud. Commendable raced throughout the summer but never duplicated his winning Belmont form.

The trainer also suffered through a terrible meet at Saratoga. On a single afternoon in July, one Triple Crown hopeful, a $1.95 million colt named Yonaguska, finished second in the Sanford Stakes to a horse that had cost $9,000; and yet another $2 million colt finished ninth in another race. None of this seemed to faze Lukas. Neither did finishing ninth with a colt named Scorpion and twelfth with Yonaguska in the Breeders' Cup Juvenile race.

"I'm still bringing contenders up from the farm, and there's a lot of time to get these horses in shape before next May," Lukas insisted.

Lukas had a good Breeders' Cup day anyway. His filly named Spain won the Distaff, and Surfside, running her second race since the spring, finished second. Hard as it is to believe, Lukas gave bettors another big surprise: Spain was a 56–1 long shot and returned $113.80 for a $2 bet. The trainer has no plans to retire.

"I'll probably fall off the pony, they'll harrow me under, and that'll be that," he said.

The early favorite for the 2001 Kentucky Derby is the Juvenile winner, Macho Uno, from the connections of Frank Stronach, Joe Orseno, and Jerry Bailey of Red Bullet fame.

"He has a lot to learn, and I'm hopeful he'll have learned it by May," Orseno said. And Red Bullet? The Preakness victor returned to the track on July 9 to finish third in the Dwyer Stakes at Belmont Park, before being turned out at Stronach's farm in Florida for the rest of the year. Red Bullet was plagued by a virus and leg troubles and may yet turn out a one-race wonder.

Behind Orseno's Macho Uno and Baffert's Point Given, a colt named Street Cry finished third. He is owned by Godolphin and Sheik Mohammed al-Maktoum and was bred by one of the Sheik's brothers. The Maktoums are as committed as ever to winning a Triple Crown race.

And the big horse, Fusaichi Pegasus?

In August, at the National Museum of Racing in Saratoga Springs, Neil Drysdale was inducted into the Hall of Fame. He offered a concise and poignant acceptance speech.

"My career would not be possible without a very forgiving clientele tolerating me, and a very understanding and loyal staff," he said. "But most of all, these lovely four-legged creatures that have given my life such passion."

Earlier in the summer, the Kentucky Derby winner was sold to Ashford Stud, the North American division of the global stallion operation Coolmore Stud, for $60 million, shattering the record price of $40 million paid for Shareef Dancer in 1983. During negotiations, Fusao Sekiguchi revealed he did not entirely own Fusaichi Pegasus, after all. Before the Derby, he had sold an interest in the colt to Shadai Farm, a breeding operation based in Japan. Sekiguchi also did not buy any more horses at the sales.

After the Derby the colt raced once, on September 23, in the Jerome Handicap at Belmont Park. He won. But he was scratched from the Jockey Club Gold Cup in October after another minor foot injury. Still, the crowd made Fusaichi Pegasus the 6–5 favorite in the 1¼-mile Breeders' Cup Classic. It was the colt's last race before retiring to the breeding shed, where he is expected to command $200,000 per coupling.

Drysdale, as usual, was understated about what it meant for him to say good-bye to the horse. "He's been an interesting character to be around" is what the trainer offered.

The Classic was supposed to be a smashing farewell. Instead, Fusaichi Pegasus finished sixth.

The horse that won was also a 3-year-old, a late bloomer named Tiznow. While Fusaichi Pegasus was winning the Derby, this colt was preparing for his second lifetime start. He was bred and co-owned by Cecilia Straub-Rubens, an eighty-three-year-old Californian who had spent forty years trying to do what everyone who loves horse racing is trying to do: find the right horse.

In fact, from January through October 2000, owners spent $510,834,975 on 8,779 yearlings at auctions in the United States in the hopes that one of them was the right horse for the 2002 Triple Crown.

In Louisville that afternoon, Cee, as she was known, watched Tiznow lead the best horses in the world almost every step at Churchill Downs. The first-place check was nice—$2,438,800—but the victory was priceless. Three days later Cee died of a heart attack during surgery. She had been battling cancer.

"Those two minutes it took Tiznow to run that race were the best she had felt in a long time," said her friend and co-owner Michael Cooper. "I think it was Tiznow that kept her going. She went out in style, a true winner."